Dr. G. W. Peters

The Prospects
of Christianity
throughout the World

The Prospects
of Christianity
throughout the World

EDITED BY

M. SEARLE BATES AND WILHELM PAUCK

CHARLES SCRIBNER'S SONS ✠ NEW YORK

A series of essays
dedicated to
Henry Pitney Van Dusen

Preface

The Christian Church has determined the development of Western civilization from the beginning, not only internally but also externally. The various elements constituting this civilization have been held together by the spiritual power of the Christian religion. This is so even today, despite the fact that Christianity has become secularized to such an extent that in many parts of the Western world active Christians represent a minority. Nevertheless the impact of the Church upon human culture continues to be deep. Indeed, it is today a stronger world-wide force than ever before. It can be found in every part of the globe, molding human lives inwardly and outwardly. To be sure, it has been undergoing great crises during these latter decades: a process of gradual secularization has been undermining its strength, particularly in Europe and America, and Communism is making a formidable assault upon it, especially in Russia and China but also in other countries where it is the dominating political power.

Is it possible to say something definite about the prospects of Christianity throughout the world? Can one make definite judgments about its influence upon civilization as the various national and cultural societies of mankind are undergoing unprecedented changes?

Questions of this sort have motivated us to assemble the essays of the present volume. We have asked experienced leaders of Christianity in various parts of the world to make brief statements in depth about the prospects of Christianity as they see them in the light of their own acquaintance with the regions where they have been at work. We have given these contributors full freedom to state their views and judgments, imposing upon them neither a qualitative nor a quantitative rule or norm. We have made no attempt whatsoever to direct their thinking. On inviting them to participate in this venture, we merely have requested them to refrain from dealing too extensively with statistical facts and to concentrate instead upon an assessment of the strength or weakness of the Christian movement. Our readers will note that the liberty which we thus have granted to the authors of the several chapters is reflected in their manner of presentation as well as in their mode of argument. We have made no attempt to align the several chapters with one another through editorial interference.

We present a picture of the state of Christianity throughout the world. We are not concerned to engage in theological discussion, and nothing is farther from our intention than to promote or defend any partisan denominational interest. Our contributors belong to many different denominations. But the specific nature of their churchmanship has not determined us in our inviting them to collaborate with us. However, we readily acknowledge that, due to the circumstances in which this project originated, this volume is preponderantly the product of Christian leaders whose judgments, while in no way sectarian, have been shaped by experience primarily in Protestant church activities. They have not neglected to pay attention to Eastern Orthodoxy or to Roman Catholicism but, in the nature of things, these bodies have not received as thorough a treatment as they certainly merit.

We dedicate this volume to Dr. Henry Pitney Van Dusen. It was planned in the circle of the faculty of Union Theological Seminary, of which he was President from 1945 until his retirement in the spring of this year. Moreover, almost all contributors are in some way or other connected with the Seminary, either as teachers, guest professors, visiting lecturers, or former students. Dr. Van Dusen will, we know, derive great satisfaction from the proof which this book offers that members of the theological school which he led for so many years are active in high positions throughout the world. The world-wide outreach of Union Theological Seminary in our day is largely the fruit of his efforts. Throughout his career he has worked ardently for the realization of Christianity as an ecumenical movement; he has thoroughly studied the forces which have made Christianity a world-church in these latter years, and by his persistent support of the ecumenical movement in its various stages of development through his remarkable organizing ability, he has decisively contributed to the actualization of the universal character of the Christian religion. Therefore we think that it is appropriate to dedicate to him this volume of studies and we trust that it will find his approval.

We wish to thank our distinguished contributors for their readiness to work with us. Our thanks are due also to Mr. William Savage of the publishing house of Scribners for his never-failing support.

M. Searle Bates
Wilhelm Pauck

October 10, 1963.

Contents

Dedication

Preface
    M. SEARLE BATES & WILHELM PAUCK   7

1   *Great Britain*
    DANIEL JENKINS   13

2   *Western Europe*
    STEPHEN CHARLES NEILL   29

3   *The Soviet Union*
    DONALD A. LOWRIE   51

4   *Other States of Eastern Europe*
    CHARLES C. WEST   65

5   *The Near East*
    CHARLES HABIB MALIK   83

6   *Africa, Part 1*
    CHRISTIAN G. BAËTA   105

7   *Africa, Part 2*
    P. ALLEN MYRICK   119

8   *North America, Part 1*
    TRUMAN B. DOUGLASS   135

9   *North America, Part 2*
     Robert T. Handy   147

10   *Latin America*
     José Míguez Bonino   165

11   *Australia*
     Hayden McCallum   183

12   *Japan*
     Masao Takenaka   195

13   *China*
     M. Searle Bates   211

14   *India*
     David Gnanapragasam Moses   227

15   *Indonesia*
     Alan C. Thomson   245

16   *South East Asia*
     John R. Fleming   259

     Index   281

✠ ✠ ✠ I ✠ ✠ ✠

Great Britain

DANIEL JENKINS

DANIEL JENKINS

Daniel Jenkins, Congregationalist, is now Chaplain of the University of Sussex. In a long career as preacher, teacher, and author, mainly in Britain though partly in the United States, he has concerned himself deeply in the relation of the Churches to contemporary society and in the consultations of Churches with each other. He served on the Board of the Ecumenical Institute at Bossey, and in various Conferences on Faith and Order. As Secretary of the Christian Frontier Council, Dr. Jenkins has been heavily engaged in a study of modern education in England. Widely known for his earlier books, THE STRANGENESS OF THE CHURCH and THE PROTESTANT MINISTRY, he has recently published EQUALITY AND EXCELLENCE: A CHRISTIAN COMMENT ON BRITAIN'S LIFE, and BEYOND RELIGION: THE TRUTH AND ERROR IN 'RELIGIONLESS CHRISTIANITY'.

I

It is only very recently indeed that a relatively objective study of religious attitudes and institutions in the setting of the rest of society in Britain has begun, although, of course, these have always been the subject of lively interest in works of fiction and in journalism. An interesting series of studies of Welsh life in which religious institutions play a prominent part has recently appeared[1] and there is a full chapter on religious life in Margaret Stacey's book on Banbury,[2] while Norman Birnbaum and Bryan Wilson, both now at Oxford, have started making the study of religious institutions from the inside a major object of their professional concern. Dr. John Highet has begun studies of the Scottish Churches[3] and a few small-scale surveys have been produced of English church life, although on nothing like the same scale as for America. But, for the most part, we still have to rely in this field on history, church statistics, and ordinary observation rather than on the findings of systematic sociological enquiry.

This is the more regrettable because the religious situation in Britain is a peculiarly complex one, which can be easily misunderstood. We often speak of the proliferation of religious groups in the United States as strange, but the situation in Britain as a whole is not very different. Religious organisation in

[1] Notably, *Welsh Rural Communities* (Cardiff, 1960).
[2] *Tradition and Change* (London and New York, 1960).
[3] The latest is *The Scottish Churches* (London, 1960).

Britain is certainly predominantly Christian, with the Jews as the only considerable non-Christian minority, although the Muslims are growing, but among Christian bodies the variations between different parts of the country are considerable. We all know this in a general sense, but popular conceptions of the British way of life are so dominated by those of the London-centered English upper classes, who have long been accustomed to overlook what does not fit in with their ideas of that way of life, that it often fails to register in our minds. In this matter, more than most, we shall need to remember that the West End of London and rural England are not the whole of Britain.

II

This is not to deny, of course, that the largest and most imposing religious organisation in Britain remains the Church of England, the Established Church of England, although no longer of Wales. Between 60 and 70 per cent of the English population has been baptised into the Church of England. When Free Church and Roman Catholic baptisms are taken into account and when the entirely voluntary nature of baptism, as far as parents are concerned, is borne in mind, it seems clear that the vast majority of the people of this country still wish to retain at least a minimal connection with the Christian community. This is confirmed by other indications, such as the discovery of a survey in Banbury that only 3 per cent of those interviewed did not consider themselves Christians. Baptism alone, however, especially as it is understood by many of those who bring their children for baptism, is a far from adequate criterion of effective participation in church life and, as we all know, the numbers of those who do participate are much smaller. Only 26 per cent or so of Anglicans go on to confirmation and, it has been roughly estimated, only 9 per cent remain as regular churchgoers. The number of Easter communicants is normally taken as the best guide to the number of practising

Anglicans and in recent years it has hovered around and now slightly exceeds the 2¼ million mark.

This last figure provides the best basis of comparison, although it is far from perfect, with the strength of the second largest group of churches in England—the Free Churches, which are independent of the State and of the Church of England. By far the largest is the Methodist Church, followed by the Congregationalists, the Baptists, the Presbyterians, the Quakers, and the Unitarians. The Methodist Church has 720,000 members; the Congregationalists and Baptists have approximately 200,000 each in England but over 100,000 more each in Welsh-speaking Wales; the English—as distinct from the Scots and Welsh—Presbyterians about 80,000; the Quakers and Unitarians are very much smaller, although the former have an influence greater than their numbers would suggest.

A precise comparison of the strength of these Churches with that of the Church of England is not easy. Membership in them normally implies a more sustained commitment than Easter Communion in the Church of England, although the difference is not as great as it was. Most of them admit to full membership at a later age than the Church of England, although they have very large Sunday schools attached to them. They also often have quite faithful adherents who are not members. Again, as a very rough guide, I should say that in terms of active church members the relative strengths of the Church of England and the Free Churches as a whole should be thought of in the proportion of 3 to 2. Two more general considerations need to be borne in mind, however. One is that the diffused influence of the Church of England is far greater. It touches more people at more points than the Free Churches. It has more clergy, more chaplaincies, and closer official connections with the world of education. It also possesses the cathedrals and ancient parish churches which are Britain's chief architectural heritage and has an elusive but real measure of identification with the dominant national consciousness. In most parts of England, it is the Church

of England from which the average Englishman stays away, except for baptisms, marriages, and funerals, when it is to the
Church of England alone that he naturally goes. The other consideration is that this is a peculiarly English phenomenon. We
shall see that the situation is very different in the rest of Britain.
It is not so often realised in England that it is also very different
in most other parts of the English-speaking world. The Anglican
Church is only one of the great popular Churches of the United
States and the British Commonwealth; and it is often far from
being the strongest. The fact that largest denominations in terms
of active church members in the English-speaking world are the
Methodist and Baptist, closely followed by the Presbyterian,
is likely to become increasingly important even in our domestic
life in England as the world draws closer together. Already I
have noticed with interest that the most fashionable church for
weddings in London among diplomats of the new African states
is Hinde Street Methodist Church.

   To turn now to the other parts of Britain, the differences of
religious organisation we observe there are of great cultural
significance, especially as religious organisations play a larger
role in the life of the community than they normally do in
England. The Established Church of Scotland, with its freedom
from State interference in its internal affairs jealously safe-
guarded, is Presbyterian. With well over a million adult
communicant members in a country with a population barely
one-tenth of that of England, it is a national church in a way the
Church of England can no longer claim to be. In the absence
of a Scottish Parliament, the General Assembly of the Church
speaks for the nation in a way quite foreign to the Church Assembly of the Church of England and evokes a popular loyalty
which is not always specifically religious.

   The Roman Catholic Church is easily the second strongest
church in Scotland, with its main concentration on Clydeside.
The Churches which are strong in England have sizeable groups
in Scotland but they are minute compared to the Church of

Scotland and the Roman Catholics. There are intense, and very vocal, dissident Presbyterian groups also, chiefly active in the Highlands and Islands, of whom the "Wee Frees," the Free Church of Scotland, is the best known. These produce a fascinating subculture of their own, which should not be confused with that of the Established Kirk of Scotland. Scotland in general has a far higher level of active church participation than England. Dr. Highet estimates that 2 out of 3 adults have some real church association.

In Wales the situation is different again. Wales has been incorporated with England at least since Tudor times and this carried with it the Anglican Church establishment. The Welsh people underwent a religious rebirth through the Methodist and later movements of the eighteenth and nineteenth centuries. These welded the ordinary people together into communities who used the Welsh language as their mode of expression and who developed the characteristic modern Welsh consciousness in close relation both to the language and to their religious life. Nearly everyone except the Anglicised gentry and their retainers and some of the middle classes in the towns joined one of the Nonconformist bodies, of whom slightly the largest was Methodism in its Calvinist form, which later naturally evolved into Presbyterianism, closely followed by the Independents or Congregationalists and the Baptists. These bodies transplanted themselves with extraordinary success from rural Wales into the industrial areas with the development of the Industrial Revolution, showing rather less success in the larger towns. They were so much the churches of the Welsh people that the disestablishment of the Church of England took place in the first quarter of this century. The Church of England in Wales is now a separate Province of the Anglican Communion, with a strength roughly equal to the Presbyterian Church. The decline of church life from the exceptionally high level of participation in the last century is very marked in Wales, but the level remains much higher than in most parts of England.

Northern Ireland also presents us with a radically different picture. The country is almost evenly divided between Protestants and Catholics and few dare stand outside or between the two camps. This is largely because the religious issue has become inextricably bound up with political and cultural issues to a far greater extent than anywhere else in Britain. The Protestants are made up chiefly of Anglicans and Presbyterians, with a sizeable Methodist group and a lively subculture of small Protestant sectarian groups in Belfast. A few patient and devoted people are now trying to sort out religious, political, and economic issues from each other and to call upon the resources of a common faith to provide a basis for reconciliation.

It is appropriate to say something here about the Roman Catholic community in Britain as a whole. For a long time, Roman Catholicism has lain on the margin of British life and its main strength has been in Ireland, and elsewhere among Irish immigrants. Thus in Great Britain, Liverpool and Glasgow have been pre-eminently the places where the Catholic community is a prominent element in the local life, as becomes manifest when the Celtics play the Rangers at soccer in Glasgow. Nowadays, however, the pattern is altering. Immigration from Ireland continues but, with the shortage of labour, it is spread much more evenly throughout the country, and there has also been large Catholic immigration from continental Europe. This immigration must be the largest single factor in the great increase in the size of the Roman Catholic community since the war, although the Church's educational policy and her teaching about marriage and the family have also obviously played their part. It is now claimed that the Roman Catholic population in England and Wales is 3½ million, although it must be remembered that this includes all baptised Catholics. This means a good deal more than the comparable figure for Anglican baptisms but it is doubtful whether it means anything like as much as the figures given for active church membership of Anglican and Free Churches. What is certain, however, is that, whatever *religious* weight we give to this figure, a Catholic population of this size in Britain is a new factor of considerable social and political interest.

The one other group of Churches which must be mentioned, however briefly, is that of the smaller Protestant sects. These vary greatly both in size and in character. They range from prosperous middle-class Christian Scientists to small groups of earnest Pentecostalists in back streets. Many of the West Indian and African immigrants are Pentecostalists, although their Pentecostalism is very much their own. These sectarian groups add up to a substantial and probably growing part of the religious community, although it is hard to find reliable figures. The Salvation Army is now so well established that it probably has far more in common with the regular Free Churches than with most of these groups.

It will be clear from all this that there is a great deal of religious diversity as between the different countries or large regions of Britain. Even within these, however, there are important variations. It is true that we can make certain broad generalisations. Anglicanism is stronger in the English countryside and its market towns than it is in manufacturing towns and industrial regions. Free Churches have had a great influence in forming the cultural pattern and social attitudes in the industrial North and Midlands. Yet these generalisations are misleading unless we realise that they often require substantial qualification. Thus, Methodist influence—as you can tell by the size of the Liberal and Labour Vote—is very strong in rural Lincolnshire, Norfolk, and especially Cornwall. Some industrial areas, Durham as compared with southeastern Lancashire, for example, are much more Nonconformist than others and even in industrial towns with strong Free Churches, the largest churches are still likely to be Anglican. As we shall see in more detail later, the level of church attendance and participation varies greatly from one type of neighbourhood to another. The rule is, therefore, always to check for local variations before applying generalisations about religious allegiance to particular situations.

III

That religious institutions have had an enormous influence
upon the general shape of British common life in the past is
obvious. What their present impact is, is much harder to determine, partly because of their very familiarity and ordinariness
to most of us, partly because it is not easy to detect processes of
growth and decay while they are happening in the inevitably
slow-moving realm of people's deepest convictions, and partly
because one's evaluations inevitably depend to some extent on
one's personal attitude towards these convictions.

The most commonly accepted notion about the religious institutions of modern Britain is that, with the possible exception
of the Roman Catholic Church, they are in a period of decline.
That a large measure of decline has taken place over the period
of the last fifty years or more is incontestable, but I also think
that its nature has frequently been misunderstood and that wrong
conclusions for their present situation and future prospects are
often drawn from it.

Rowntree and Lavers in their book on *English Life and
Leisure*[4] mention surveys of churchgoing in York on similar
Sundays of the years 1901, 1935, and 1948. The broad conclusion
was that 35 per cent had attended church on the first occasion,
17 per cent on the second, and 13 per cent on the third. This
confirms the general impression that, whereas in the memory of
many people still living, churches flourished, now they frequently languish. There are, however, several considerations
which lead to a modification of this impression.

The first is that, from some points of view, the older percentage is more significant than the newer ones. I find it very
striking that in the period of post-Victorian church prosperity,
in a church-dominated city like York, only 35 per cent of the
population was in church. We can have a pretty clear idea of

[4] London, 1951.

who the majority of the absentees were. They were the urban poor. Charles Booth in his great *Survey of London Life and Labour* published near the turn of the century[5] made an exhaustive and still unrivalled analysis of the churches of every neighbourhood of London in their social context and underlined the fact that large sections of the poorer parts of the community were not to be found in the churches, although it was true—as it still is—that many of them had some contact with the churches through a church-staffed organisation. It can be said broadly that the larger the town, the more likely is this to be true, unless the large town happens to have sizeable Roman Catholic population of Irish descent.

When this is seen, the situation ceases to look like that of the mass turning-away from the churches which is often pictured, but becomes more like one in which, over a couple of generations, the churchgoing minority of the population has both failed to make headway in influencing the majority and lost heavily from among its own membership.

I want to suggest that when certain other factors are taken into account, the extent of this loss, although substantial enough in all conscience, does not appear to be quite as great as is sometimes supposed. One of the chief reasons for the relative prosperity of religious institutions in Victorian times was that—as in America today where an even greater prosperity is visible—they fulfilled a clearly defined social need in communities with a rising standard of living and growing expectations from life, communities which also still retained along with these a large measure of stability and coherence. It was this which helped to make the second half of the nineteenth century, especially among the Free Churches, a greater period of *institutional* prosperity than the first, despite the immensely powerful influence of the Methodist and Evangelical revivals in the earlier period. The First World War represents the decisive break with the social situation which made this institutional prosperity possible. A whole generation

[5] London, various editions 1889 to 1902.

was uprooted from its accustomed way of life. It lost its bearings and many of its members failed to find them again, not merely in relation to religion but also to many other matters. The difficulty was intensified by the Depression and, to a much lesser extent, by the coming of the Second World War in almost the same generation. It was in the 1920s, running into the early 1930s, that the Churches reached their lowest point. After that, the story begins to be one of slow revival, although this in its turn is complicated by the upheaval of the Second World War. The statistics partly conceal this fact because, with institutions to which most people bear a lifelong allegiance, it takes a very long time for either decline or renewal to become statistically visible in any striking way. But it was in the 1920s that theology became most confused and the Churches sounded their most uncertain notes. The Churches survived the Second World War much more effectively than the First; and although the social upheaval created by the war meant a further diminution in membership, the fifties have seen the beginning of a slight rise in institutional strength. It is probable that surveys made in 1958 would show a small increase in church attendance as compared with 1948.

This rise is the more impressive, small though it is, when it is borne in mind that in this period Churches, like other deep-rooted institutions, have had to contend with extraordinarily rapid social changes. If you were to ask me for the chief reasons for the decline in church attendance as compared with the pre-1914 world, I do not think I should put changes in intellectual climate first. Such changes have certainly taken place, but they have not all been negative from the Christian point of view. It is an illusion that men have ever found it easy to believe, although social convention has made formal religious profession much easier in some circumstances than in others. I think the chief reasons for the *institutional* decline of churches have been the movement of population and the decline of settled communities in which churches were strong, and the advent of the private motor car and of popular leisure-time distractions, of which the latest and most powerful is television. Church allegiance is a deeply personal thing, closely linked with family loyalty and the pattern of life of particular neighbourhoods. It requires not only strong conviction but a considerable measure of social confidence to enable people to form new church connections in new and unfamiliar places. When middle-class people move from one suburb to another, they often manage to do this. Simpler people are apt to find it much more difficult and retreat into their family circle and into anonymous weekend distractions like driving cars or, most tempting of all to the person in a strange environment, watching television. A survey of what happened to Welsh people who have moved into the Birmingham area showed that, whereas 60 per cent of them had had church connections in their Welsh homes, only 3 per cent formed them with the Welsh-speaking congregations in the Birmingham area. These statistics are misleading: many people probably had gone to English churches because the Welsh churches were few and inaccessible, but undoubtedly the drop was very great. I am sure that this kind of wastage has taken place all over the country. It is only slowly, and often only through their children, that many of these people come back into churches.

The result of this uprooting and these distractions is to make the British, and particularly the English, to be very bad joiners. They may not go to church much, but where else do they go? They certainly do not go to political meetings. Politicians in these days speak with awe of the size of the audiences at religious gatherings as compared with political ones. I do not derive much comfort from this about the state of England but it suggests that what is most impressive about the Churches is not that they are weaker than they were but the extent to which they have resisted the general decline of institutional life.

This suggestion is reinforced by two other considerations, one more familiar than the other. The first is that along with the relative decline in the traditional forms of religious life there has gone a marked increase of religious activity in other

ways. All-embracing communal institutions have a difficult time
at present but specialised ones often flourish, and in these specialised institutions religious influences have become more
marked. This is true in the world of education but it is also true
of industry and the professions, and the influence is often of a
predominantly lay character. Well-known clergymen find themselves embarrassed in these days by the number of invitations
they have not merely to speak in schools and colleges but also
to preach at the official service of, for example, the Institute of
Personnel Managers or the Commercial Travellers' Association.
Religious broadcasts have large listening figures and the number
of religious books certainly does not diminish. The proportion of
actively committed Christians in public life as distinct from conventional churchgoers seems to be as large as it has been for a
long time.

The other consideration is that churches are at their most
successful today in the newest and most characteristic parts of
modern society. Dr. Gibson Winter in his book *The Surburban
Captivity of the Churches*[6] points out how churches—he speaks
primarily of America but it applies to Britain also—flourish in
the suburbs but neglect the metropolis and the inner city. He
is right to insist that a purely suburban ministry is dangerously
inadequate, but it is important not to minimise the significance
of the churches' suburban prosperity. If anything is certain, it
is that with growing prosperity more and more people are going
to lead a suburbanlike existence, even in renovated areas of the
inner city. If churches prosper most in such places, they are
not likely to continue to decline all along the line in the next
generation.

IV

What can be said about the future of the British Churches?
Anything said must be qualified by the recognition that there
may be a sudden and unforeseeable alteration in the spiritual

[6] Garden City, N.Y., 1961.

climate which will upset all our calculations. But given peaceful development along present lines, perhaps we can say these things.

First, unless new factors do enter the situation, the institutional decline of the Churches in those older neighbourhoods of Britain which are themselves declining will continue. Most rural areas and many parts of South Wales and the industrial North show evidence of this decline. Some of these places have in the past been among the best seed-beds of intellectual and spiritual vitality in this country and we shall have to think hard about how they can be revivified and about what can take their place.

Secondly, we can now look forward with some confidence to a period in which major realignments will take place among the Churches. In particular, many long-estranged denominations will be reunited or enter into much closer relations. The old Anglican-Free Church, Cavalier-Roundhead division in English life will not disappear—nothing ever does in England—but it will be overcome in very large and significant areas and a division which has poisoned and bedevilled English life for many long generations will be removed. When this happens, it will have beneficial effects throughout not only the whole of Great Britain but also of the English-speaking world.

Third, it has been suggested by more than one perceptive observer that we may be on the eve of a period of renewed religious institutional prosperity. This suggestion is made on analogy with American experience, where church membership is a concomitant of rising standards of living and of education. To put the argument in purely sociological terms, churchgoing is largely a middle-class habit. As the community becomes more and more middle-class in outlook, it is not likely that churchgoing should increase? I think that to argue thus is over-simple, especially as in England large sections of the middle-classes no longer go to church. But in some places it may very well happen. Already there are signs of its beginning to happen in those ever growing suburban areas where moderately prosperous younger people with growing families are concentrated.

Fourth, and finally, even if this renewed institutional prosperity comes, it will not do a very great deal to alter the shape of British life in the years ahead unless it moves out from the family circle and leisure-hours occupation into the places where public decisions have to be taken. The weakness of modern English life has been its undue concentration on the domestic virtues and its too limited view of the possibilities which modern technology can provide for the fresh development of communal life. I should be the last to deny the importance of the domestic virtues and it may be a necessary stage in community development that so many previously poor people should discover a pride in their homes and their families. But I am alarmed that so few of those who have the resources and opportunity to take an active part in public affairs do so. Our Churches have shared too long in this backward-looking cosiness. In our own time, the ecumenical movement has called them out of this attitude to serve the wider world, in the same way that the missionary movement, the greatest glory of nineteenth-century England, did in previous generations. The Churches of Britain are showing signs of responding to this call. The great question before them is one which confronts us in so many parts of our life in Britain: will they do too little and do it too late?

✦✦✦ II ✦✦✦

Western Europe

STEPHEN CHARLES NEILL

STEPHEN CHARLES NEILL

The Right Reverend Stephen Charles Neill is, since 1962, Professor of Missions and Ecumenical Theology in the University of Hamburg. He served as a missionary in India 1924-45 and was Bishop of Tinnevelly in the last six years of that period. Assistant Bishop to the Archbishop of Canterbury 1947-50, he was also Associate General Secretary of the World Council of Churches 1948-51. Bishop Neill was General Editor for ten years of that unique series from which translations have been made into a wide range of languages: WORLD CHRISTIAN BOOKS. Holder of frequent lectureships and visiting professorships, Bishop Neill has written THE CHRISTIAN SOCIETY, THE UNFINISHED TASK, and many other books. He was joint editor, with Ruth Rouse, of the official HISTORY OF THE ECUMENICAL MOVEMENT 1517-1948; and, with H.-R. Weber, of THE LAYMAN IN CHRISTIAN HISTORY. Bishop Neill is editor of a third volume of ecumenical import, TWENTIETH CENTURY CHRISTIANITY.

II

Viewed from either Russia or the United States of America, Western Europe presents itself as a unity. And indeed there is much to be said for this judgment. The whole of Western Europe has been profoundly influenced by the Christian tradition in all its complexity, deriving as it does from the Hebrew experience with its vivid sense of the unseen and of the significance of the divine dimension in relation to all human experience, from the Greek with its restless curiosity in regard to both man and the world in which man dwells and its unfailing sense of proportion, from the Roman order with its stress on the rule of law and the place of justice in all human affairs. The visitor from another world of culture, such as that of Islam or of Hinduism, finds himself confronted in every part of Western Europe with the same basic structure of society and with essentially the same understanding of the meaning of human life.

Yet the moment we begin to consider Western Europe from within, we become aware of strange variety. Political organisation is most diverse. Of the countries of Western Europe, seven are limited and constitutional monarchies: the United Kingdom, Norway, Sweden, Denmark, the Netherlands, Belgium, Luxembourg; two are uncomprising dictatorships: Spain and Portugal; one is a republic verging on dictatorship: France; seven are republics deriving in greater or less degree from the principles of the French Revolution: Italy, Switzerland, Austria, Finland, Iceland, Ireland, Western Germany. Almost all these countries have in some measure maintained the medieval tradition of association between Church and State; they wish to be regarded as in some sense Christian countries. Spain is probably the nearest of all the countries of the Christian world to a theocracy, in which the Church is a determining factor in the whole life of the State. Elsewhere the association varies from the State Churches of Scandinavia through the national Church of England to the comparatively free association which exists in some of the cantons of Switzerland. But within varying degree the principle of religious liberty has been slowly accepted in all these countries, and other Christian Churches and the adherents of non-Christian faiths have the right to the free exercise of their religion.

Where the varieties are so great, the difficulties in the way of brief delineation are considerable. But there is one deep and apparently irreducible division which must be reckoned with at the outset—that between the countries with a large Roman Catholic majority and the countries of the Protestant world. With the Peace of Westphalia in 1648 and the end of the creative periods of the Reformation and the Counter-Reformation, the lines of division were laid down and they have hardly changed in more than three centuries. The Netherlands is the only country in which the ancient balance has been seriously disturbed by a steady increase in the proportion of Roman Catholics as against Protestants. In Great Britain the percentage of Roman Catholics is a good deal higher than it was a century ago (now perhaps 7 per cent of the whole); but this is due much more to the steady streams of immigration from Ireland, and at an earlier date from Poland, than to accessions by way of "conversion" from other forms of the Christian religion. Rather more people seem to leave the Roman Catholic Church than join it from other confessions. In Western Germany, the influx of about ten millon refugees from eastern regions has resulted in a new and interesting mixture of populations in areas where earlier only one of the great confessions was represented, but without seriously affecting the total number of adherents of one or the other. In Switzerland, the progress of industrialisation has led to the growth of considerable Protestant communities in what were traditionally Roman Catholic cantons; and the influx of Roman Catholics into Geneva has led Protestants to view with some anxiety the future of the city of Calvin as a bulwark of the Protestant form of the Christian faith. But the general balance between the confessions in the country as a whole has hardly been affected.

This being so, it will be convenient to allow this major distinction between the confessions to form also the major division in our survey.

I

Few things in the history of the modern world are more remarkable than the astonishing vitality displayed by the Roman Catholic Church. Its nadir was reached, perhaps, during the Napoleonic wars. At that time a number of intelligent observers concluded that it need no longer be taken seriously as a factor in human history. Such predictions were quickly falsified by events. A notable series of Popes over more than a century have won back for their Church esteem and influence in every corner of the world. Who would have supposed that, on the election of a new Pope in 1963, one of the first to hasten to send a message of congratulation would be the head of a Communist state?

Outsiders are always impressed by the "monolithic unity" of the Roman Church; and it does indeed derive great advantages from the centralisation of its affairs in Rome, and from the increasing control that the head is able to exercise on every part of the body. In point of fact, however, even within the Roman Church account has to be taken of differences which are no less remarkable for remaining most of the time unseen. The early sessions of the Second Vatican Council (1962) revealed in startling fashion the divergence between the more conservative and the more liberal elements in the Roman Catholic world.

South of the Alps, in Italy and in Spain, the Roman Catholic Church enjoys almost a monopoly. Ireland, traditionally the island of the saints, is in a similar situation. In these countries the Church is extremely conservative and traditional. The medieval ideal of a docile people, obedient to their priests and not asking too many questions, seems still to prevail. Education is largely in the hands of the Church; its influence penetrates to every corner of the life of the country.

In this situation it is difficult for the principles of religious liberty to assert themselves effectively and to be recognised. Spain has had a particularly bad reputation in this matter; it is hardly possible to speak of a persecution of Protestants; yet discrimination against them has been the rule, and life for a Spanish Protestant has in many ways been extremely hard.

Happily the situation seems to be changing for the better. Ireland has an impeccable tradition; and, though there may occasionally have been cases of anti-Protestant prejudice, the government throughout the forty years of independence has shown itself a most scrupulous guardian of the liberty and rights of all its citizens. The day before these lines were written news was received from Spain of the opening of several Protestant churches which had been closed for some years. A number of Spanish Roman Catholic leaders have in recent years demanded in the name of liberty better conditions for the Protestant fellow citizens, of whose principles they do not approve, but whose right to exist they do not wish to deny. In Italy, religious liberty was firmly written into the constitution which came into force after the end of the second World War; there was a danger that this might remain a dead letter. The Supreme Court of the country has, however, made it clear by a number of decisions that the constitution means what it says.

The outward prosperity of the Church in these countries is very great. It may be doubted, however, whether the appearance and the reality correspond. Italy, the central home of the Roman Catholic Church, has a far larger Communist minority than any other country in Western Europe, and in the last election the Communists increased their votes by more than a million. What does this mean? In Spain, any criticism of the regime or of the Church is dangerous; but it seems more than likely that the bitter hostility to the Church, which during the Civil War found expression in the destruction of churches and the assassination of priests and nuns, still exists not far below the surface. There are many indications that these countries are now beginning to face the problems which smote the churches north of the Alps with such force a century ago. All the statistics seem to show that in Roman Catholic countries, as in all others, church attendance varies inversely with the progress of industrialisation. In the villages the sway of the Church is almost uncontested; in the great conurbations of the industrial world the working man of the modern age seems even in the first generation to disappear from the Church. This is a problem for which none of us as yet has found a solution.

Once we pass to the countries north of the Alps, we encounter an entirely different situation. The Roman Catholic Church is face to face with a strong and vigorous Protestant minority; it cannot remain untouched by its surroundings. In France, Belgium, the Netherlands, and to some extent in Germany, we encounter a much more liberal kind of Roman Catholicism, which is not content merely to repeat the formulae arrived at centuries ago, is keenly interested in the modern world, and is eager to enter into contact with it. The complex and flexible movement of renewal may, for the purposes of a brief survey, be considered under four heads:

1. The movement of biblical theology is a growing power in the Roman Church. The modernist movement of the early years of this century produced a crisis which was met with stern measures of repression and condemnation. In this period of uncertainty Roman Catholic scholars hardly ventured to express themselves on any theological problem, and tended to concentrate on such safer but marginal fields as biblical archaeology.

A notable easing of this tense situation came with the publication of of the "liberating Encyclical," *Divino Afflante Spiritu* (1942); this wise utterance of Pius XII stressed once again the authority of the Scriptures as divine revelation, but encouraged scholars to go forward in the spirit of reverent enquiry to a new understanding of their meaning. Naturally Roman scholars must turn for help to the works of their non-Roman colleagues; the Society for Old Testament Study is one of the fields in which cooperation between the learned men of all confessions has been most happily worked out.

One of the results of this biblical movement has been the appearance of translations of the Bible into various European languages. The so-called Jerusalem translation into French has won widespread acclamation both for the excellence of its scholarship and for the purity of its French style. Through such work interest in the Bible has spread far beyond the ranks of the clergy; for a parallel to this rediscovery of the Scriptures by the laity it would perhaps be necessary to go back to the sixteenth century and to the days of the Reformation. It is hard to set limits to the effects that this biblical renewal may have on the life and the thought of the Roman Catholic Church.

2. A number of teachers have been turning away from the old scholastic methods in both dogmatic and moral theology, and asking whether theological formulations do not need to be radically redrawn to meet the needs of the modern world. Professor Aubert of Louvain has written amusingly of "those who were troubled to find moral theology reduced to a series of Byzantine discussions as to the best method of dodging the regulations of the Church without positively breaking the rules" and of the help troubled minds have received from the work of such scholars as Bernhard Häring, who in his book *Das Gesetz Christi* (The Law of Christ, 1954 ff.) has tried to relate Christian ethics at every point to the actual situation of man in his world and in his daily life.[1] It is true that Pope Pius XII in the Encyclical

[1] R. Aubert, in S. C. Neill, ed., *Twentieth Century Christianity* (Garden City, N.Y., 1963), p. 87.

Humani Generis uttered grave warnings against the dangers of too great or too rapid a departure from the traditional lines of thought and teaching; but such words of caution are often intended rather to control than to inhibit new movements of thought within the Church.

3. The Liturgical Movement is perhaps more widely known and in the end more influential than any of the other movements of renewal. A young Belgian Dominican Dom Lambert Beauduin became convinced, rather more than fifty years ago, that it was both the right and the duty of the laity to participate intelligently in the liturgy. By means of booklets, distributed each Sunday at the door of the church, containing the text of the Mass for the day in French with brief explanations, he began a campaign of education, the results of which were so sensationally successful that imitation followed in almost every country in the world. No permission has yet been given for the celebration of the Mass in a modern vernacular.[2] But in Germany and France, it is a common thing today for the entire Mass, with the exception of those prayers that are said secretly, to be repeated audibly in French or German from the pulpit while the celebrant is saying the Latin Mass at the altar.

Liturgical reform is one of the central issues at the Second Vatican Council. Bishops who had never left Europe were astonished at the strength of the feeling of many missionary bishops on this subject. It is impossible to say at the time of writing whether any breach will be made in the entrenched fortress of Latin as the liturgical language of the West; but history suggests that, when a movement has grown strong enough on the periphery, Rome at the centre will in the end yield to the desires of the faithful.

4. Lay movements of every kind are characteristic of life in the Roman Catholic Church today. In earlier times the distinction between the teaching Church and the learning Church, be-

[2] This sentence and the next three were written months before the promulgation (December, 1963) of a papal constitution authorizing the use of living languages for the administration of the sacraments and for portions of the Mass.

tween the priest in whose hands all authority was concentrated and the layman whose only business was to listen and to obey, was very strongly marked. This distinction is still made. But much recent Roman Catholic theological writing has endeavoured to interpret the specifically priestly ministry within the context of a body which itself and as a whole is priestly.

There has been a tendency for the clergy to regard lay movements simply as docile auxiliaries to the work of the priesthood, to be kept strictly under clerical control. The official recognition by the Vatican of lay movements, which found expression in the first World Congress for the Apostolate of the Laity held in Rome in 1951, was certainly of value. But it made plain the danger that official approval might in fact stifle the spontaneity on which lay movements depend for their life.

By reaction against this danger of clericalisation a number of Roman Catholic laymen have felt that their best service could be rendered not within such movements but in a more adventurous going out from the Church to meet the world where it is and to find the sphere of their apostolate precisely in their place of business or of professional activity. The parallel to the Protestant understanding of lay activity in the world will immediately be observed. In several countries, Roman Catholic lay activity has found expression in the formation of specific political parties; that this has its dangers is evident to a number of Roman Catholic thinkers. If the Church is identified with one political group, opposition to that political group and its policies must inevitably appear to be opposition also to the Church.

The development of a new ecumenical sense in the Roman Catholic Church is worldwide. Yet it will hardly be denied that Western Europe has taken the lead in Roman Catholic ecumenical development. Among Roman Catholic writers who have taken up a notably ecumenical position, the mind turns at once to the Belgian Gustave Thils, to the Frenchmen Yves Congar and Maurice Villain, to the German Father T. A. Sartory, and in recent times especially to the Tübingen theologian Hans

Küng, whose writing on the Vatican Council and related themes has created such excitement both inside the Roman Communion and beyond it. The fruit of the work of those who have laboured patiently over many years, sometimes in the face of considerable official opposition, has been seen in the strength of the liberal wing at the Council, a strength apparently far greater than had been foreseen by those in whose hands lay responsibility for the organisation of the Council. Since the writing of this chapter began, a new Pope has been elected. Paul VI has declared that a major part of his work will be the carrying to completion of the plans made by his predecessor for the Council; this means that he is committed to the great task of adapting the Roman Catholic Church to the claims of the modern world, of which the Council is one expression, but an expression which has drawn to itself the eyes of the whole world.

II

When we turn from the Roman Catholic world to the mainly Protestant countries of Europe, the answers to all questions must be hesitant and in part negative. Industrialisation came early to this part of the world, and with it all the dark and difficult questionings arising from the developments of modern science and from the materialistic explanation of the world and all things in it. A number of observers have reached the conclusion that the Christian faith is gradually and irreversibly disappearing from the northern European scene. We shall not find so pessimistic a conclusion necessary; yet a calm survey of the facts suggests that such a view may arise from honest anxiety rather than from malice.

The situation varies a good deal from country to country. It will therefore be convenient to follow a geographical method of description.

1. *Great Britain.* A good case can be made for holding that the Christian faith is in a bad way in Britain. Statistics of church

attendance show that not more than about 10 per cent of the population is likely to be in church on any given Sunday. There is widespread ignorance of the Christian faith. Recent painful events make it plain that, in influential circles in the country, any idea that Christian principles could influence conduct has long since been ruled out as antiquated and absurd.

Yet this superficial view may not in the end be the right one. In no country in Europe is there more residual Christianity—semiconscious, muddled, inarticulate, but a very real force in the minds of ordinary men and women. Two-thirds of the babies born in England are baptised in the English Church; slightly more than half of the marriages are solemnised by priests of that Church. There is a small section of the population which is anti-Christian by conviction. The majority wishes to remain in some kind of connection with the Church, provided that not too many demands for faith and action are made upon it. The remark of Professor D. W. Brogan, that the Englishman likes the Church of England to be there for him to stay away from, is as true as when he made it twenty years ago. The recent reaction of indignant outrage in the face of scandals in moral and political spheres will no doubt be classed by many as just one more example of the illimitable capacity of the British people for hypocrisy. This would be a sadly facile judgment. There is still a sense that right is right and wrong is wrong, even among them who would not feel themselves bound to live in accordance with the Christian law.

It may well be said that this residual Christianity does not amount to much, and is no guarantee for the survival of the faith. This is true; but it is the background against which certain more encouraging signs have to be considered.

It cannot be said that British theology has been exciting in the last few years. No new writers with the popular appeal of C. S. Lewis and Dorothy Sayers have been discovered. On the academic side, British scholarship continues to produce works of sober, reliable erudition such as the *Commentaries* of Professor C. K. Barrett on the Gospel of John and on the Pastoral Epistles.

Anglican scholarship, as always, is particularly strong on the side
of Patristic study and the history of the Church; the *Lexicon of
Patristic Greek*, now being published after many years of preparation, is a monument of precise and accurate scholarship, than
which nothing more distinguished has appeared in this century.
And when theology does descend from the study into the
market place, it is clear that the public ear is alert and attuned to
anything that it is able to regard as a new and challenging voice.
When the Bishop of Woolwich wrote a book with the title
Honest to God, his publishers printed 6,000 copies. Within a
few months of publication, 280,000 copies had been sold, an all-
time record for a theological publication other than the Scriptures. Certainly many readers of the book are anxious to be
assured that the Christain faith is not true, and hear with enthusiasm that at last this idea is discussed by a Bishop. But
many others turn to the book in the hope that it may enable
them to see how a man can be true to himself and to the convictions which he holds in other spheres of life, and at the same
time continue to be a Christian.

The British Churches have always taken a leading part in
the ecumenical movement. Not unnaturally they have been led
to seek for unity among themselves. A recent attempt to bring
together the Anglican and the Presbyterian Churches was rather
roughly rebuffed by the General Assembly of the Scottish
Church. Negotiations have been renewed but have not so far led
to anything. More impressive was the development in 1962 of a
complete scheme for union between the Church of England and
the Methodist Church. There is naturally much criticism and
some strong opposition; but if this union were to be brought
about, the effects of it would be felt through the whole of the
worldwide Anglican and Methodist Communions.

Plans for unity are not necessarily signs of life. But, though
the general picture in Britain is dark, there are factors in the
situation which may serve as grounds for modest hope for the
future.

There has probably never been a time when religion had a stronger hold on the universities of the land. So many of the leaders in the life of the country come from the universities that what today is only student religion is likely in time to exercise very extensive influence.

The community of Iona in Scotland, with its serious purpose to bridge the gap between the Church and the working-class, has proved an inspiration to many.

Industrial chaplaincies seem to have come to stay in many cities, notably Sheffield, and to provide a place where the Church can enter into living contact with men in their place of work.

The "house church" experiment, the small intimate neighbourhood group, has seemed to many to be the answer to the loneliness and anonymity of life in a great city, and to offer a warmth of fellowship which is often lacking in the larger worshipping group.

The list could be made much longer. None of these experiments has developed into anything like a nationwide movement. Yet singly and together, they make it plain that there is life in the churches, and that British religion is still inventive, self-critical, and ready for new adventures in a changing world.

2. *The Scandinavian Countries.* The situation in Scandinavia is not unlike that in Britain, though alienation from the Church seems to have gone further.

The peculiar feature in these countries is that the Lutheran Church has almost a monopoly of Christian existence in all of them. The strenuous efforts of the Roman Catholic Church to secure a foothold have met with hardly any success at all. Yet these countries have been the scene of revival movements in rather sharp contrast to the traditions of the official Churches. In Norway, the movement associated with the name of Hans Nielsen Hauge has remained within the national Church; but has produced the curious phenomenon of two theological faculties in Oslo, with a far larger number of students in the unofficial than in the official faculty. In Sweden, the various revivals have led to the formation of a number of separate Churches, the Pentecostalists having a considerable following.

The Scandinavian Churches have been State Churches in the full and strict sense of the term. This may have been a strength in the past; probably most Scandinavian churchmen today would feel that the advantages have been outweighed by the drawbacks; a Church which is so completely dependent on the State tends to lose the sense of its nature as Church and to become too tamely dependent on the inheritance from the past. Sweden had retained the Church-State connection in so rigid a form that it was scarcely possible to speak of religious liberty or equality in that country. The legislation of 1953 removed many of the inequalities, gave a greater measure of recognition to religious bodies other than the State Church, and made it possible for citizens to withdraw from the Church without prejudice to their civil status. In point of fact, however, comparatively few availed themselves of the new freedom; the Church remains the Church of the vast majority of the population.

Here we encounter the paradox of the Scandinavian situation: An admirably developed and creative theology (the contribution of Scandinavian theologians to Old Testament study is on the highest level), a strange deep regard for the Christian tradition; and at the same time empty churches, widespread disregard for Christian laws of morality, a high suicide rate despite great prosperity. Almost all young people in the Scandinavian countries undergo careful and thorough preparation for Confirmation, and this corresponds to the wishes of their parents. The majority of young mothers in Sweden, for example, pray with their children. There are few signs, if any, of hostility to the Christian faith. Yet only in the case of a small minority does this rather vague and remote loyalty rise to the level of personal religious conviction or practical action.

3. *Switzerland* presents many of the same features as Scandinavia. The thrifty Swiss, with few natural advantages, have produced a prosperous and orderly, if slightly unadventurous, community. The peaceful co-existence of two races, four official languages and two great religious confessions in a single country is an example to the whole world. With Karl Barth, Emil Brunner and Oscar Cullmann among its teachers, Switzerland has made a contribution to modern Christian thinking out of all proportion to its size. Yet even in the city of John Calvin not more than 5 per cent of the Protestant population will be found in church on a Sunday morning.

"The good Swiss bourgeois believes in some way in the good God; but he doesn't quite know what to do with Jesus Christ." So remarked a very intelligent Swiss to the writer. This seems to be true. And perhaps this sage remark sums up the whole problem of the Protestant world; we have made for ourselves a monistic or unitarian image of God, as one, remote, incomparable; and then we find it impossible to fit Jesus Christ into the image we have made. Religion has been transposed into a vague metaphysic, to which a reduced code of ethics has become attached. It is no more a matter of redemption, of personal devotion, of the quest for holiness, of lively adventure; it is hardly surprising that the busy man of the world finds little to interest him in the Christian faith as he has come to understand it.

4. *France.* France holds the largest Protestant minority to be found in a mainly Roman Catholic country. The long and agitated history of the Huguenots falls outside our scope, but is the unforgettable background of the French Protestant consciousness to day. Two changes in recent times may briefly occupy our attention.

To-day, happily, almost all the Protestants in France, with the exception of the Lutherans who are strong in Alsace-Lorraine, are to be found within a single Reformed Church. After the separation of Church and State in 1905, tension between the conservative and the liberal wings of French Protestantism became so acute that the Church became outwardly and inwardly divided. The recovery of union in France as elsewhere was a slow and difficult business. Here alone, among the many histories of Church union in the twentieth century, the theological issue played the leading part; questions of faith had divided the Reformed Churches, only through an agreement in faith could they come together again. And here alone the development of the Ecumenical Movement directly served the cause of reunion. The first Faith and Order Conference held at Lausanne in 1927 played a decisive part in setting in motion the process which in 1938 led to the union of Methodists and other Free Churches, relatively small, with the two wings of the Reformed Church.

Protestants in France have always been very unevenly distributed. Their great strength has lain in certain comparatively small areas, notably such regions as the Cévennes. The shift in population from the villages to the towns has led to many grave problems. The most promising young people tend to disappear from the old centres, leaving behind an aging population; in the cities to which they move they do not always find their way readily and at once into the Church of their fathers. As elsewhere, the Church feels urgently the need of greater flexibility, yet is not always able to find the method that is appropriate to a new and unfamiliar situation.

Protestants make up not more than 3 per cent of the population of France. Yet through industry, integrity, and a certain international sense, they have acquired more influence in the life of the country than their numbers would suggest. From the beginning, their contribution to the Ecumenical Movement and their faithfulness to its ideals have been beyond praise.

5. *The Netherlands* is a land of paradoxes. A greater proportion of the population than in any other European country declares

itself in the census returns to belong to no religious community
at all. Roman Catholics are now almost as numerous as Protestants. In some areas a chilly liberalism has emptied the
churches. In others, the old solid Calvinist tradition lives on;
for all the austerity of Calvinist worship, the churches are
crowded, and the worshippers listen with every appearance of
attention to long and deeply theological sermons. In the Netherlands alone family worship has survived as self-evidently necessary in every family that makes any claim at all to be regarded
as Christian.

The loss of Indonesia same as a tremendous shock to the
Dutch people, and especially to the Christian section of it,
which had come to regard the evangelisation of Indonesia as the
special task which God had given to the Dutch people. A widespread reconstruction of thought, as well as of economic policies, has now been carried through, and the Dutch churches are
ready to look out on the world with new eyes, and a readiness
to find new answers to new questions.

The many divisions in Dutch Protestantism are a great
source of weakness. As an eminent Dutch lady once remarked
to the writer, "Every Dutchman is a theologian, and every
Dutchman wants to have his own church." Many have suc-
ceeded in attaining to this ideal. Yet in no country in the world
is the ecumenical ideal a more living reality. No two men in
this century have more deeply impressed themselves on the
thought of the Christian world than Dr. W. A. Visser 'tHooft,
General Secretary of the World Council of Churches, and Dr.
Hendrik Kraemer, missionary statesman, church reformer and
apostle of the layman in the Church. It would be possible to
mention a half dozen others who have played notable parts in
the development of the ecumenical movement in its present
form. This spirit has spread to the younger generation; there is
today more friendly exchange between Protestants and Roman
Catholics than perhaps at any time since the Reformation;
young people in the Netherlands seem determined to break
away from the restricting traditions and suspicions of the past.

6. *Western Germany.* In matters of religion, as in all else, Western Germany remains the great question-mark of Europe. Which way will it go, and what influence will it exercise on the life of the rest of the world?

In the years immediately following the war, it seemed that the German Churches might be entering on a great period of renewal. But the initial impulse appears to have died away. The power of tradition in these highly organised Churches is immensely strong; almost all of them seem to have settled down to keep everything exactly as it was in the days of old. No strong prophetic voice is to be heard from the Churches. The great days of Martin Niemöller passed with the period of crisis. Bishop Dibelius of Berlin is old, and no one has come forward to fill his place.

As always, German theology is of the greatest importance to the rest of the world. The crisis arising from Rudolf Bultmann's proposal to demythologise the New Testament has set echoes ringing around the world. Readers in the English-speaking world are beginning to be aware of the movement among the followers of Bultmann to set out on a new quest of the "historical Jesus." Through translations the names of Gerhard Ebeling and of other younger scholars are becoming known. German New Testament scholarship is moving away from the highly negative position maintained by Bultmann; yet it must be regarded as doubtful whether even in its more positive forms this theology can provide a gospel which can be preached with power, and by which the Churches can be renewed.

In one field Germany has given a lead to the Churches of the world. The Evangelical Academies, of which there are now more than a dozen, in a unique way are providing meeting points for the coming together of the Churches and of those who at present stand outside them. Not all are equally effective; but all stand as symbols of the concern of the German Churches to reach out beyond themselves and to make themselves at home in the new and estranged world of the twentieth century.

Since the Reformation, the German Churches as such have taken a very small share in the missionary work of the Church; the work has been done by voluntary missionary societies. This year for the first time the EKD, the Evangelical Church in Germany, is appointing an official committee for missions, to serve as a link between the Churches and the societies, and to express the new sense of responsibility felt by the Churches for this part of the Church's life. Germany should be able to provide a great many more missionaries than it now does, and Germans are acceptable in some parts of the world where others are not. An awakening of missionary enthusiasm would certainly react favourably on the life of the Churches at home.

The prospect for Christianity? Our survey can end only with a kind of yea-and-nay evaluation. It cannot be said that the prospects are bright. An immense amount of ground has been lost. The adversaries of the Church are numerous, vocal and well organised. There are no signs of a great revival of spiritual life; nowhere have the Churches broken through on a broad front into the newly paganised world. There is much perplexity as to how the gospel should be preached, indeed as to whether the Church has a message at all for the man of today. But to present only the dark side would be to falsify the picture. The European Churches all have a long history. There have been dark and lifeless periods in the past, yet again and again the new inspiration has come, and the Church has manifested a strange power of renewal and recovery. In our day there is a great deal of quiet faithfulness and unobtrusive service. The Churches are penitent rather than arrogant. Many thoughtful men and women are asking new questions, and in the attempt to find an answer are being driven back on the basic elements in the gospel. Interest in religion is far from being dead. Some striking experiments and many successes on a small scale light up the general picture of dull mediocrity. Best of all, perhaps, is the openness of mind of the younger generation. Even those who are not convinced that religion has any message for them are prepared to listen and to think; they are more likely to be reached by a quiet and patient appeal to mind and conscience than by the more aggressive methods of evangelism which were so successful in the past. Indeed it is doubtful whether the recovery of faith will come anywhere today through methods of mass evangelism; the peoples of Europe may have to be won back one by one through the quiet testimony of individual believers and of lives in which the likeness of Jesus Christ is unmistakably seen.

✦ ✦ ✦ III ✦ ✦ ✦

The Soviet Union

DONALD A. LOWRIE

DONALD A. LOWRIE

Donald A. Lowrie, member of the Orthodox Theological Academy in Paris, served with the Y.M.C.A. in Russia 1916-20, in Czechoslovakia 1922-30, in Paris with its Russian Department 1933-40; and from 1945 to 1954 was Director of the Y.M.C.A. Press, Paris, devoted to the publication of Russian books. Now retired, he continues to be active in the United States in private and group study of the Russian Church and nation, and in publication of valuable articles and pamphlets in this field. Among his books are to be noted several volumes translated from the works of Berdyaev; and the widely acclaimed biography of that great Russian thinker, REBELLIOUS PROPHET: A LIFE OF NICOLAI BERDYAEV.

III

*F*or nearly a thousand years the empire of the Czars was an officially Christian State. Since 1917 it has been ruled by a government officially and militantly atheist. The extent to which the Communists have now eliminated religion from society and some prognosis of the future of Christianity in the Soviet Union is the subject of this chapter.

Save for two feeble church magazines, all "religious" news coming out of Soviet Russia is intentionally and intensely one-sided. In fact the greatest amount of printed information about religion must be gleaned from between the lines of the extensive atheist literature, books and pamphlets and journals, pouring copiously from the Soviet press. Visitors to the Soviet Union, usually guided, receive only stereotyped answers to questions asked of church people, and Russian visitors to the West are equally tight-lipped. In both cases, tactful inquirers know better than to press questions too far. News of Christianity in Russia is like news of a city under siege.

To be sure, tourists in the Soviet Union may learn some facts from simple observation: crowded churches, the number of young people in the congregations, church buildings transformed into offices, storerooms, or cinemas. But no statistics are obtainable in this fashion. The only over-all census of the Soviet Union that included a question about religion, revealed such a percentage of believers in God that it was never published.

For obvious reasons, Christian Churches do not maintain an exact count, but the consensus of Orthodox and Protestant opinion is that in the Soviet Union there are today more than forty million active church members. In the order of size, they are the Russian Orthodox, the Armenian Orthodox, the Roman Catholics, the Lutherans, "the Evangelical Christian Baptists," the Reformed, and the Adventists. All these are officially recognized by Soviet law. Besides, there are minute but often "fanatically" active groups like Jehovah's Witnesses and certain Pentecostalists. The Russian Orthodox form at least eight-tenths of the total; therefore we often speak of the Orthodox as "the Church." What happens with them is typical for all.

Under the Czars, the Orthodox was the State Church to such an extent that it was almost an arm of the government. It maintained the civil registry of births, deaths, and marriages. In czarist Russia to be legally married outside the Orthodox Church was most difficult. Generously supported by the State, it manned half the schools in the whole country. It maintained four theological academies of university grade, and a theological seminary in almost every diocese. It carried on an extensive publishing program and gave broad support to Orthodox mission churches abroad. There was scarcely a village or a government office without its own church or chapel, not to mention thousands of private chapels in homes or on great estates. It was almost true that to be Russian was to be Orthodox.

Under the Communist regime Christianity is enemy No. 1 of the Party, which is in effect the government. One of the earliest Soviet decrees separated the Church from the State and the school from the Church. Since the revision of the constitution under Stalin, Communists point with pride to "the equal privileges" granted to religious and nonreligious persons: freedom to practice religious rites and freedom of antireligious propaganda. At this writing there are two academies and four seminaries, recently reduced from eight. Where once theological students were counted by the thousands, now they number a few hundred. Instead of the rich theological literature of pre-revolutionary days, Christian literature in the Soviet Union consists of two monthlies, the *Journal of the Moscow Patriarchate* and the Baptist *Fraternal Messenger*. The Orthodox Church has published a half dozen books, among them a collection of sermons by the late Metropolitan Nicolai, and issues a Church calendar each year. During the forty-five years under the Soviets, the Orthodox have been permitted to print 25,000 Bibles and the Baptists 10,000—35,000 Bibles for an estimated forty million church members.

As the State Church the Orthodox was truly dominant. It was unfriendly to all other Christian bodies, this attitude extending toward persecution for the Protestant groups. Lutheranism was tolerated, Roman Catholicism recognized but distrusted. Now the pressure of persecution has brought all faiths, Christian and others, into more sympathetic relationships than before the Revolution, and a general spirit of cooperation among Christian groups reigns. Although it officially recognizes some of them, the Soviet government never conceals its ultimate aim of putting an end to their existence. Unrecognized sects are actively pursued by law.

The reasons why the Soviet government aims at abolishing all religion are clear. The basic motive, never acknowledged by the Communists, is that Communism is itself essentially a religion. Except for the fact that it recognizes no divinity (although Lenin, enshrined for adoration in the Red Square, has almost been deified), Soviet Communism bears most of the marks of a religious faith. To assure world domination by Communism, all other faiths must be exterminated. As Lenin said, "Marxism is materialism, and . . . is merciless toward religion."

The official reasons advanced for fighting religion are both ideological and political. Religion is assailed as unscientific and a-social, a hold over from the past. Throughout the Christian era, the Communists claim, religion has struggled against science. But "the deeper man penetrates the mysteries of nature, the less place there remains for belief in God." "Religion is a vestige of earlier unscientific times." Moreover, religion beclouds men's minds, makes them inattentive to the building of Communism, that sublime goal toward which all citizens strive. Marxist theory teaches that religion is a product of the class struggle: "The social principles of Christianity preach the necessity of classes—the dominant and the oppressed. . . . they exalt cowardice, disdain humility, while the proletariat has daring, a sense of personal worth, pride and independence." Communists claim that this a-social phase of religion has always been used by the "exploiting class" for its own sinister purposes. Behind the mask of religion, say the Marxists, workers rising against their oppressors were cruelly suppressed, crusades against the young Soviet republic were organized.

A recent article in the official atheist monthly, *Science and Religion*, presents another charge: The Church teaches that man's goal in life is "blessedness in the next world, rather than happiness on earth." But, "hope in God is only a comforting delusion. . . . The Church and the sectarians, calling people to believe in God, are injecting their faithful with unbelief in their own powers, and dooming them to fruitless searching. . . . This faith demagnetizes believers, undermines their will and decision in overcoming difficulties, gives birth to despair and pessimism." The Communist's faith "is rooted, not in God, but in his own strength, not in a figment of imagination, but in knowledge. . . . The means of attaining our goal is not prayer, but stubborn struggle for the high ideals of Communism."

One other fact conditions this official hostility toward religion. Religious bodies, particularly the Christian Churches, are the only social institutions surviving from before the Revolution. This makes the Churches suspect, and still to a certain degree feared. A dictatorship always requires an enemy. Since religion is the only phase of life the Communists do not themselves operate, the Churches automatically become enemy No. 1. All of which explains the affirmation of *Science and Religion* that the "struggle against religion is the urgent task of our time." The Party Program of 1961, replacing that of 1918, reads: "For the first time the Party assigns to itself the task of liquidating religious prejudices in the mind of every believing person."

The means by which liquidation is to be achieved vary between outright violence and the most subtle philosophical and psychological approaches. In the early days of the Revolution, churches and monastic institutions were closed by force, thousands of clergy imprisoned or executed, church services invaded by gangs of "hooligans." Had these measures continued much longer than the point where Stalin made his concordat with the Churches in 1942, all church organization would probably have been wiped out. To assure popular support for the war effort Stalin restored some of the Church's rights, and persecution was almost stopped. Under Khrushchev, however, the pressure against religion has steadily mounted, with every means at the government's disposal. Among these are the press with thousands of books and pamphlets as well as periodicals, chief of which is *Science and Religion* published monthly in Russian in 150,000 copies. The press feeds the whole state educational system. In theory and now almost completely in fact, every subject in every class, from kindergarten through all institutions of higher learning, must be taught from the atheistic viewpoint. Hundreds of manuals are at teachers' disposal on how to present history, science, literature, mathematics, for the advancement of godlessness in any given grade. Millions of lectures in all sorts of places, village halls, factories, collective farms, are provided by the official "Society for the Diffusion of Political and Scientific Knowledge," the Khrushchev era's successor to the Union of Militant Godless, abolished by Stalin as part of his agreement with the Churches. Films, dramas, and radio programs also play a significant role in the over-all effort to crush religion.

Living under a regime that aims to eliminate all religion, how has the Christian Church reacted? Both Orthodox and

Protestants have evidenced a marked conservatism. Its whole activity limited to the conduct of services, the Orthodox Church has moved to increase their beauty and impressiveness, by the upkeep of the church buildings left to them, by maintaining the elaborate ancient ritual, and by return to the earlier church music that in the latter half of the nineteenth century had been overlaid with "Western," "concert" modes. Both Orthodox and Baptists deprecated the appearance of a modern translation of the Russian New Testament, now in process as a project of the British and Foreign Bible Society. Both Orthodox and Baptists insist upon using the Orthodox version made over a century ago.

For decades, like the rest of the Soviet population, Christians lived under complete quarantine from the rest of the world. In the fifties Baptists were permitted to send delegates to Baptist world conferences. In 1948 the Moscow Patriarchate convened what it hoped would be the first pan-Orthodox conference in centuries, but some of the national delegations, Greeks, Constantinople and others, refused to agree with the carefully considered condemnation of the World Council of Churches. This attitude was reversed in 1961 when the Orthodox and most of the other Christian bodies in the Soviet Union were received into membership in the World Council. Previous to this time, the Orthodox Church had participated in international gatherings of "The World Council in Defense of Peace," a Communist-inspired organization, which repeated the Soviet government propaganda for "total disarmament." Within the Soviet Union, Christian bodies have participated in government-organized conferences of all religions—Muslims, Jews, Buddhists —"for the defense of peace."

Considerable criticism is expressed by some members of both Orthodox and Baptist Churches because of the churches' use of their large incomes. As never before the Revolution, Christians give most generously. In the largest Orthodox church near Moscow that "stands" ten thousand, two services were held on Trinity Sunday 1957. The priest in charge of this church told me the collection and candle sales that day amounted to 40,000 rubles, $4,000 at the current tourist rate. With education, social service, and philanthropy forbidden to them, with practically no possibility of publishing, churches show a tendency to pay high salaries to clergy, and in the case of the Orthodox, to maintain the hierarchy in residential state almost like that under the Czar. The man in the street holds it against the clergy in general because many of them now own their own cars.

Under the Czar, Christianity had no effective rival in Russia. Christianity permeated all of public life. The Church calendar regulated most peoples' schedules; a peasant ordered his sowing and harvest by the appropriate saints' days. The Russian language is full of Gospel allusions and Christian proverbs. And even "Mr. K." occasionally lapses into a "God give you health" or "God forbid." Every Russian has a thousand years of Christianity in his blood.

Over against Christian revelation, Communists put the complete and "scientific" truth revealed by Marx and Lenin. The dogmatic acceptance of this doctrine is as obligatory for Communists as the Nicene Creed is for Christians. These dogmas inspire in Communists both messianic hope and missionary zeal: Marxism is to be spread throughout the world, where necessary by force. This means crushing all other religions, by all possible methods. In the Soviet Union force has been employed with varying intensity throughout the past forty-five years. As a result, the Church in Russia has known an army of martyrs unsurpassed in modern times. When violence proved not to be completely effective, the Soviet government officially decried its use. Besides insisting that schools should produce young people who are militant atheists, the government attacks religion from the "scientific" angle, from the philosophical viewpoint, with all the classical arguments in the history of free thinking rehashed again and again.

In the Soviet Union, Christianity has one ideological rival buttressed by all the power of the world's second most powerful state. Against this rival, the Church dares not utter a public word. What is the Church doing to maintain its existence under such pressure?

Since church services are legal, most public effort must be exerted there, in more impressive services, in the depth of piety, the directness of sermon appeal. Sermons are part of every service in all churches, Orthodox or Protestant, and are of course carefully watched by Soviet censors. With organized religious instruction of young people under eighteen forbidden by law,[1] clergy have occasionally conducted children's services, or preached children's sermons, but this is illegal, and involves the preacher in danger of arrest. The Orthodox theological seminaries say that they teach Apologetics as well as the Soviet constitution. And we have the atheist press to thank for information that clandestine manuscripts "adapting the Christian faith to science" are in circulation. A recent pamphlet explains the situation: "Religion neither sanctifies nor regulates state forms or social-economic relationships in our country. . . . It no longer has the possibility of regulating the activity of a believer, can not pretend to be the spiritual tutor of society." But what remains to the Church, the writer continues, is "the possibility of placing its stamp on the attitude of the individual toward society, labor, the family—the stamp of suspicion toward society, of pessimism, of despair."

The fact that Churches in Russia live under pressure so continued and so vicious, conditions their activities, as this atheist pamphlet says. In several ways religion has been driven underground. Priests that served churches closed by the government make their living by clandestine services in churchless towns and villages. Baptisms, and funerals, and other services are performed in homes by laity who know the rituals. No Communist may attend church without grave censure by Party leaders, and other state employees (and under a socialist regime

[1] Article 227, Law Code of the Russian Soviet Federal Socialist Republic, July 25, 1962.

all but the clergy are state employees) risk public censure or loss of jobs by being seen in church. But despite recent cases of prison sentences for priests who performed "illegal" baptisms, Soviet authorities admit that perhaps 80 per cent of all children are baptized. In the early years, it was easy to eliminate millions of "paper" Orthodox from church rolls, but later years have seen less success in the war against religion.

Only within recent years has atheist propaganda concerned itself with the philosophical bases of Christianity. Beginning with the first recognition in thirty years of Russian Christian philosophers living abroad, Communists now attack Christian philosophy in detail. From the Christian standpoint this has certain positive effects: First is the recognition that there is a Christian philosophy, thus largely refuting the old argument that only aged and ignorant people are believers. Second, in attacking Christian doctrines these must be stated, thus offering the other side of the argument although it must be admitted that in such philosophical articles, as in much atheist propaganda, false premises, allegedly Christian, are frequently set up to be knocked down by atheist dicta.

To the aid of philosophy, the Soviet atheists are now bringing psychology. They discover that religion is something of the emotions, and are demanding closer study of the nature and cause of this feeling, and how it may be equally well induced by Communist means, such as "stories or films of the beautiful Soviet actuality."

Facing this subtle and all-pervasive effort, the eventual survival of Christianity in Russia may be said to depend upon the grace of God and grandmothers. For the past few years anti-religious agitators have been tracing the origin of individuals' Christian faith back to Christian families. The press is filled with pitiful stories of parental effort to maintain children's faith against the impact of ubiquitous atheist education. Where parents are indifferent, grandmothers insist upon having children baptized. Now we are witnessing what might be called a children's crusade in reverse. Teams of investigators visit schools and try to trap children into admitting that they participate in religious observances at home, say prayers, wear a baptismal cross. No child risks wearing it at school, affirms a magazine article, but many put it on at night. Children admit that they celebrate religious holidays. *Science and Religion*[2] tells of one such study in the second and third grades where the teacher asserted that none of her class believed in God, and of the discovery that many do. There is a sickening account of "difficult talks" with an eight-year-old, to bring him into the atheist position.

As a result of this new approach, Soviet law has been reinterpreted and propagandists are urged to force themselves into Christian homes to root out religion. Newspapers report parents sentenced to forced labor for "illegal activity." Up to the present most believers arrested were charged with "crimes against the State," such as refusal to do military service or forbidding children to join the Communist youth organizations. In the current phase, since "religion teaches passivity, lack of self-confidence, indifference to the life of society," propagating it is illegal and "government organs are obliged, and have the right, to stop such activities and call those guilty to account."[3]

It is a crime "to diffuse religious ideology, either in preaching or in religious services outside the church," or to bring youth and children into church. Parents found guilty of giving their children religious instruction may be sentenced to prison and have their children removed from them for education in state boarding schools.

Confronting such attitudes and measures, how can Christians react? There is an increasing emphasis, in all Churches on the inner life of the individual himself and of the Church. Official attitudes toward the Church being what they are, one who attends church does so out of sincere conviction, thus pro-

[2] February, 1963.
[3] *Science and Religion*, May, 1963.

ducing a congregation that is a religious elite. No Christians from abroad can fail to be impressed by the depth of devotion and the profoundly emotional impact of church services, Orthodox and Protestant alike.

Outside their churches Christians in the Soviet Union bear daily witness by their lives. Baptists report that one of their chief sources of new converts is conversation at the workbench or in the field. Even the atheists have to admit that Christians are good citizens and good workers. Taking the cue from them, Communist authorities have now ordered their members to be friendly to others, to be kind to neighbors in distress, "since that is the way Christians ensnare people in their nets." Monks torn from their cloisters for torture and death, though being dead, yet speak, and with no small voices.

Under increasing peril, the Church persists, and even, according to atheist asseverations, is increasing in membership beyond the estimated forty million. Church leaders tell us of slow but steady influx of young adults whom the religion of Marx can no longer satisfy. Small incidents noted with alarm in the atheist press are significant. "The young intelligentsia are becoming increasingly interested in philosophy and the Christian life." "In the Kirovgrad church the priest is twenty-seven, the parish chairman is an engineer, and in the parish council are a doctor and the chief book-keeper of a factory." Two students of a technical institute registered in a theological seminary and the other students knew of this, but did not report it to the authorities. "In the Baptist churches all sorts of Soviet specialists preach: engineers, doctors, teachers. They are also very active in refuting materialistic doctrines." *Science and Religion* inveighs against Christians in official positions, and against Communists who participate in religious festivals, who permit their children to be baptized, or even have church marriages.

Pravda cites incidents where the children of parents who "do not believe in God" go to church, fulfill religious rites, are baptized. Church rites are carried out "even by members of the Communist Youth League. Last year many hundreds of young people were married in the church."

Does this present offer any prognosis for the future? We may not anticipate any relaxation of the steady antireligious pressure by the State. There are signs, now, that the Churches are better able to resist atheist doctrine than under the early attacks. In Orthodox and Baptist bodies the emphasis is now on youth; men in their thirties are bishops and leading officers. And in view of the past forty-five years' pressure we may be sure that most of these young men are not engaged in the service of the Church from other than veritable motivation by faith. The Soviet press is constantly criticizing official atheist propaganda because of the increasing number of believers, "particularly among the Baptists." This is probably due to the conspicuous fact of adult baptism, as well as to the more active evangelizing effort by individual church members. On the other hand, most of the examples cited of intelligentsia as active in the Church are Orthodox. All this contradicts the Communist claim that only old people are interested in "that relic of the past, religion." Christians know that no persecution in their history has ever been able to crush the Church or quench the Holy Spirit, and this recent story from Moscow appears symptomatic. A nine-year-old coming home from school inquired, "Mother, we don't believe in God, do we?" "Of course not," his mother replied. A pause—then, "Mother, does God know we don't believe in Him?"

Russian Orthodox living abroad have expressed fears that the relentless power of the Soviet state might finally crush the Church. When I told a venerable Russian priest of this, he replied, "Never fear. For a thousand years the Church has been preaching the Gospel in Russia. She will be preaching the same Gospel a thousand years from now."

✳ ✳ ✳ ✳ ✳ ✳ IV ✳ ✳ ✳ ✳ ✳ ✳

Other States of Eastern Europe

CHARLES C. WEST

CHARLES C. WEST

Charles C. West, Professor of Christian Ethics at Princeton Theological Seminary is an ordained minister of the United Presbyterian Church in the U.S.A. Theologically trained in Union Theological Seminary, New York and in Yale Divinity School, he served as a missionary in China 1946-50 and as a fraternal worker with the World Council of Churches in Germany 1950-53. Dr. West was Associate Director of the Ecumenical Institute, Bossey, 1956-61. In these positions and in his studies, he has been persistently concerned with the theological problems and activities of Christians living under Communist rule or otherwise confronting Communism. Dr. West's major book is COMMUNISM AND THE THEOLOGIANS. He addressed Christian students in OUTSIDE THE CAMP: THE CHRISTIAN AND THE WORLD; and he translated and wrote the introduction for Johannes Hamel's A CHRISTIAN IN EAST GERMANY. Dr. West is widely known as lecturer, consultant, and author of many articles in the field of his experience. He serves the World Council of Churches in its Committee on Missionary Studies.

IV

Three vignettes may suggest the complexity of our problem:

1. The scene is a Sunday morning church service in one of those lands where the Churches of the Reformation have been for centuries a part of the established social order, whether dominant as in Eastern Germany or an entrenched minority as in Czechoslovakia, Hungary, and Romanian Transylvania. The service goes on as it always has, supported largely by old people, and by the dwindling band of children preparing for Confirmation. The locality has always been Protestant, but the village church is now much too large for the remnant gathered there. A neighboring church has closed for lack of support but the few recruits from that area have not helped much. The spirit of the people is low.

The reasons for this state of affairs are two. The first is obviously pressure, unrelenting, all-pervasive, operating through every agency which a total government controls to organize the whole life of every active citizen and to push religious practice to the outer periphery. Every worshiper in the pew knows several other Christians who would be there if circumstances permitted: farmers or shopkeepers whose business has been collectivized, thus forcing them to move elsewhere to find work; employees in collective farms and factories who have found it wise not to jeopardize their jobs or their advancement by being seen in church or by sending their children to Confirmation.

But the second reason is even more oppressive because it lies within. It is the creeping paralysis of the spirit—nihilism it would be called if it were a philosophy, or despair if it were an acute feeling—which makes one person after another resign from the effort of responsible living. This mood has its ups and downs. Today it is acute in East Germany as a reaction to the Berlin wall, which forced the people to face the awful finality of their separation from their brothers and sisters in the West. In Hungary it is somewhat in abeyance, for conditions have improved after the acute bitterness which followed the suppression of the 1956 revolt. But its ongoing essence surrounds this church service, as it surrounds every Communist-sponsored gathering as well, like a chill damp fog.

"You Westerners romanticize everything that goes on in our countries," protests one of the congregation on the way home from church. "You see terrible oppression, with secret police, midnight torture, and concentration camps one day—and wonderful breakthroughs of humanity and freedom the next. You regard us as corrupted tools of a Communist conspiracy with one eye—and as heroes of resistance with the other. In reality our life is nothing like this exciting variation; it is gray. It is a dull, hopeless routine of shortages, inefficiency, shoddy goods, ill-conceived planning, and empty propaganda. It is a life in which one spends countless extra hours day by day just buying and cooking three meals, because nothing works as it should. It is a life where no one cares, no one takes initiative or responsibility because it would only lead to danger and frustration, where every man, even the Communist official, protects what little private life he can against the powerful and capricious system while conforming as far as he must with its demands."

So what is the point of going to church? Is it not a futile gesture? Does it offer any hope to balance off the risks involved? Small comfort that every mass organization, even the Communist Party itself, faces the same predicament. The problem is the decay of humanity in an empty and hopeless world.

2. Let us shift the picture. A sincere young Communist, a lecturer in philosophy at the University of Prague, is addressing an international conference of Christian students. This in itself is a surprising event. But more surprising is the content of his remarks. He characterizes the Western critique of Communism fairly: monolithic order, ideological dogmatism, inhumanity, bureaucracy, and materialism. He confesses a degree of truth in these criticisms, and even that "our movement has sinned, particularly in the Stalinist era." But the heart of Marxism and the source of its power, he maintains, is its devotion, in theory and practice, to the "real destiny of living human beings, and the struggle to make their living conditions more human." Humanism is the heart of Marxism; materialism is only a way-station.

"We Marxists," he continues, "understand the struggle for Communism as a struggle, on the one hand, for the maximum development of man's scientific and productive powers and abilities and, on the other, for maximum recognition of each individual and the harmonious development of his emotional and intellectual faculties. The meaning and aim of all our efforts is man, not only his well-being but especially the complete fulfillment of his life."

This is his measuring rod for Christianity and his reason for rejecting it. Christianity has not fulfilled its highest ideals for man. It has used dependence on God and submission to him as a substitute for human responsibility. At the same time this young philosopher reads modern theology with intense interest, because he sees in the thought of Dietrich Bonhoeffer and others a new concern, a "nonreligious" one, for man. He invites his Christian hearers to an open competition: "I wish that in the future we might struggle to surpass one another in readiness for sacrifice, in creative work, in the development of the classical values of true humanity. . . . May a sincere fair struggle decide who wins the prize, in other words, who first gets close to man and stands up for him."[1]

[1] Milan Machovec, "Marxism and Christianity—A Marxist View," in *Student World*, No. 1 (1963), pp. 79-83.

The reaction of several theological students from Eastern Europe is enthusiastic. "This is a challenge which opens new fields to us," says one. "Never has the dialogue between Christians and Marxists been so active and so free." Of course it has not penetrated the higher levels of the Party or the government. But increasingly in Eastern Europe outside of Russia the reaction against the dead hand of Stalinism takes the form of exploring the whole humanist tradition of the Western world, including those theologians who have something significant to say about man. More and more young Communist intellectuals are discovering that there are Christians alongside them, who do not look back to the pre-socialist era but who differ with them ideologically, and have another idea of what it means to be human. "Once they understood that we accept socialism as a radical but necessary step toward justice, and are not hidden enemies of the whole social order," explains a young theologian, "they come to us for companionship and for advice. They listen to our insights into what it means to be human in the light of Christ."

"But are you not still opposed to the lack of freedom, the arbitrary power and total control of life which is part of your socialist system?" asks the doubter.

"Of course. But the transfer to socialism was historically necessary to sweep away the decadent injustice of centuries of 'Christian culture.' Now that we are free to preach an unencumbered gospel we must work to build respect and freedom for the individual on top of the socialist achievement!"

3. A final picture. A group of young Christians, some students, some employees of collectivized enterprises, is gathered in Eastern Germany for an evening of Bible study, worship, and the sharing of each other's experience. This gathering is the deepest nourishment of their spiritual life, far more important to them than the Sunday services of the Church. Each in his or her way knows the anxious insecurity of Christian living in a society where the pressures are against it. One lost a year of schooling

for refusing to take part in the "Youth Dedication" ceremony. Another works in a menial job where his advancement is blocked because his faith is known. A third has served a prison term for expressing himself indiscreetly about the "achievements of the people's democracy." More than one of them has been grilled at one time or another by the police. They are discussing a recent incident which rocked the self-confidence of the government of the German Democratic Republic to its foundations. Sixty-two young Marxists had been hand-picked from the leadership of the Free German Youth, every one a proved activist in the building of a socialist society, to attend the World Youth Festival in Helsinki, Finland. Thirty-four of them defected to Western Germany.

"That's the difference between us and the Communists," one of the young Christians reflects. "If a similarly picked group of us had been sent abroad, every one would have returned. This is the country where God has placed us in order that we may love it and serve it, not the way the Communists do, but the way He does."

Every one of these pictures is true of the life of the Christian community in the Communist-controlled lands of Eastern Europe. Is there an underlying truth which includes them all? This is not an objective question to be answered by description. It is a historical, and at heart a theological, question. The crisis and calling of the Church in these lands today consists in the fact that both the Communists and the Christians are groping for new answers, and in the process are beginning to confront one another. To understand it more deeply we must look at the history of this encounter.

I.   *The Churches*

To speak of the Protestant Churches in these lands as in many others is to refer to a dual, well-nigh contradictory reality. On the one hand the Churches of the Reformation, like the Roman Catholic Church, and like the Orthodox Church in

Russia, Romania, and Bulgaria, belong to the traditional religious establishment of Christendom. In Eastern Germany the one Evangelical Church (Lutheran and Reformed) embraced five-sixths of the population at the time of the Russian invasion. In Hungary and Transylvania about one-third of the people have maintained their Lutheran or Reformed identity over the centuries despite Roman Catholic oppression, until in recent years their Churches too were granted official status. Only in Czechoslovakia is Protestantism still strongly marked by its five-century struggle, along with the Czech nation, against the Roman Catholic culture of the Holy Roman (and later the Austro-Hungarian) Empire. In the mid-fifteenth century 90 per cent of the Czech nation belonged to the Church of the Hussite Reformation—a Church which later received both Lutheran and Calvinist influences into its life. Present-day Roman Catholicism, embracing about five-sixths of the population, dates from 1615 when the Hapsburg emperor conquered Bohemia and drove out or forcibly converted the people. The liberal Joseph II granted official toleration but it was not until the Republic was established in 1918 that Protestants again enjoyed full equality. Meanwhile, however, Czech nationalism flourished in Protestant soil even though, under Jan Masaryk, it took a liberal humanist direction. The establishment of which Czechoslovak Protestantism finally became a part was a secular post-Christendom, with religious overtones and a socialist direction that remained nevertheless middle-class bourgeois. This uneasy flowering in the twilight of a Christian culture may help to explain why the theology most positively oriented toward the Communist revolution has emerged in Czech Protestant churches.

Thus the social reality of Christianity, massively opposed for social and cultural as well as for theological reasons to the Marxism-Leninism of the Communists and the revolutionary spirit of the working class. The resistance of Protestantism, however, has never been quite the same as that of Catholicism or

Orthodoxy because of a second reality to which its message bore witness, even when its life did not. The Churches of the Reformation have always understood themselves not as sacred institutions, but as creatures and servants of the free word of God. This has been their strength and their weakness as the world evaluates these things. Whenever they have been tempted to glorify their inner life, or to provide religious sanctity for the society of which they are a part, their own message has risen up to remind them that man is justified by the grace of God alone and that the Church like the rest of the world is moving toward its meeting with its Judge and Savior. The strength in this position has been most eloquently expressed by Josef Hromadka:

> The Church of the Reformation desired nothing more, but also nothing less, than to be a communion of pilgrims proceeding from their house of bondage, from the land of Egypt to the promised land. . . . The Church of Christ is strong because she clearly realizes who her Lord is, and whom she would obey above everyone else. And she is free because she does not depend on human orders, she does not depend on worldly goods, but desires only to give the testimony of the living God, serve and help the people no matter what may happen in this world.[2]

And it has been repeated countless times in the forthright declarations of the Evangelical Church in Eastern Germany to the State on matters affecting the common life. "The Church," wrote the bishops of this church to the Soviet military governor in 1948, "has received a definite commission from its Lord Jesus Christ. It must proclaim the Christian Gospel and it alone, by word and by deed. It must proclaim this Gospel in the form given to it in Holy Scriptures. It is bound only to its heavenly Lord in carrying out this commission. It can accept no directions from any human authority concerning the content of

[2] "The Church of the Reformation Faces Today's Challenges," in *Theology Today*, VI (January 1950), p. 448.

its message, not even from the state or from a political party."[3] The weakness however is the obverse of this very bondage to Christ alone. Because Christ is its Judge it is not enough for the Church or the culture it shares in Protestant understanding to be relatively better than its critics and enemies. Rather it feels called to read the events of world history in the light of God's call to repentance and new life, including those events wherein the Communist power has established itself. For this reason the Protestant Churches as a whole have not presented the massive resistance to every encroachment of Communist power which has characterized the Roman Catholic Church where it was dominant (though not, be it noted, in Eastern Germany where it was in the minority). The Lutheran and Reformed Churches in Hungary for example were unable to muster the confidence of Cardinal Mindszenty and his hierarchy that every acre of church property and every churchly privilege which tradition had bestowed, was a matter of divine right. Nor has Protestantism preserved as full and attractive a liturgical life within the walls of the Church as has Orthodoxy, for it has no final confidence in the value of such a life. Where sermons are preached which ignore the pressures and tensions of Communist society, and where prayers are offered which repeat old formulae, the congregation dwindles away. A Protestant church has no option: it cannot place another world alongside of this one. Whatever the risks, it lives by seeking and proclaiming the word of God to and in Communist society.

This, then, is the Church which faced the oncoming wave of Communist power in 1945. It was a culture-bound Church, but one already aware through its own theology that there is a judgment of God even on the Church itself, and that the way to the future lies through repentance. It was a Church freighted with social prestige and privilege, yet conscious by the very word proclaimed in it that the only power it could count on is that of a Lord who reigns from the Cross.

[3] *Kirche im Kampf der Zeit*, Die Botshaften, Worte und Erklärungen der evangelischen Kirche in Deutschland und ihrer östlichen Gliedkirchen (Berlin, 1955), p. 100.

II. *The Communists*

In one sense the whole history of the years 1945-61, in the countries we are considering, could be said to have taken place regardless of this inner drama of the Church or the needs of society. Events took place according to the plans and analyses of the strange and dogmatic ideology of Marxism-Leninism which created a fantastic world of its own. Into this world, beset with its own fears and hopes, all other reality was distorted to fit. The juggernaut of collectivization and propaganda rolled on regardless of obstacles save for an occasional change of pace which international politics required. Yet in another sense these were years of dramatic encounter between Communists and Christians, precisely because both were caught in forces which often neither controlled, and they were compelled to confront one another with pure witness of faith.

The basic confrontation was ideological. Despite the many efforts, no words on paper can reproduce for the outsider the atmosphere which Communist power produces when it takes exclusive hold of propaganda and educational power in order to "change the consciousness" of its subjects. Yet this, and not the external facts of political tyranny and economic collectivization, is the first reality of the Marxist-Leninist world. It is rooted in the working belief of every Communist that "social existence determines consciousness." With the "liberation" from Nazism and bourgeois and feudal capitalism, a new era in society has begun, in which the "people" led by the working classes are fundamentally in control, and peaceful progress will be made toward a socialist society. To this new society a new social consciousness corresponds. It is the function of all education, indeed of every agency of thought and public opinion, to bring the people to inward appropriation of this consciousness, that is, to "ideological maturity." Yet this, for the Marxist, is not an arbitrary *tour de force*. He is simply laying, as he sees it, a "scientific" foundation for knowledge in a socialist world, one which will unite theory and practice and present facts—the unpleasant facts of present poverty for instance—in the light of their future dialectical development toward a prosperous and happy society. To this picture belongs of course the "struggle for peace." Marxism-Leninism, and the present tactical requirements of the "fight for peace" led by the Soviet Union are not, for the Marxist mind, one philosophy or one point of view among others. They are the state of consciousness of a democratic society on the way to socialism. They are the science of existence.

For the Protestant Christian, accustomed to the demand that he respond to the grace of God's word by the faithfulness of his own words, this raises with peculiar poignancy the problem of truth. This in fact has been the fundamental issue in Eastern Germany. It is raised daily in countless subtle ways. It is at stake when a teacher distorts the facts of history in order to keep his job, lest when he leave it some irresponsible ideologue take over. It arises for the pupil who learns one truth from his family and another from his school until he learns to juggle both, being responsible for neither. It is at issue every time an ordinary citizen confronts a Communist official, knowing that if he is honest—if he tells the Communist the truth—it may mean the loss of job or possibly of freedom. It permeates the factory, the office, and even the neighborhood where a man must pretend to be what he is not except among his most trusted friends lest some informer raise trouble for him. Whence does a man get, in the words of Johannes Hamel, "the courage to be truthful"?[4]

The experience of the Church in Eastern Germany would seem to suggest two answers. The first was given by Hamel himself, in the lecture cited above, to the students of the University of Leipzig. Truth is not in the first place a set of propositions at all. "Truth is no thing. God himself is the truth, and this truth became man in Jesus Christ." To stand in this relation is to be true, and to act toward others as neighbors with whom the same Christ has to do, is to be true to them. This truth, the Christian owes also to the Communist: not to write

---

[4] *A Christian in East Germany* (New York, 1960), pp. 87 ff.

him off, not to protect oneself against him as an enemy, but to
seek him out as a helpful friend who has his deepest interests at
heart, to forgive him and to seek with him the true problems of
his life which underlie those his ideology presents to him. A
thoughtful book of essays and sermons by East German pastors
calls it "Christian Pro-Existence."[5]

The second answer is inseparable from the first. The Christian has no ideology, no total system of truth, not even a
Christian one, to defend. But just because of his freedom he is
the custodian of those relative human truths which ideologists
of all sorts neglect and distort. He is called to confront his
neighbor—the same neighbor to whom he owes that truth which
is called love—with these truths as he is given to see them. This
applies first of all to the Communist. One does him no service
if one leaves him encased in the illusions of his world-view. One
is not truthful if one leaves him with a false idea of his relation
to other men and of the facts of life. But it applies equally to
the fearful, the resentful and hate-filled opponents of the Communists, for whom nothing that happens in a socialist state can
be human, just, or hopeful. An example will illustrate the point.

A pastor receives a call to come to the police station to
explain some irregularity in his conduct of the church—perhaps
a meeting he had not registered in advance. Such calls can be
ominous. A charge, however ill-substantiated, may mean years in
prison. It turns out, however, that the police officer is using the
veiled threat of such a charge to press the pastor into a public
statement in favor of Parents' Advisory Councils for the schools,
to which there had been much Christian opposition in the town.
He dwells on the supposed irregularity for some time. He leaves
the pastor sitting for more than an hour without explanation.
Finally he returns with his most accommodating air. It can all
surely be arranged this time, he assures his anxious victim, but
there is this important matter of the schools.

[5] *Pro-Existenz: Verkündigung und Fürbitte in der DDR*, vorgelegt von
Elisabeth Adler (Berlin, 1960).

"Don't you realize," replies the pastor, "that Christian parents can hardly be expected to support a school where the truth about the world and Christianity is systematically distorted in the classroom?"

The discussion goes on for three hours longer. Gone are the police threats. The surprised officer has become a human being in honest argument over a public issue, during which he hears things no one had ever dared tell him before—because he has met a man whom he could not manipulate, and who treats him as a neighbor. As the pastor rises to go, the officer offers his hand: "Thank you for your sincerity," he says. "Not even my own colleagues speak the truth to me as you have."

It need not be a pastor. The schoolboy or girl who finds a way of expressing the truth and of thinking straight, knowing that he may at any time be expelled for it; the professor who maintains the integrity of his subject and offers critical advice on public policy related to his field; the ordinary citizen who questions the speaker in the meeting of his mass organization and so deflates one more bit of propaganda—these and many others peppered through Communist society constitute the Church's witness to the truth which is for the Communist even while it deflates his ideology.

The second great confrontation of the years 1945-61 was economic-political. It centered in the determination of Communist power to destroy every form of private enterprise and to substitute the structure of "People-owned Industries," "Rural Production Cooperatives," and a State retail-wholesale trading monopoly. In Eastern Germany this process was most ruthless. In Czechoslovakia it came about more quietly but no less completely. In Hungary there are large numbers of private farms to this day. The German situation therefore poses the problem most sharply.

If the issue in the ideological conflict is truth, the issue in the collectivization drive is responsibility. There is no theological reason why a Protestant Church should espouse either private enterprise or a socialist system in itself, nor have any official

Church statements tried to do so. The problem lies rather at two other points: (*a*) the manner in which collectivization was carried out, and (*b*) the hopeless inefficiency of total planning, and the irresponsibility which it breeds. Doubtless Protestant farmers and businessmen would have fought collectivization under any circumstances. But it was these two points which brought theology itself to their side and turned repentance into further resistance to Communist revolution as long as it was possible. The Communists never made the collectivization of farms, shops, or of industry into a law. After the first confiscation of large industry and land holdings in 1945 they used economic sanctions, propaganda, and sometimes political threats to accomplish their purpose by attrition. High quotas for production or trade were set on private businesses and farms. Failure to deliver could mean heavy fines or imprisonment. Raw materials, feed grain, fertilizer, and the like were delivered to private enterprises only after orders from collectives had been filled. Limits were set on employment in the private sector. And when this did not drive the farmer and the shopkeeper into the cooperative, arbitrary arrests and heavy sentences for minor or nonexistent infractions were tried. Finally a large part of Communist officialdom was organized to put personal pressure on the farmer in his field, his home, and wherever he went, until he finally gave in. All of this the Church protested step by step in the name of sheer humanity.

Christian vocational responsibility, however, posed and still poses the deeper problem. It was obvious to every non-Communist analyst of Eastern Germany's economy that she was sustained in the first years after the war, in spite of heavy reparations to the Soviet Union, by the productivity of her private enterprise. There alone standards of efficiency, service, and workmanship were taken seriously, a condition not unrelated to the traditional Lutheran concept of the place of work as the place of divine calling. As more and more of the economy was collectivized, however, the crisis of the private farmer and businessman grew more and more acute. No longer was the work profitable;

it was exhausting, debt-ridden, and increasingly dangerous, haunted by the awful insecurity which Communist power had deliberately created. What was the use of going on? What use, especially, in view of the probability that in a very few years the Marxists would have worked their will and no private enterprise would be left.

To this the Church has found two answers, one which has played its historical role, and another which points the way to the future.

First, to serve one's neighbor in the private sector of a collectivizing economy is a clear, God-given responsibility as long as it is possible. This is so because private businesses and farms serve as yardsticks to the whole economy, maintaining in it some standards of productive efficiency and some flexibility over against the total plan. But it is so as well because these private places of work provide a haven from the incessant pressure of ideology on people's lives. Here are places where human relations can be natural and free.

Second, when the time comes that the responsibility which the private sector imposes is forcibly taken away, a new place of service will be given, within the collectivized socialist system, where God can also be served. The end of economic freedom is not the end of vocation or responsibility, nor is it the end of the rule of God over the economy or of His promise that the earth will be fruitful.

A small village in Saxony held out against land collectivization to the very end. In 1960 it became clear however that the end had come. Flying squads of Communist officials were invading villages, bullying, cajoling, threatening, subduing one after another. The community therefore notified the government that it was ready to collectivize of its own free will. A deputation came to arrange the transfer of property. They arrived to find the whole village decked out in Sunday clothes in the square. The transfer was made and the crowd burst into the hymn they had chosen for the occasion, "A Mighty Fortress Is Our God." It ends:

That Word above all earthly powers,
No thanks to them, abideth;
The Spirit and the gifts are ours
Through Him who with us sideth;
Let goods and kindred go,
This mortal life also:
The body they may kill:
God's truth abideth still,
His kingdom is forever.

III. *The Future*

The story of collectivization is over. The sharp struggles and poignant defeats of those years are temporarily obscured by the general *détente* between East and West. Even Communist authorities are talking in Eastern Germany about "trustful co-operation" with the Church. But the basis of this is the accomplished fact of a totally planned socialist economy. The ideological struggle continues, but it is far less acute. Contemporary Eastern Germany and Czechoslovakia, at least, seem to be moving into a secular technological age in which not only the ancient forms of the Christian Church, but the relatively more modern forms of Communist organization and propaganda are becoming less effective and relevant. In this situation it is perhaps no surprise that each is in a self-critical mood, and that they are slowly beginning to talk to each other.

What are the bases of this future conversation, and of the Protestant Churches in at least these Communist lands? We suggest, in conclusion, three.

1. The power relations between the Christian Church and the Communist Party remain what they have been from the beginning, but today they are clearer than ever before. Provisionally Christians live in a State where power is held by the Communists and where the structure of society is collectivist socialism. They have been given this living place by God himself in order that they may "seek the welfare of the city where I have

sent you in to exile and pray to the Lord on its behalf, for in its welfare you will find your welfare" (To the captives in Babylon, Jeremiah 29:7, R.S.V.). It is not permitted them to hope for another city; but it is commanded them that they shall proclaim to this Communist authority that it is in the hands of the Lord Jesus Christ and will be judged by him for its treatment of the human beings in its care.

2. The form of the Christian community is changing radically in response to the needs of a collectivized society, but the Church is discovering therein the form which her own message decrees, the form of Christ, in the modern world. While traditional parishes are dwindling, new groups are springing up in factory and on farm, meeting not in churches but in living rooms or empty offices. Yet they are also the Church, and they know it. While the traditional pastor's office diminishes, new ministries are taking shape: theological resource man for a factory congregation, lay group leader for a community dedicated to conversation with Communists, and a number of others. They arise out of the needs of the Church itself as it takes seriously the Communist philosopher's challenge to "get close to man and stand up for him."

3. The form of Christian service and witness in Communist society has changed with the opportunities, but its basic character remains the same. *Pro-Existenz* describes it as "objective witness"—appropriate to the matter at hand, the sober reminder to an ideological world of what it means to be a neighbor, and to serve one's neighbor effectively with the resources that are to hand. The range of possibilities may not be as great for a Christian in a collectivized system as they are in a more flexible society, hence the responsibility may be differently expressed. But the neighbor is there, and in need, whether he be the Communist or the Communist's victim. Christian service has never depended on worldly resources; it is a service "made perfect in weakness" because its essence is the service of Christ.

✦ ✦ ✦ V ✦ ✦ ✦

The Near East

CHARLES HABIB MALIK

CHARLES HABIB MALIK

Charles Habib Malik, member of the Greek Orthodox Church, Patriarchate of Antioch, is Distinguished Professor of Philosophy at the American University of Beirut. Native and citizen of Lebanon, he graduated from the University in which he has taught much of the time since 1927, serving also for a time as Dean of Graduate Studies. He earned the master's and doctor's degrees in philosophy at Harvard, and studied in Freiburg. Author of more than a hundred articles and essays in English and in Arabic on philosophical, religious, and international subjects, Dr. Malik has recently published two important books, CHRIST AND CRISIS and MAN IN THE STRUGGLE FOR PEACE.

Charles Malik is an international figure, recognized by forty-five honorary degrees from American, Canadian, and European institutions of higher learning; and by decorations from a dozen governments. He was Lebanon's Minister and Ambassador to the United States 1945-55; and, between 1956 and 1958, served terms as Minister for National Education and the Fine Arts, and as Minister for Foreign Affairs of the Government of Lebanon. Dr. Malik's manifold prominence in the United Nations is represented in his service as Rapporteur of the Commission on Human Rights and as its Chairman; as President of the Economic and Social Council; as three times President of the Security Council; and as President of the General Assembly.

V

By the Near East I mean Turkey, Iran, Israel, and the Arabic-speaking countries east of and including Egypt and the Sudan. Statistics, especially in this area, are difficult to come by, and when found, they are not reliable; but the total population of the Near East is roughly of the order of 120 million people, of whom not more than between six and eight million are Christian. Thus the Christians of the Near East constitute between 5 per cent and 6.7 per cent of the total population.[1] The Copts of Egypt are the largest group, but they form a distinct minority of the total population of the country, as is the case in Syria. The ratio of Christians to non-Christians in Lebanon is roughly 6 to 5. The Christians of the Near East outside Egypt, Lebanon, and Syria constitute very small minorities of the countries to which they belong. Protestants and other Christians of Western rites are tiny minorities of the Christian population, but economically, culturally and even politically, their importance is out of proportion to their numbers. The overwhelming majority of the Christians of the Near East are either Catholics with Syriac or Byzantine or Armenian rites, or Greek Orthodox, or Christians with other Oriental rites, such as the Orthodox Copts or

Editor's Note:
   Dr. Malik wrote a more extensive text on the subject of this chapter, but having regard to limitations of space in relation to the other contributions, we print here a slightly condensed version, with the approval of Dr. Malik.
[1] Lower figures in the *World Christian Handbook*, 1962, are inadequate; and, in the important case of Egypt, as also in others, obviously dubious.

Armenians, who for centuries have not been in communion
either with Orthodoxy or with Catholicism.

II

Since the advent of Islam in the seventh century conversion
has virtually always been one-way, namely, from Christianity to
Islam; so that apart from slight Crusader infusion the existing
Christians of the Near East are on the whole remnants of pre-
Islamic Christianity. With very few exceptions, a Christian in
the Near East can with certainty claim that his religious lineage
mounts to the early centuries of the Christian era. Christianity
in the Near East, then, is historical and traditional, overwhelmingly dependent on liturgy, and quite conscious that it is but a
leftover from the Islamic onslaught. It is not a Western importa-
tion, however the West may have discovered, aroused and challenged it in Crusader and recent centuries; it is fully rooted,
racially, culturally and ecclesiastically, in the Orient; it is what
has survived of the Church of the East from the ravages of time,
with all the original splinterings and marks of this Church.

III

The Christians of the Near East have preserved the faith
they received from their fathers. This in itself is a great achievement. Much of this faith is embodied in custom, ritual, art,
song, and ceremony. These devices, besides being great artistic
creations, are often excellent conservers—better than what the
word alone can carry—of what is under attack; they embellish,
cover, and conceal it enough to make it appear relatively harm-
less and unprovocative. But underneath the artistic imagery,
sometimes most beautiful in itself, stands the core of the faith
in perfect formal completeness. All that it takes to discover that
this faith is there and is absolutely intact is to unmask the song
and ritual and penetrate to what they say and mean. By attending most carefully to every intonation and every gesture, and by

taking in the majestic sweep of the total ceremony, one can read the whole content of the faith, in fact the whole cumulative history of the Church, from a single celebration of the liturgy. The liturgy is a special instrument whereby the Church has been providentially saved by the Holy Ghost under special circumstances over the centuries.

When the Church is driven into the catacombs, whether physically or socially and spiritually, it ceases to be evangelical save unto itself; it turns then liturgical, preserving the entire deposit of faith behind symbol and song. It dies, so to speak, that the faith may live. "Being-evangelical" is not the only mode of existence of the Church. Under certain conditions, when the principalities and powers of the world have taken, whether in the name of society, or in the name of some abstract system of thought, or from demonic motives, or even in the name of God, a consciously militant attitude against it, "being-liturgical" is the only possible mode of existence for the Church. It then suffers patiently and in silence, it bides its time, until the word is freed and the heart and mind can sing and shout again in open exultation.

But faith overflows also in cultural bearing and general outlook. While the Christians of the Near East share with their non-Christian fellow citizens the economic, social, and political life of their respective countries, they tend on the whole to manifest a distinctive intellectual, moral, spiritual, and personal existence. At least in theory, at least in the intent of their mind, their view of morality, woman, family life, the sanctity of children, freedom, the human person, personal responsibility, universal human nature, reason, the possibility of regarding all men as human beings, tolerance, and trust; their being open to all truth wherever it is found, their participating unapologetically in the positive, cumulative Western tradition of science and thought, and their founding social and political existence more on consent than on coercion: all this appears, in their actual life and conduct, distinctively and unmistakably Christian. It often brings upon their heads misunderstandings, trials, and sufferings

of the crudest or subtlest sort, but the fact that they have survived all these things measures how much they have borne.
Thus, only God knows how and how much this struggling handful of Christians in the Near East has served over the centuries
as an awakener, a stimulant, and a leaven; only God knows how
and what the Near East, and indeed the world, would have been
without them.

IV

The Christians of the Near East are conscious of their
minority status. Their entire attitude and mentality reflect this
minority consciousness. The Lebanese Christians are only a partial exception, because they too, when they mentally set themselves politically within the context of the larger Muslim world
of the Near East to which they belong, automatically fall into
the strange unauthentic workings of the minority mind. The
Christians of the Near East develop a dual soul, with a terrific
inner tension, often also exceedingly comic, and they suffer
under a pathetic sense of insecurity. They will not let go their
Christianity, but at the same time they must do nothing that
will offend their Muslim world. They do not want to betray
their Christian heritage, but neither do they want to prove
traitors to the Muslim world to which they belong economically,
socially, politically. In many fundamental interpretations of
man, history, and destiny, Islam and Christianity do not see eye
to eye; in fact, in some instances they hold contradictory positions; and so the poor Christian is torn between the inner world
of his fundamental Christian convictions and the overwhelming
outer Muslim world of his social-political existence. He is called
to endure, and be not unfaithful to both of these worlds; and if
he succeeds in the teeth of the apparent impossibility of this
task, no achievement anywhere is more glorious than his. He has
kept his integrity, not vis-à-vis something neutral and uncommitted (e.g., the pagan world), but vis-à-vis something that has

arisen in the first place precisely on the basis of a self-conscious position toward what he stands for. And since Christianity is a universal religion, since therefore he is necessarily in communion with other Christians all over the world, establishing all sorts of spiritual and temporal associations with them, and since there have been for centuries, going back to the original wars between Christendom and Islam, passing through the Crusades, and culminating in the "colonialism" and "imperialism" of the nineteenth and twentieth centuries, most important economic and political conflicts and complications between the "Christian" West and the "Muslim" Near East, the Christian of the Near East is always under suspicion that he might be, or is strongly tempted to become, an agent or a "lackey" of "the imperialists," and a traitor to his own country and people.

A strange type of soul often arises under such conditions. The term "Levantine" has been aptly used to denote it. Living in two worlds at the same time, the Christian and the Muslim, without fully belonging to either; appropriating from one world a spiritual-moral-existential content and from the other only formal aspects of its economic-social-political existence; compelled to "belong" to the two worlds, on the one hand by the force of spiritual inheritance, and on the other by sheer physical-geographical-social necessity; finding itself quantitatively overwhelmed by one world while being fully convinced in its heart that the other world to which it does not also quite fully belong is nevertheless qualitatively superior; profoundly attached emotionally and existentially to its soil and country, and yet feeling somewhat of a stranger in its own land and among its own people; resigning itself to a permanent status of social and political inferiority; therefore turning its energies, not to the creative responsibilities and decisions of history, but to commerce, shopkeeping, speculation, smuggling, "reporting," "interpreting East to West and West to East," and the dark, shady world of entertainment and pleasure; reducing everything to the common denominator of money and gain; crafty, sensuous, wily,

calculating, sly; stopping in the midst of a sentence and changing its tack when it suddenly realizes that the audience is
"mixed," containing representatives of both worlds; developing
a strange kind of "eye" whereby audiences are canvassed and
cautiously weighed in advance; living in whispers, doubletalk,
ambiguous phrases, esoteric meanings; boastful, unreal, given to
exaggeration and dreams; with a truncated sense of history
whereby it shies responsibility for great causes in which it may
be called to fight and die for something; sponsoring, when it
realizes the unsufferability of its condition, all sorts of national,
Arab, Pan-Arab, socialist and Communist causes, thereby escap-
ing from the burden of its Christianity and creating a convenient
common platform with the Muslims in which they too escape
the burden of their Islam; often unable to discriminate between
truth and falsehood, or willfully slurring over such discrimination; taking childish pride in the most elementary virtues if it
ever actualizes them, such as being "sincere" and being "frank";
looking on rather than acting, waiting for salvation from outside
rather than relying on its own resources, receiving and following
rather than giving and taking the lead—such is the characteriza-
tion of the Levantine soul in general.

I need hardly reassure the gentle reader that I am here
neither thinking statistically nor fastening on particular individuals or groups; I am only asserting that such is the Levantine
character however and wherever it arises, and that, by reason of
the hard conditions of their life, the besetting temptation of the
Christians of the Near East, unless they are most careful, is
precisely to develop such a character.

V

The phenomenon of Levantinism is not confined to urban
existence in the Near East. Wherever man lives in two civilizational worlds at the same time without fully belonging to either,
one world overwhelming his existence quantitatively (e.g., economically, socially, politically), the other determining it quali-

tatively (e.g., personally, spiritually, genetically), he is likely to become Levantinized. In varying degrees and under diverse modalities the phenomenon of Levantinism appears under three other conditions besides the Near East. There are distinct traces of it among populations in border areas between large cultural or national concentrations. It appears, in the second place, wherever there are sizable immigrations of peoples with diverse backgrounds into settled societies with a strong cultural consciousness. This is true all over the Western Hemisphere. Thus nowhere is Levantinism more rampant than in New York, although the phenomenon there appears under a special modality.

Third, one of the subtlest forms of Levantinism appears whenever people think for a long time internationally and interculturally, or whenever they expose themselves in international conferences for a long time to clashing points of view. You begin to see *some* "good" in the other point of view and you gradually lose hold on your fundamental principles. There is no *good-in-itself*, no transcendent judge. Everything can be compromised, everything can be accepted if seen or taken "from the right point of view." "Survival at any cost" becomes then the overriding principle: there is nothing worse, nothing to be dreaded more, than death, and therefore under the threat of extinction everything is justified. There is no truth or cause for which one would gladly die, no evil which one would rather not live than take part in or embrace. In internationalist or interculturalist existence you will find softness, sandiness, perpetual yielding, "peaceful coexistence." You will find fear of force, but not fear of the Lord; fear of not-being, but not fear of being. You will find "tolerance," not in the sense of genuinely "respecting" the other fellow for the good that he has without ever letting him down with regard to what he has not and is not, not in the sense of loving him and seeing him in the light of the good that he may become, not therefore in the sense of judging him in terms of his potentialities, not therefore because you yourself are in touch with a real good absolutely independent of you and him in the light of which and by the power of which you judge and see him and yourself, but in the flat, stale, and static sense of patting him on the back, of appealing to him to "live-and-let-live," of not wanting to challenge him at all, of thanking God and laughing in your sleeve if you are only permitted to coexist side by side with him.

Since, then, the world has incredibly shrunk into a neighborhood, since the problems of war and peace and of human community are on everybody's mind, since we must not only understand but also agree with one another to be able to live together without destroying one another, and since this understanding and agreement necessitate that we live at least intellectually in one another's world, then the whole world has become a sort of Levant where nobody can afford to live smugly in his own world alone. What the Levant by reason of its geographical necessities went through over the past millennia, the whole world is now suddenly forced to go through.

Christianity is not a matter of social adjustment or cultural civilizational necessities, although it has a great deal to say about these things. Christianity arose at the heart of the Levant when the temptation of Levantinism was perhaps at its intensest. Its affirmations and claims are altogether independent of any sociological or worldly cultural determinations. Therefore, Christians, whether Copts of Upper Egypt, or merchants of Damascus, or landowners in the Syrian countryside; whether among the ruling classes of Lebanon, or the shrewd businessmen of Beirut, or the sturdy peasants of the wonderful villages of the Lebanese hills and mountains; whether between the Slavic and Western cultures of Europe, or at the various points where the Eastern Church meets the Western Churches; whether as minorities in Asia and Africa; whether as immigrants in the Western Hemisphere in the midst of overwhelmingly dominant alien cultures; or whether, finally, discharging international or intercultural tasks, or simply concerned about how understanding and agreement, and therefore peace, may be brought about;

Christians of any description who are especially subject to the Levantine temptation, and who fall into this temptation, have thereby ceased to be Christian. The most superficial reading of the New Testament, let alone the doctrinal and living traditions of the Church and the great affirmations of liturgy, reveals that One, Jesus Christ, made absolute claims about Himself, about man and about history, claims that no modernism, no scientism, no rationalism, no liberalism, no "pluralism," no pathetic personal escapism, no "higher criticism," no Levantine necessities, no requirements of peace and international concord, can possibly obliterate or explain away. Therefore Levantinism in the foregoing sense in *the religious sphere* has nothing in common with Christianity.

VI

The Christian communities of the Near East have performed a splendid task of preservation. Every conceivable material and mental device has been used by them. In their whole existence they embody a sort of sedimentation of centuries of suffering and experience. They know the catechism and they teach it to their children. Grandmothers play an important role in the transmission of the faith. They piously cross themselves, and their daughters wear necklaces with a beautiful pendant golden cross. There are crucifixes in their homes and icons and pictures of saints. Every rite has its own resplendent liturgy coming down from the early centuries and containing, among the Orthodox and Catholics, the wholeness of the faith.

Signs and symbols of Christianity are found everywhere: in their homes, in their morals, in their customs, in their language, even in their names. Religious ceremonies—baptisms, weddings, funerals, the Holy Mass—are most colorful and packed with meaning and memory; and the solemnity with which they are performed leaves an indelible mark upon those who attend or participate in them. They are an education by themselves, so that a child who goes through them several times, even if he received no formal religious education of any kind, has had the substance of the faith imprinted on his soul. There are thousands of church buildings, some very old, throughout the Near East, with characteristic Oriental cupolas; and the Holy Eucharist has been celebrated for centuries, in some every morning, in others certainly every Sunday. Practically every hilltop in Lebanon displays an imposing monastery or some religious institution; and all along the road in the countryside are little niches, beautifully lit at night, with madonnas or icons or pictures of particular saints, and whenever the faithful pass these symbols, their hearts brighten or they cross themselves.

Who can measure how much society in the Near East, both Muslim and Christian, especially in Lebanon and Syria, owes to the selfless works of charity of wonderful dedicated Sisters, belonging to diverse religious orders, and of other Christian religious communities, in raising homeless children, abandoned babies, unfortunate girls? No sound in Lebanon is more distinctive and more evocative of profound nostalgia than the rhythmic chimes of churchbells floating across hill and dale, at dawn or dusk, from churches or monasteries. The great feasts of the Church (in Lebanon, especially Easter, Christmas, the Feast of the Assumption of the Virgin, the Feast of the Transfiguration of the Lord, the Feast of the Cross, and the Feasts of particular Patron Saints) are occasions of great joy and celebration, preceded for the more pious by special acts (including strict fasting) of mortification and penance.

I do not believe church attendance in the Near East is below that in any other part of the world. There is a distinctive Christian Arabic poetry and literature, especially in Lebanon. The Bible, Homer, and the *Summa Theologica* of St. Thomas Aquinas were translated and published in Lebanon. There are Lebanese religious orders, some sending forth dedicated missionaries.

All this struggling faithfulness, all these movingly stubborn remnants of what was once a most creative spirituality to which the whole Christian world owes so much, are absolutely wonderful. Let no man belittle the preservative achievement of the Christianity of the Near East. When I observe the readiness with which Western Christianity, in the face of less trying odds, lapses at times into secularism, liberalism, humanism, relativism, materialism, Marxism, Communism, and immanentism, I humbly conclude that the achievement of the Christianity of the Near East, in the eyes of the Lord and so far as the "book of life" is concerned, is not altogether null.

VII

Eastern Christianity cannot afford to look forward only to the accomplishments, great as they are, of transmission and preservation. It must be more original, more daring, more confident, and more creative in its dreams of itself.

1. The Christians of the Near East must never separate themselves from the social, intellectual, and national stirrings of their world. When they cannot lead, they must nevertheless take as active a part in these movements as possible. Certainly the living Lord has a special will, often quite unknown and to be sought with tears, for the economic, social, and political orders emerging in the Near East. There are two dangers of the most tragic character which face the Christians of the Near East in this regard: (a) to identify themselves with these movements at the price of their Christianity; or (b) to interpret their Christian identity in such a way as to become virtually excluded from any effective participation in these movements. No general rule can magically or mechanically save one from adventure, experimentation, and suffering. The fundamental regulative principle is: Never be disloyal to Christ, never detach yourself from the movements stirring your people at their depths; and where the two injunctions conflict, seek the will of Christ for that occasion

with total abandon, and accept any suffering with which He may wish to visit you. There is no drab *modus vivendi*: in the rapidly changing Near East, changing often in mysterious ways, every morning the challenge faces you in ever fresh forms.

2.   The Christians of the Near East have a special intellectual-spiritual vocation. They must never weaken in holding up the highest standards of scholarship and learning. They must be absolutely convinced that in the bosom of the Eternal Logos all truth safely and certainly and joyously discloses itself. Upon the advent of Islam it was from their forebears that the adherents of the new faith first obtained an inkling of Greco-Western thought. If certain of their present scientific-historical findings concerning the original relations of Islam to Christianity and the subsequent development of Islam cannot now be published, they should not on that account lose interest in fundamental historical research: on the contrary, they should work out the truth in the fullest detail, and leave it to the safe-keeping of future more enlightened generations. They should impart to their world the ideal of absolute dedication to the truth, above all self-interest and all emotion. They should keep in the closest touch with Western higher centers of learning and develop such centers themselves. They should stress not only science and technique, but above all the liberal arts, the power of reason in all spheres of human existence, the cogency of argument, philosophy, fundamental ideas, the compulsion of the universal, the value of fundamental research in all realms, the original potency of the spirit. In these domains if they do not endeavor to lead, in the face of all hardship and misunderstanding and no matter at what cost, nobody else in the Near East can and will lead.

There are great intellectual-spiritual achievements in the classical Muslim tradition—in poetry, in literature, in positive science, in jurisprudence, in philosophy, in Muslim theology, in art, and above all in Sufi writings—that the Christians of the

Near East can appreciate, rejoice in, and help to discover and elucidate. Canon Kenneth Cragg has been pioneering, especially in his *Operation Reach,* in the field of what he calls "the positive content of Islam." Thus he writes:

> There is in many quarters a will to understanding and a patient search after the ear at least of thinking Muslims by a careful concern for the positive content of Islam. Themes like sovereignty, God in his signs, the Names of God, man in nature and man in sin, the mystery of idolatry and its antagonism to Divine Lordship, the meaning of Divine unity, are being more deeply studied in Christian circles, in the belief that through these areas of common ground witness to the Gospel may more truly penetrate the Muslim mind with those themes, like the Cross, the Incarnation and the Holy Trinity, which have been too long imprisoned in, and ill-served by a barren controversy. It is not that controversy is finally avoidable, but that it must be set in those realms which the issues of it really concern and where the answers can most blessedly arise. There is no front of Christian witness where the art of communication is a more urgent field of loving study and spiritual attainment than that on the Christian frontier with Islam.[2]

I completely endorse these words, and I believe that the Christians of the Near East should join with Western Christians in lovingly exploring "the art of communication . . . on the Christian frontier with Islam." Much more than they have dared to do so far, the Christians of the Near East can make the world of reason, study, thought, and books their world, and through it they can perform a unique service in which nobody else can replace them.

3. The Christians of the Near East should "revive" their own glorious religious past. This means, among other things, vital reacquaintance with the great Greek Fathers, especially Chrysostom, Basil, and the Damascene, with St. Ephraem, with Pseudo-

[2] *World Christian Handbook,* 1962, p. 37, in an introductory article entitled "The Muslim World."

Dionysius, and with the great hermits, ascetics, and anchorites of Egypt, northern Syria, and the desert. Circles of study, courses in schools, sermons in churches, celebrations of feasts, topical retreats for the faithful, exposition of the liturgy that everybody knows by heart—all these things can sensitize living Christians to an integral deposit that arose and matured in their own lands and under their own skies, a deposit on which the whole edifice of Christian doctrine and life, both in the East and in the West, has been built. With the humanism and immanentism of this age, in which man and history are conceived as wholly self-sufficient and paradise on earth as attainable through revolution, social change, and unaided human effort, nothing is more needed to remind mankind that it must first "give God the praise" than the original transcendental spirituality of the Near East. God is Creator and Wholly Other (there is here a fruitful "common ground" with Islam), history and man are wholly in His hands, and man can be mystically united with his Creator (again a "common ground" with the great Muslim mystics) through absolute detachment from all creatures and through seeking His face alone. This independence and otherness of God, His free Majesty, are wonderfully represented in the Eastern liturgies; the sinner attending Mass completely forgets about himself and his miserable sins and loses himself in the Divine Majesty; he experiences a "lift" of freedom from himself, because nothing that is said touches his particular personal sin, the entire drama depicting God, Heaven, the Angels, Christ, the Cross, the act of salvation, the Mother of God, the divine economy, the mystical coming of Christ in person right there in the Bread and Wine on the Holy Table, as though he and his stupid sins did not exist.

Original Oriental mysticism has much to say to the complacent, pagan, modern world, so wrapped up in itself, so entangled in its own self-analysis. When vigorous Christian communities in the West, forgetting this original impulse to which in the end they owe everything, have had a thousand years of trials behind them, they will then rediscover and feel at one with the Christianity of the Near East; they will find that its conclusions are not much different from theirs; and in the achieved unity of history they will become humble. If the Christians of the Near East knew how to "revive" this original mystical spirituality, they would help considerably both in correcting the progressivism and immanentism of this age and in reestablishing the unity of history.

4. The Christians of the Near East owe a great deal to Western Christian missionaries: American, British, French, German, Italian, and Russian—Protestant, Catholic, and Orthodox. The direct Christian impact of this mighty movement of the Spirit during the last century and a half upon the Muslims of the Near East has been negligible, Islam as such being quite resistant to Christian conversion. The ultimate reason for this resistance is that Islam, as it first formed itself, took a final, clear-cut, conscious stand about Christianity, and once such stands have absolutized and established themselves, their change becomes humanly impossible. But if the direct Christian impact of the missionary endeavors upon Islam has been almost nil, the indirect impact, through contact and association, hospitals and education, books, acts of charity, and the revitalization of the native Christian communities themselves, has been enormous. I am of the opinion that no sacrifice has been a waste, no tear has been shed in vain, no sigh or suffering has been of no avail. The story of how much the Christians of the Near East owe the great Western missionary movement, not only spiritually but in every other way, will fill volumes, and in its exact total scope it can never be written: it is known only to God.

Some Western missionaries have been turning over their responsibilities lately to native forces, but of course they cannot altogether disinterest themselves in what they have created and left behind. Three problems arise: (*a*) how each missionary enterprise may continue to relate itself both to its product and to the old Churches of the Near East; (*b*) how the scandal of rivalry, suspicion, and division, both among the Protestant missionary enterprises and between Protestant and Catholic missions, may be ended; and (*c*) how the *Kulturkampf* among the diverse home cultures as the various missionaries carry them over to the field (e.g., among the Protestants, between British and American, and between German and Anglo-Saxon; and among the Catholics, between French and German, and between European and American) may be softened. These three problems are among the determinants of the future of Christianity in the Near East; for the Near East, more than any other region in the world, faithfully mirrors the state of the world, both the degree of unity or disunity prevailing, particularly in the West, and the scandal of Christian disunity.

5. The Christians of the Near East are gradually discovering both one another and the Christian world as a whole. Unless they understand, love, help, and cooperate with one another, they cannot pass, Christianly speaking, from the old virtue of conservation to the new path of creation. Partly as a result of the present ecumenical impulse which I do not believe is a passing phenomenon and which has certainly reached the Near East (the spirit of Pope John XXIII has virtually wrought a revolution), partly by reason of other processes, pressures, and compulsions, a wonderful new spirit has come upon the scene. There is less acrimony and mistrust than ever before; there is a new openness of spirit, a new creative tolerance, a readiness to listen and learn, a genuine longing for fellowship and unity. Christians feel one another's stimulating and sustaining presence more than ever before. The liturgy is not as repulsive to Protestants as it was only a generation ago; Orthodox are not as suspicious of Catholics as they were only a decade ago; and Catholics enter into creative conversations on questions of doctrine and unity, with both Orthodox and Protestants, more than they used to do only two or three years ago.

If this spiritual *rapprochement* continues under the Holy Ghost and as He wills, and if the underlying subtle *Kulturkampf* is reduced to manageable proportions, then wonderful creative days lie ahead before the Christianity of the Near East. But two conditions are absolutely necessary: more calls for religious vocations, and constant touch with the sources of the streams of ecumenicity in the world, particularly at Rome, at the World Council of Churches, and with the Russian Church. The Christian world cannot be indifferent to the fate, both spiritual and temporal, of the Christians of the Near East; and the Christians of the Near East cannot remain isolated from the stirrings of the Holy Spirit among their fellow Christians throughout the world.

6. The Christianity of the Near East depends to some extent on the fate of Lebanon. It is not correct to say that Lebanon is a Christian country, because about half of its population is non-Christian—Muslim (Sunni and Shii) and Druse. But it is correct to say that Lebanon is a country in the Near East in which the Christians are, or should be, as free as they are, and feel, or should feel, as much at home as they do, in Rome or Paris or Munich or Madrid or Manchester or Boston. The Muslims too are, or should be, as free and happy as they are anywhere else in the Muslim world. The uniqueness of Lebanon is that *both* Christians and Muslims feel, or should feel, perfectly at home in it. If you ask a Lebanese Muslim: Do you want a Lebanon in which a Christian does not feel perfectly at home? he will emphatically answer you, No. And if you ask a Lebanese Christian: Do you want a Lebanon in which a Muslim does not feel perfectly at home? he will also emphatically answer you, No. There is, then, a free, equal, self-reliant, self-respecting, historically rooted, unoverwhelmed, distinctive, *Christian* culture in Lebanon. Its value is appreciated almost unanimously by Christians and Muslims in the Near East. Any political arrangement with respect to Lebanon may vary, and any person or

regime is expendable, but what should be looked upon as fixed and invariable is the concept of Lebanon as wholly dedicated to the human person, a country in which the truth, at every level of existence, may be freely sought and found, and wisely declared, a country in which human rights and fundamental freedoms are held sacrosanct, and therefore a country in which both Christian and Muslim can live happily and creatively side by side in peace. It is obvious that Lebanon does not wholly fulfill this ideal, but it is this ideal nevertheless that justifies Lebanon. The Lebanese themselves are of course primarily responsible for translating this ideal into working, stable arrangements, but the world, both East and West, both Christian and Muslim, is also responsible. Nowhere else can concerned outside forces have more creative relevance and bear more certain fruits, in the service of man, truth, and freedom, than in Lebanon.

7. The fullest identification with the aspirations of the people, the most vigorous intellectual leadership, the most intensive effort to "revive" the tradition of the Fathers and Saints, the closest cooperation among themselves and with existing missionary activities, the most sincere participation in the promising ecumenical movement of this age, and the brightest prospects for a free, independent, and secure Lebanon—all this is not enough to cause the Christians to move from the preservative to the creative stage of existence. They are excellent preparations, but without the independent, free, sovereign, additional agency of the Holy Ghost, no creation is possible.

What is needed is effulgence of light and power, the peace of being that freely creates, the certainty of the hand of God. God Himself must bless and act. Without godliness, saintliness, and holiness, without the victory of the Cross and the joy of the Spirit, nothing is possible save staleness and repetition. The Christians of the Near East cannot just "resolve" one morning to pass from conservation to creation and then the creation will forthwith ensue: it may be that God does not want them to create; it may be that their utmost task now is only to conserve. To be in a position to create, the Christians of the Near East must once again affirm in their own life the mystery of "suffering for His name's sake." They are actually suffering in all sorts of ways, but somehow the suffering is not counted to them for righteousness: it is a cosmic waste. That is why they do not "count" in the total Christian scale; that is why there is no inspired Near Eastern Christian literature read in Helsinki and Paris, in Burma and Buenos Aires. There are a number of causes under consideration in the councils of Rome, but the cause of the Maronite hermit Sharbel Makhlouf appears to be more advanced than the rest. If this man of God is declared saint, it will be a great day in the modern history of Near Eastern Christianity; it will signify that God has once again deigned to call men to suffer creatively and "countingly" for His name's sake on these shores. Man can only suffer: it is God alone who can transfigure suffering into glory. Man can only accept the Cross: it is God alone who can raise from the dead. Absolute detachment from the world and all its deceitfulness; dying to self; treading under foot the ugly face of the Devil through the power of the Cross; repenting, confessing, sharing, trusting, expecting; absolute nearness to the heart of Christ; the sanctification of whole actions and institutions; simply letting the Holy Ghost guide, lead, and direct; entering into the glorious company of the saints through contemplation and ardent prayers of intercession; the quiet of eternity; loving and obeying unto death—you can pray and yearn for these things; you can reject them when they come your way; but one thing you cannot do: you cannot produce or create them. They are the free and independent gift of the Holy Ghost. The question is whether it is in the design of the Holy Ghost to grant them to the Christians of the Near East.

✦ VI ✦

Africa, Part I

CHRISTIAN G. BAËTA

CHRISTIAN G. BAËTA

The Reverend Doctor Christian G. Baëta, O. B. E., is Professor and Head of the Department for the Study of Religions in the University of Ghana, and is a member of the Ghana Academy of Sciences. Dr. Baëta used well the advantages of the Mission Training School at Basel. He earned the B. A. and B. D. degrees in the University of London; and later the Ph.D. degree for his interpretation of field studies published under the title, PROPHETISM IN GHANA. Dr. Baëta served in the Gold Coast Legislative Council.

Christian Baëta was Synod Clerk of the Evangelical Presbyterian Church of Ghana, and is an elder statesman of that body as well as of the Ghana Christian Council in which he has been Chairman. He was Henry W. Luce Visiting Professor of World Christianity in Union Theological Seminary, New York 1958-59. He has been Chairman of the International Missionary Council, presiding over that body in the important period of its integration with the World Council of Churches. He has also been active in the Council of the Churches on International Affairs and in various units of the World Council; in the Theological Education Fund Committee; and in the All Africa Church Conference.

VI

M̲y consideration of Christianity's present position and future prospects in the newly independent countries of sub-Saharan Africa will discuss the internal adjustments made incumbent on the Church by the whole movement of African emancipation, some difficulties which arise for the Church's full witness from certain events and facts of the situation, and my reading of the way ahead in the light of the "signs of the times." The term "Church" is here used to signify the Christian presence, whichever the organisation(s) representing it might be.

There appears to be a great need for Christians to understand the shift that has taken place, since colonial days, in the position occupied by the Church within society. Despite some restrictions usually placed upon its operations in Muslim areas, purely for reasons of politics and of good order, the Church under the outgoing regimes enjoyed a position which in many respects was a privileged one. That was so not only because it represented the religion of the ruling powers but also, and even more, for the reason that it was acknowledged by all, rulers and the enlightened among the ruled alike, to be a good, indeed an indispensable influence in the life of the peoples. Christian missionary agencies participated to a certain extent in the civilising aspect of colonial rule. For example, old mission-station records of my own home area reveal that the travelling missionary was constantly warning local chiefs that if, by his next visit, they failed to supply at least ten children to attend the

newly established village school, the matter would be reported
to the Government District Officer. (I first came upon these
records at a time when my own problem, as Synod Clerk of my
Church, was precisely that several of our members were threatening to leave the Church because we could not find places for
their children in our schools!)

The Church was held in high regard, and deference to its
dignitaries came naturally to most government representatives as
a result of their upbringing. On State occasions Church leaders
were given places of honour and their counsel and cooperation
were sought in difficult emergencies of all kinds. Of course
there were also dissenters from the general attitude, and it is on
record that some administrators used their position to pay off
old resentments against the Church, which they had brought
with them from home. But whoever might be concerned, and
whatever his own private views on the subject might be, so
universal and well established was the favourable general opinion
of the Church that overt hostility to it was both ill-advised and
ineffective. For the Africans the Church was the major agent
transmitting the benefits of Western civilisation, and membership in it was a mark of personal "progress" in life and of
enlightenment, even a step up on the local social ladder.

It would appear that the majority of Christians on the
continent, both Africans and expatriates, still continue to assume this climate. It was recently said of a leading churchman
that he firmly believed three things: that the Church was the
most important factor in the life of the nation; that his own was
the most important Church; and that since he was the head of
his Church, he was the most important person in the nation. I
remember how inconsolable distress was caused to a friend of
mine because at a State banquet, contrary to the practice on
previous such occasions, no grace was said.

Recently in one of the countries, the early-morning short
broadcast of praise and prayer on the National Broadcasting
System was shifted to a later hour, so that workers who had

been in the habit of listening to it before setting out could no longer do so; then also the total time for religious broadcasts was curtailed. Upon widespread and insistent public demand a delegation of Church representatives waited on the minister of State concerned, to request the restoration of these services. He pointed out that the time previously made available had been out of all proportion to the relative size of the Christian communities within the population; that he was deluged with requests for time on the air from all sorts of bodies including medicine-men and fetish-priests who, after all, represented the aboriginal, and still the majority, religious group: all these people believed themselves to have something of value to offer and were very eager to instruct the public; it was his business to see to it that a just and fair share of opportunity was given to all.

In point of fact this particular matter has since been straightened out satisfactorily so that it is no longer an issue, yet it is still noteworthy that the reaction of these church people who learned of the minister's reply was one of stupefaction and blank dismay. I have cited this case because the minister's reply is symptomatic of the new order, and the reaction of shocked surprise and horror which it evoked is also entirely typical for similar situations. As the process of shaping the new way of life develops, the discovery that the Church does not in fact possess the influence over the State that had traditionally been held to belong to it as of right, as well as anything emerging which seems to contradict Christian policies or to represent a setback for the Christian position, tends to call forth almost paralysing alarm and near despondency.

In this way the proposed or effected transfer of some Church schools and hospitals to public agencies, as well as the indication that this development (dubbed "encroachment") is likely to continue, has occasioned much chagrin. Of course any diminishing of the accustomed opportunities of service is rightly a matter for deep regret; also, indeed, the concern felt is a thoroughly genuine one based, as it is, on the not unreasonable fear that, once pushed out of the arena of public service the Church would lose significance and consequently become less effective even in its own spiritual sphere. However, is it the facilities thus on loan to it from external sources (which can therefore be withdrawn again at any time) that undergird the Church's life? Does it not rather live by the grace of God and depend upon the personal devotion of its members to their Lord in response to His love? It appears indeed unseemly to insist upon retaining any vested prerogatives whatsoever, and the Church must learn to carry on its work unimpeded, entirely from its own resources.

Again, faithfulness to the Cause is too largely identified with simply holding on fast to past practice in the Church's ways of self-expression: in organisation, worship, music, manner of life and work, and even in such externals as dress and the architecture and decoration of church buildings. After a discussion in which more use by the Church of African music and dance had been urged, a participant whispered to another, "You may say and do what you like, but the great universal Christian hymns will not only be sung to the end of time, they will continue to be sung in heaven." Said the other, "I'm sure you are right, but why not some African music *as well?*" Back came the slightly irritated retort, "But why all these new-fangled ideas and innovations when we have never felt that anything was lacking?" It cannot be surprising that a frankly negative attitude to African ways of self-expression nowadays merely courts reactions which deliberately emphasize the foreignness of Christianity.

Quite often, particularly in smaller groups and informal gatherings, protest demonstrations and strong public statements of condemnation or prophetic warnings have been urged. Now without a doubt some occasions have already arisen on which such a course was indeed justified. But the question is precisely whether the real demands of our day are not better met in less panic-stricken or spectacular ways. The Cause could hardly benefit by mere righteous indignation or rash public protests made for insufficient or wrong reasons. In these matters the development of a defeatist attitude or of a general persecution and fear psychosis must be avoided at all costs, especially as (at least so far) there appears to be no justification for any such thing.

Precisely because a far more serious situation might well evolve; because a real religious disagreement with the ruling authorities and the consequent disobedience towards them, however undesired and even feared, may again at any time become an unavoidable duty for Christians; precisely because the point may again be reached, at any time, when, like the Apostles before the Jewish authorities, there is nothing else that Christians can do but to say, "We must obey God rather than men," and humbly suffer the consequences; and because all such situations are tragic in the extreme and may even prove disastrous to the Cause, at least temporarily, it becomes an imperative obligation upon the Church, with all Christian realism, calm, and levelheadedness, to come to a clear view not only of where a breach would become inevitable but also of what constructive, happy, and mutually helpful relations might well be established.

It is earnestly to be hoped that all Church leaders have by now adjusted their minds sufficiently to accept African governments fully as the equals of their predecessors in every way, and to give them the same deference. This did not always come easily or as fast as it might have, partly due to the fact that mental attitudes and habits change slowly, and partly because the new governments themselves are in large measure even as yet rather inexperienced in their job, and for sheer lack of better-prepared human material must carry much inefficient personnel. However, care must be taken that the Church does not lag behind but rather leads the way in this important matter of giving honour where honour is so rightly due.

So a herculean task is crying to be done in clarifying the true position and function of the Church in society today, in distinguishing the essentials from the trimmings, in discovering a sounder basis for the Church's stand and a maturer approach to its witnessing in the world. The inheritance of the past and the pressures of the present make this an extremely delicate and hazardous undertaking, but there is no way of circumventing it. I strongly believe that this effort must include taking in hand at long last, within the Church, the magical understanding of religion generally prevalent in the African continent, which regards it as a supernatural means of purveying benefits rather than as a God-given capacity for deepening the human spirit.

II

One of the most obvious duties of a Church caught in a wave of intense and impatient "nationalism" is, of course, to maintain a constant reminder, not only of its own essentially universal character but also of the common humanity and brotherhood of the people concerned with all the rest of the world. The African revolution necessarily has racial undertones since the wounds inflicted by racial discrimination have been and in some areas still continue to be principal scourges of African life. Indeed "nationalism" in our context really means the active rejection of white supremacy, tutelage, leadership, or even influence. It would therefore seem to be a plain Christian duty to do everything possible towards ensuring that the end of imperialism does not mean merely the emergence of yet another exclusive and hostile bloc but rather a further step toward the integration of mankind.

However, also in this respect the odds against the Church are very heavy. Whereas there must be many non-Africans who genuinely welcome the African transformation, this is by no means a universal attitude. Africans who would fraternise and advocate frank, amicable, and trustful relationships with foreigners believed to have been converted from colonialist intentions, have found themselves confronted with a whole range of very ugly contrary facts. This makes their position not only slightly ridiculous but also suspect in the extreme to their own compatriots. The spectre of neo-colonialism is by no means a mere phantasy but rather a very powerful and effective force; witness its operations in the Congo. Hardly less discouraging are the constant warnings issuing forth about the dangers of rapid and full African liberation: of possible racial discrimination in reverse; suggestions that the faults and wickedness are not all on one side; that whilst the end of freedom may be a good thing in itself it could be a great evil to hurry it; that time must be allowed for the practice of the Christian West to catch up with its own conscience, etc. When there are beams to be removed, it is unconvincing to be drawing attention to motes, and people in the grip of a life-and-death struggle for a worthy existence too long denied, can only understand such complacency as just another form of plain opposition. The conclusion has to be that, while the Church must certainly keep flying the banner of universal brotherhood and seize every suitable opportunity of witnessing to it, so long as the danger of sabotaging the freedom movement persists, it should be circumspect in reacting to self-protective government policies or actions appearing to be unfriendly to aliens, whether in our midst or abroad.

III

Certain African governments have already publicly declared their official stand in the matter of Church-State relations. In Ghana, in a speech delivered on the occasion of the presentation to him of the Lenin Peace Prize, the President praised "the practice of Secular Democracy" as a useful factor in the peaceful coexistence of nations, without saying definitely that it was the policy to be applied in the country. In societies in which people profess several different faiths and some no faith at all, this principle would naturally commend itself to sound commonsense, and it must be quite safe to assume that it will in fact generally be the basis for these relations. The term "Secular State" has been variously interpreted as meaning "a state which is neutral to the influence of religion" and "a state which welcomes religion, but does not give a preferred place to any particular religion." In any case all the basic religious freedoms appear to be guaranteed under it. Doubtless emphases in practical application will vary from place to place, but so long as there is no radical departure from the doctrine itself, things cannot go very far wrong, and in my opinion the Church does well to adopt a positive attitude towards it and to plan its witness within this framework.

The Church will need to be constantly on guard against unwarranted extensions of the meaning of "Secular Democracy" to suggest that the State regards religion as undesirable or unimportant or untrue; or that its aloofness from religion is in some way or other an indication of its hostility to it or of its preference for godlessness. In loyalty to the accepted principle the Church must refrain from offensive assaults on other faiths or on irreligion merely as such, and should rather seek amicable relations with all, showing readiness to learn from all. But, in view of atheist propaganda it is necessary to warn simple believers against being taken in by insinuations as if godlessness were more "scientific," or had a greater guarantee of truth, or were entitled to more rights, or had in any other way a higher standing than faith. Rather, atheism must be seen for what it is, namely, a speculation like any other speculation, and one which still has to offer evidence that it can shed a better light upon human existence than we have had, or in some way more greatly enhance human living.

Attacks on the Church in Africa usually start with criticism of the missionary efforts of the past, which are discredited to the point of denying them any useful or constructive achievement whatsoever. The usual procedure is to weld Christianity's early conflicts with African culture and the worst errors committed in its name in Asia and elsewhere, into one massive indictment which, however, bears but little relation to the facts of the actual situation in Africa. That is not the way of truth, and the truth is unlikely to come to light so long as writers on these matters as a rule merely indulge in generalisations based on vague, subjective impressions, with hardly any real documentation. In this connection the recent formation of an African Church History Society is greatly to be welcomed, as it promises to furnish detailed, scholarly studies of specific topics in this field. The Church owes it to its past to make the facts available.

Far more important than the Church's acceptance, under the principle of the "Secular State," of an equal place with other religious bodies and voluntary organisations vis-à-vis the State, will be its readiness to renounce all use or seeking of worldly power. Its true assignment is to nourish the law of God as written on men's hearts; its point of departure is the knowledge that God has made man in such a way that, given favourable conditions, he will respond to God's call. The Church's only power is the power of powerlessness and its method only that of service and the persuasion of love. It must plainly be seen to be well content with this task and with this mode of its performance. While it must without ceasing witness to Christ, in both private and public matters, by throwing intelligible and well-informed light upon the things in our actual condition and in our planning which fall short of the best that they might be; and by pointing to the ways of righteousness as well through its proclamation as through its own manner of life and work, it must be at great pains to resist the temptation of trying to exert influence where it is not competent to do so.

Always under the reservation that man's first loyalty is to God, and that therefore he must have freedom of conscience with which to exercise it, it is necessary to emphasise the rights of the State in its own sphere. If the Church was instituted by God for man's redemption, so were the ruling authorities (i.e., the organised civil government) instituted by God to make human living in community possible. Thus the State in this sense is the prior institution because without the necessary basis of good order and peace which it provides, the Church could not exist. The self-evident justification of its God-ordained existence makes obedience to it a moral duty.

The new African governments are doing God's business also in another, very special way. Apart from fulfiling the normal functions of government they have to educate their citizens into real possession of their newly found freedom and nationhood. In spite of many evil and unworthy things happening at the same time, the coming of a greater measure of human dignity to Africans, of larger opportunities for work, for personal self-advancement and self-realisation in life, for development as fully responsible human beings, for higher living standards and a more commodious style of existence altogether, must be seen as the work of God. If that is so, then the Church should be in the front line of those who give these new governments the most genuine and unfaltering support, whether by cooperation in service, or by showing sympathetic understanding for their diffi-culties, or by instructing Church members to do their duties of citizenship with the faithfulness required of those under the discipline of Christ.

As regards public declarations of support, Christian good sense and taste must steer a middle course between the Scylla of being only a prophet of gloom and the uplifted warning finger, forever denying needed encouragement, and the Charybdis of joining in the shrill, extravagant, and for that reason somewhat indecent, adulation (often quite insincere) that has become common in our day.

Once the autonomy of the proper respective spheres of Church and State is recognised and each has firmly renounced any acts or pressures that might violate the other, their relation-ship need no longer be that of mutual indifference or cautious suspicion. Rather, since they complement each other for the true welfare of the people, it should be one of active and trustful contacts, a relationship which might well be described as "Positive Coexistence." Church and State are both deeply engaged in the search for the new values and standards which will lend quality, integrity, and genuineness to personality under the circumstances of today. New African governments have not hesitated to appeal to religious authorities for assistance with issues concerning public morality, standards of good behaviour, philanthropy, youth or child welfare, and the like. The continuance of religious teaching in the public educational system is another example in point, as the presence of Departments for the Study of Religions in the new African universities is yet a further indication of the positive attitude of the governments towards this whole area of life which is the Church's special concern, demonstrating their willingness to make available to the people the constructive forces which a sound and competent study of this subject can release.

Whatever the difficulties, there should be no thought of the Church's withdrawal from intimate involvement in any sector of the national life where good is being done or evil eliminated. Such voluntary abdication of duty does not even take the Church into a catacomb existence, it merely leads it into a ghetto, which is the last sort of place where it should be. God Himself did not abandon the world to its own devices because it was difficult or even wicked, rather He sent His Son into it to redeem it. Indeed the Church of Christ cannot live without rendering needed service, and if some of the social assistance it has traditionally given must now be surrendered, that is only a challenge to the imagination to discover new forms of service. As the late Pope John XXIII pointed out in a message to a Catholic Youth Conference recently, even in the Welfare State there are endless opportunities for Christians to minister to urgent human need, particularly on the local and personal levels. While the Church may never come to look upon its humanitarian work as its sole *raison d'être*, it must continue uninhibitedly to ask for, to accept and utilise faithfully to the best of its ability, all the facilities and opportunities that may be willingly placed at its disposal by the State for the service of the people.

The African revolution has indeed only just begun. It has yet to develop a culture, an adequate, meaningful world-view, an ethos, a scale of values, a general mode and style of life, an "African personality" that shall be worthy and shall serve the best interests of our peoples. I am convinced that in all this the African Church has a vital role to play. Whatever the Church's failures may have been in other parts of the world, I am sure that its record in Africa fully supports its claim to a share in this great enterprise. But it pleads for a fair chance to participate, not on these grounds but for the reason that nonparticipation would be abandonment of all that it stands for, and a threat to its own life.

My opinion is that the Church in the newly independent countries of sub-Saharan Africa is in quite good heart, and that it is here to stay. However, it may not be taken for granted as an ensured heritage, but must be constantly nurtured, cultivated, watched over, striven for. Provided that the newly inaugurated All Africa Churches Conference will receive the equipment necessary for it properly to fulfill its functions: of keeping the Churches in touch with one another and with the ongoing changes in their own situations; of recommending priorities for their activities; of helping to find the necessary resources to carry out their plans, etc., it should become a key factor in the future scene. Someone has said that a master, good or bad, can be chased away at any time, but nobody drives out a good servant. Said the Lord Jesus: "I am among you as one who serves" (Luke 22:27).

✦ ✦ VII ✦ ✦

Africa, Part II

P. ALLEN MYRICK

P. ALLEN MYRICK

The Reverend P. Allen Myrick, member of the United Church of Christ in the U. S. A., is a missionary of the United Church Board for World Ministries. He is now lecturer in Old Testament in the Federal Theological Seminary of Southern Africa, located at Alice, Cape Province, Republic of South Africa. The Federal Theological Seminary is the chief institution in South Africa for the training of Bantu ministers, supported cooperatively by Congregational, Presbyterian, Anglican, and Methodist bodies and serving students from a still wider range of Churches. Mr. Myrick received his theological training in Union Theological Seminary, New York. He has served in South Africa since 1958, beginning at the Adams United Theological School, then at Modderport in the Orange Free State but now forming one of the denominational colleges participating in the Federal Seminary. Mr. Myrick's relationships in South Africa during the formation and development of the Federal Seminary have aided him in gaining a wide and sound understanding of the Churches.

VII

Southern Africa may be distinguished from the rest of the continent by the fact that here large number of Europeans have settled permanently. Most of them are Christians, and for several generations they have supported missionary work among the native African people. Consequently, there is a larger Christian community in this region than in any other part of Africa. Statistically, the Republic of South Africa is the most significant country in this area, and we shall devote most of our attention to it. About 90 per cent of the three million whites are Church folk; about 50 per cent of the eleven million nonwhites are connected with the Church in some way, although a minority of these are full members. Protestantism is dominant and the Roman Catholic Church relatively small. In Southern Rhodesia the population numbers over two million, and about 250,000 of these are Protestants. By contrast, in the Portuguese territories of Angola and Mozambique the Roman Catholic Church is the strongest Christian body. Angola, with a population of 4,750,000, has about 1,500,000 Roman Catholics and just over 500,000 Protestants. In Mozambique, out of a population of more than six million there are approximately 300,000 Roman Catholics and 50,000 Protestants.

The greatest issue confronting the Church in Southern Africa is that of race relations. And nowhere is this problem so acute as in the Republic of South Africa. We shall, therefore, analyze this country's dilemma in some detail, and make only brief reference to the other nations of the area.

Built into the heart of South African life, conditioning every political, social, and economic circumstance, is the fact that the white man rules. Furthermore, he is convinced that he must rule indefinitely. This is not a new belief. It can be traced back through the recent decades of tension to the Anglo-Boer War (1899-1902), back through the life of the Boer Republics to the Afrikaners' Great Trek away from British rule (beginning in 1836), back into the eighteenth century when the Afrikaner soul was formed, with belief in white supremacy as a basic ingredient of that soul.[1] The Afrikaner Nationalist Party came to power in 1948 on a platform of white supremacy, summed up in the slogan *apartheid*—separation. In the years since 1948, law after law has been enacted to undergird and extend white supremacy. Residential segregation has been made universal; the little nonwhite representation which remained in Parliament was removed; African education was made the instrument of white supremacy; wide powers were granted to cabinet ministers to imprison or restrict suspected persons without warrant or trial. As African nationalism has grown, so has the power of the police, and white South Africa has armed itself in fear of revolution. Increasing tension has driven a growing number of whites into the Government camp. And the main Opposition party, which claims nearly all the remaining votes, also defends the ideal of white supremacy.

In such a setting, the Christian Church faces a cruel dilemma which impinges upon every aspect of its life. Most white South Africans are Christians, and the institutional Church is heavily dependent upon their support; while some denominations have a nonwhite majority, in most cases the bulk of the leadership and financial resources comes from the European community. Yet these same people firmly believe in a

[1] For a fuller discussion of these issues, see C. W. De Kiewiet, *A History of South Africa, Social and Economic* (London, 1941).

white supremacy which threatens men's liberty, hinders the spread of the Gospel, and jeopardizes the whole future of the Christian faith. Furthermore, African nationalism, spurred on by its victories in the lands to the north, is growing rapidly, and many African Christians sympathize with it. Thus at the precise moment when the nation needs a clear Christian witness in race relations, the Church is ruinously divided on this issue. Unless it honestly faces this predicament and works it out with courage and love, its future prospects are bleak indeed.

In analyzing this dilemma, we shall speak first of some general historical and theological factors, and then of the three major groups within the Christian community: the Afrikaners, the English, and the native Africans.

The Christian witness on race relations has been seriously hampered for a number of reasons. Chief among these is the fact that the Europeans have been white men before they have been Christians. They have inherited a culture technically superior to that of the Africans, and this has made them dominant in every phase of political, social, and economic life. This dominance they have made an article of faith; and like every ruling class, they passionately resist any suggestion that they should share their power with their less privileged brethren. At the same time, currents of thought which have worked for social justice in much of Christendom have passed South Africa by. In its geographical isolation from Europe, South Africa was relatively untouched by the Enlightenment philosophy and its passion for the "Rights of Man." The Industrial Revolution, the abuses of which stimulated the Christian concern for the "social gospel" in Europe and America, came very late to South Africa; when it did come, few Europeans suffered deprivation, and the white Christian conscience rested content. Calvinism, which in some circumstances in Europe and America contributed to a zeal for liberty and social reform, was used by Afrikaners to build an authoritarian state upon the premise that they were an elect people. And a strong strand of pietism led many Christians to dissociate religion and politics altogether. Thus until 1948, when the Afrikaner Nationalist Party began to implement its *apartheid* policy, little was said or done by the Church in the field of social ethics. Since that date, moreover, this concern has grown but slowly.

The Afrikaner people have traditionally been devout church-men, and the vast majority belongs to the Dutch Reformed Church. This Church has contributed much to the rise of Afrikaner nationalism, and most of its members support the ideal of white rule. To authoritarian Calvinism the Church has added an element of pietism, so that social action committees are chiefly concerned with problems of family life, alcoholism, Sunday observance, and the like. As Parliament has steadily eliminated men's civil liberties, the Dutch Reformed Church has scarcely ever publicly criticized the Government. Some Dutch Reformed leaders explain that rather than making public statements, they prefer to meet privately with Government offi-cials to influence legislative and executive action. Yet while this Church is silent on most *apartheid* legislation, it protested vigorously and publicly when Parliament considered a bill which it believed to be in violation of Christian principles: a measure permitting Africans to purchase alcoholic beverages. The bill passed anyway.

A few Dutch Reformed leaders have, of course, opposed *apartheid*. This criticism came to a head in 1960, when eleven Dutch Reformed ministers published a book of essays entitled *Delayed Action*, calling upon the Church to reassess its position and to abandon its support of white supremacy. Then in De-cember, 1960, the World Council of Churches convened a meeting of its South African member Churches at Cottesloe, Johannesburg, to discuss the Christian attitude toward race rela-tions. All of the Afrikaner, English, and African delegates en-dorsed the *Statement* which was issued, with the exception of the members of the conservative Hervormde Kerk. (The Moder-ator of this Church, which split off from the Dutch Reformed

Church in the last century, is reported to have said later, "What does the Gospel have to do with land and food and drink? It is the message of forgiveness of sins.") The Cottesloe *Statement* declared that racial discrimination must be abolished, and criticized many of the Government's policies and actions. Perhaps most significantly it said that ". . . a policy which permanently denies to Non-White people the right to collaboration in the government of the country of which they are citizens cannot be justified."[2]

When the Cottesloe report was released, the Afrikaans Churches reacted most negatively. In the synodical meeting of 1961, *Delayed Action* and the Cottesloe *Statement* were sharply criticized. Those bodies which were represented at Cottesloe (The Cape Province and Transvaal Synods of the Dutch Reformed Church, and the Hervormde Kerk) withdrew their membership from the World Council of Churches. Great pressure was brought to bear upon liberal members, and efforts were made to reduce their influence in the Church. One *Delayed Action* contributor was tried for heresy by the Hervormde Kerk. Since 1961 this pressure has been reinforced by political events. The danger of violence has grown appreciably, and whites of all views are drawing together in self-defense. In such an atmosphere, the handful of liberal Afrikaners seems to have adopted a "wait and see" attitude. A few of them have cooperated with some English-speaking ministers in the publication of an excellent monthly journal of liberal Christian opinion, *Pro Veritate*. Some continue to support the interracial ecumenical study groups which meet in several cities. But on the whole any movement for a more decisive witness on race relations seems to have lost momentum, and the prospects for the liberalization of Dutch Reformed attitudes are not good.

Most English-speaking Christians also defend the status quo. To be sure, here one detects a growing concern for the im-

[2] World Council of Churches' Consultation, Cottesloe, Johannesburg, Dec. 7-14, 1960: *Statement*, Part II, Section 15.

provement of race relations, but it has a very long way to go. In recent years some denominations have been more critical of Government policy, and resolutions condemning discriminatory legislation are published occasionally. The social action commissions of the Methodist and Presbyterian Churches have inaugurated new programs of study on Christian citizenship and race relations. Some Anglican and Roman Catholic bishops and clergy have given creative leadership on such issues. But these are small beginnings, at a very late hour.

At the local level, the English-speaking churches rarely witness to the unity of all men in Christ. Assuredly, such witness is more prevalent than it was a decade ago. In sermons and study programs, race relations is dealt with from time to time. But here a liberal minister must tread carefully, lest his congregation repudiate him altogether. A Methodist minister faces a congregation nearly 60 per cent of which is of Afrikaans descent, in a denomination which has strong pietistic leanings and tends to dissociate religion and politics. Most Anglican ministers were born and educated in Britain, and their views are not always those of their native-born white congregations. Thus many Anglican laymen have deeply resented the outspoken attacks upon the Government by the Archbishop of Cape Town and the former Bishop of Johannesburg. Baptists have little concern for political and social problems, stressing that the salvation of individual souls will solve all difficulties. Other denominations are likewise reluctant to undertake the task of reconciliation in divided South Africa. The judgment of a distinguished analyst of South African affairs is apt: "The weakness in my own church [Anglican] and I imagine some others is the lack of a clear-cut challenge from the pulpit on grave questions of the day which affect Colour. . . ."

Interracial fellowship is a rarity in the English Churches. Occasionally white and nonwhite Christians meet together for a social gathering or a special service of worship. It is unusual, but not unique to find a white congregation inviting an African minister to preach from its pulpit. Most Anglican and Roman Catholic cathedrals are open to members of all races, and some white churches will occasionally permit nonwhite visitors to worship with them. A small (Presbyterian) interracial congregation has been established in East London. On the whole, however, the little interracial fellowship which occurs does so on a firmly paternalistic basis. Many white congregations have "adopted" a nonwhite church nearby and helped it with food, clothing, financial grants, and advice. Some Europeans may visit the non-European church for the children's Christmas party. But rarely does one find deep fellowship across the color line.

This same problem prevails on the national level as well. Most denominations have both white and nonwhite members, and delegates from both groups usually sit together at regional and national assemblies. (In this respect also the Afrikaans Churches go their own way, for they have established separate "mission" synods for their nonwhite members.) But almost always the Europeans are represented out of all proportion to their numbers; for example, 75 per cent of the Methodist Church is African, but Europeans have a small majority in the supreme governing body, the Methodist Conference. In most Churches the majority of the committee chairmen, district superintendents, and executive leaders are Europeans. The Anglicans have consecrated only one African (assistant) bishop, the Roman Catholics two. For the past four years in succession an African has been narrowly defeated in the election of the Methodist Conference President; many fear that if an African were to be elected large numbers of Europeans would leave the Church and form their own separate body.[3] Finally, one might note that the salary scales of European and non-European ministers are sharply divergent. And so the *apartheid* which reigns in the world permeates the Church as well.

[3] Editor's Note. In October, 1963, the Reverend Seth Mokitimi was decisively elected President, by a vote of 4 to 1.

The African Christian community is large and complex, and generalization is hazardous. We can pick out only certain aspects for attention here. Everywhere in Southern Africa the traditional African tribal culture is disintegrating. Western government, education, and industrialization have produced rapid social changes which have cut Africans loose from their old ways and plunged them into a wholly new world. Any such rapid change creates confusion, anxiety, and widespread immorality. If the African Church had only these problems to deal with, it would still face an immense task. In such circumstances, the indigenization of theology, liturgy, and church order, the pastoral care of a troubled people, and the conversion of the heathen are all made the more difficult. Yet as the African enters the white man's world he encounters the further complexity of racial discrimination. Having rejected the old world, the African is himself rejected in the new.

Faced with this dilemma, African Christians have responded in at least four ways:

1. Many have a pietistic faith which stresses the emotional and legalistic aspects of Christianity and has little concern for political and social righteousness. The Christian must obey the laws of the State and endure what suffering may come, knowing that at least he is a citizen of the Kingdom of Heaven. This attitude is very widespread among African Christians.

2. A good many Africans, especially those with some education, are leaving the Church altogether. They repudiate the Church for its failure to champion racial justice, and their rejection is reinforced by the Government's claim to be the bulwark of "Christian civilization." The Christian ministry to African intellectuals thus becomes increasingly difficult. Many of them become thoroughly nihilistic in outlook. A growing number support African nationalist movements with which the Church has little contact. Probably a few become Communists, but Communism appears thus far to be very weak.

3. Some abandon the white-ruled churches and join one of

the "separatist" churches. There are now more than two thousand of these entirely African bodies, some large and well organized, some consisting of no more than one congregation. Many are thoroughly Christian in faith and order, having broken away from a traditional church because of the white rule there (and often for other, less respectable reasons) but retaining the essential features of the parent body. Others, craving both independence and a more indigenous spirit, are clearly syncretistic, and cannot rightly be called "Christian" at all.[4]

4. A growing number of African Christians, while remaining within the traditional churches, insists that the social dimensions of the Gospel must be made plain. Many favor vigorous Christian opposition to *apartheid,* in deed as well as in word. Some have even come to advocate the violent overthrow of the present Government. Within the past two years this conviction has spread and it may be of considerable significance in the years ahead.

The ecumenical movement, an effective stimulus to social thought and action in much of the world, has been particularly weak in South Africa. In the face of such immense social and political problems the Church needs all possible unity. Yet the walls between denominations are strong and high. The Christian Council of South Africa lost the membership of the Afrikaans Churches shortly after its establishment in the 1930s, and many other members have considered it ". . . just another of those outside committees on which we elect our ecumenically minded ministers."[5] A large proportion of its funds comes from overseas. For years it had only a part-time secretary, and several Churches recently refused to free a minister to serve as full-time secretary. The Council has made some useful statements on public issues, but usually on its own behalf alone, without the active support

---

[4] The best study of the African separatist church movement is B. G. M. Sundkler, *Bantu Prophets in South Africa.* (2nd. ed., London, 1961.)

[5] Christian Council of South Africa, "Memorandum on the Reorganisation of the Christian Council of South Africa," prepared by the Secretary, Basil H. M. Brown, February 1962.

of its member Churches. The Council has recently accepted the principle of reconstituting itself as a national council of Churches and linking itself more directly with the World Council of Churches. The resultant revision of its commission structure may encourage more vigorous action. In making this decision, the Council will render more difficult the task of reconciliation with the Afrikaans Churches; but recent experience has clearly demonstrated that harmony with Afrikaans Christians *and* the unity and social witness of the other Churches cannot be achieved simultaneously.

Efforts for church union move even more slowly. No significant union of Churches has occurred in South Africa. Various bodies within the same denominational heritage cooperate more fully today, and some are at last working on organic union: three Congregational groups plan to unite, as do three Presbyterian Churches. Anglicans and Methodists (representing the two largest Churches, each with over one million adherents) have met informally to explore the possibilities of union, but no specific action has been taken. Similar talks continue between Anglicans and Presbyterians. Such discussions are complicated by the fact that the Anglican Church is uniformly "high church" in character. Many other denominations are jealous of their particular heritages, and loath to compromise for the sake of wider union. As a result, each follows its own course in relation to the developing racial crisis. When, for instance, in the interests of white supremacy the Bantu Education Act of 1953 transferred the control of African education from Churches to the government, some denominations tried to make a united stand; but the inertia of separation was too great and the will to a united witness too weak. As a result, each dealt with the Government separately, and its position was correspondingly weakened. One by one, all of the Churches surrendered, some willingly and others reluctantly; and "Bantu Education" is today a powerful instrument of Government policy to "keep the Native in his place."

In a few cases, progress has been made in ecumenical ventures. A number of fruitful interracial ecumenical study courses have been held. Wilgespruit Fellowship Centre, near Johannesburg, welcomes Christians of all races and communions to use its conference facilities; and its interracial workcamp, to which about twenty-five young people come each winter, is a powerful instrument of reconciliation. The newly established Federal Theological Seminary trains nonwhite students from Anglican, Methodist, Presbyterian, and Congregational Churches, and the unity which is begun there may bear fruit in the work of its graduates. These and others are small beginnings, but they hold some promise for greater unity and strength.

In Southern Rhodesia, Angola, and Mozambique the Church is also challenged by the injustices of a white supremacist government. With the triumph of African nationalism in Northern Rhodesia and Nyasaland and the dissolution of the Central African Federation, the small white minority in Southern Rhodesia may stand closer to losing its supremacy. Under such pressure, the Church there has moved rather farther than its South African neighbor in the direction of interracial fellowship and African responsibility. Church leaders are increasingly aware of the need for a more emphatic witness, and African participation in Church councils and committees is growing. But Europeans still control most positions of authority, and most white Christians defend the status quo. As the African political consciousness develops, African Christians are relating their faith more directly to political and social problems, even though at times this means an uncritical endorsement of nationalist movements. One observer comments: "My summary of the situation is that the direction is right, the speed is slow, and the prospects of an increasingly effective role good."

In the Portuguese territories, the dominant Roman Catholic Church has tended to support Government policy, and the "League of Throne and Altar" is probably more intact there than anywhere else in Africa. Protestant leaders, under severe

pressure from both an unjust administration and a bigoted
Church, have had little opportunity to oppose national policy,
and have largely confined themselves to looking after their own
flocks. In Angola, however, certain changes have taken place
recently. In 1961 a full-scale war, precipitated by Portuguese
oppression, broke out in the northern districts. The authorities
have blamed Protestant missions for this violence, and Methodists, Baptists, and others have suffered severely as a result. This
has led some Christians publicly to attack Government policy.
British Baptists have broken their long silence and made known
to the world many facts about Portuguese rule, as have American
Methodists, their chief neighbors in the regions most involved.
In a pastoral letter several Roman Catholic bishops deplored
African violence, but pleaded for reforms.[6] Other leaders have
preferred not to speak publicly, but have given creative guidance
to their people in the emergency. Many African Protestants have
stood firm and faithful: some, when arrested, have refused to
yield to police pressure falsely to accuse their leaders of sub-
version; others have made great sacrifices to keep churches,
schools, and hospitals open. As war continues, doubtless much
suffering lies ahead for the Church in Angola.

The future prospects of Christianity in southern Africa
are most difficult to assess. They are profoundly influenced by
the course which white and black nationalism will follow in the
coming years, and this course is impossible to predict. If the
white rulers of Angola, Mozambique, Southern Rhodesia, and
South Africa should forge a strong alliance for mutual defense,
white supremacy might continue in this bloc of states for years
to come. In this case, the progressive denial of civil liberties and
silencing of criticism seems certain. A Church which faithfully
witnesses to the sovereignty of God over national life and the
unity of all men under God would be increasingly a suffering
Church. Thus far, white Christians have proved most reluctant
to accept the role of suffering servant, but there are a few hope-

[6] Thomas Okuma, *Angola in Ferment* (Boston, 1962), pp. 95-96.

ful signs that African Christians are beginning to embrace this calling. The longer the Church dissociates itself from the cause of racial justice, the more in doubt its future becomes. It might retain its white membership, but it would be less and less the Church of Jesus Christ, and the judgment of one Afrikaner minister upon his Church would become true for all: "Jesus Christ is no longer the head of my Church. The Afrikaner *volk* is." At the same time, its African membership would either dwindle away, sit quiescent and irrelevant, or split off to form separate bodies.

If the rising tide of African nationalism conquers southern Africa by violence, however, the prospects for Christianity are somewhat different. A racial war would be fought with intense bitterness on both sides, as the Angolan experience has shown; the bloodshed and anarchy would be fearful. In the ruins following an African victory, the Church would face a staggering task of service and reconstruction which might exhaust its resources for years to come. If African extremists won power, their nationalism might be as demonic as the white man's, and a witnessing Church might well be persecuted. In the light of the Church's recent record, the elimination of white rule would mean the repudiation of the Gospel by many Africans, and the Church might lose millions of followers. Already reluctant to relate itself to political issues, the Church under such pressure might be tempted to retreat into a ghetto and concern itself only with the "spiritual" life of the faithful. At the same time, the Church would have a great new opportunity. As a new African society emerged, Christians high and low would be called to guide the nation into paths of justice and peace, and to be God's leaven in the new institutions which were formed.

Victory for either extreme, white supremacy or black nationalism, would only be won at appalling cost. Surely Christians must work and pray that a compromise between these may be found. A variety of forces—sabotage, the threat of revolt or invasion, world criticism, economic boycott—might force the present rulers to accept a multi-racial government. However, the intractable prejudice of whites and the long-standing bitterness of blacks would still be formidable obstacles to peace. In such circumstances, the Church would again be called to banish from its midst the demon of racialism, and to accept the task of reconciliation which it has refused in the past. Upon its response to this call, much of its future health and power would depend.

··*·* VIII *·*·*·*

North America, Part I

TRUMAN B. DOUGLASS

TRUMAN B. DOUGLASS

The Reverend Doctor Truman B. Douglass is Executive Vice President of the Board for Homeland Ministries of the United Church of Christ in the U. S. A., continuing for this union of the Congregational Christian Churches with the Evangelical and Reformed Church the service he began in 1943 as head of the Congregational Christian Board of Home Missions. He is therefore deeply concerned with policies and activities in such areas as the development of new local churches, race relations, higher education, publishing, welfare services; and has been a pioneer in church use of the radio. A member of the General Board of the National Council of Churches of Christ in the U. S. A. and of the Board of Managers of the Council's Division of Home Missions, Dr. Douglass also serves on the Information Committee of the World Council of Churches. Well-known as a lecturer and as contributor to periodicals, he has published several books including PREACHING AND THE NEW REFORMATION and MISSION TO AMERICA.

VIII

$\mathcal{A}$s the Church moves toward the final third of the twentieth century of the Christian era the task of appraising Christianity's prospects in North America becomes increasingly complex. One set of measurable facts seems to contradict another (though less ponderable) set of facts. On the one side, by most statistical standards of judgment the Churches in North America are in a period of extraordinary health and vigor which shows no signs of declination. Yet there has never been a time when the leadership of the churches has displayed more symptoms of self-doubt, uncertainty, and profound questioning concerning the future.

This statement can be swiftly documented. Membership in religious bodies in the United States has passed one hundred million and is at the highest level, both numerically and proportionately, in the history of the nation. In March, 1957, two out of three persons fourteen years of age or over reported themselves as Protestants and one out of every four as Roman Catholics. Only 3 per cent stated they had no religion, and only 1 per cent made no report of religious affiliation.

Membership in religious bodies has been growing faster than the population. It is estimated that in 1900 the membership of the Churches now reported in the *Yearbook of American Churches* totaled 36 per cent of the population. In 1960 it was 63 per cent. During the fifty years following 1906 the population of the United States increased approximately 100 per cent. Dur-

ing that same period the membership of religious bodies showed
a gain of about 190 per cent.[1] In Canada the ratio of religious
affiliation is even higher, perhaps above 80 per cent.[2]

In the United States financial support of the Churches and
their programs now approximates three billion dollars a year. A
billion dollars a year are spent for new church buildings. For the
past several years new congregations have been established at the
rate of about ten thousand per year. More than five hundred
institutions of higher education are related to organizations of
churches and synagogues—approximately one-quarter of all colleges and universities in North America. Church periodicals have
a circulation of about twenty-five million—a "mass circulation"
of no small dimensions.

Despite these outward manifestations of abounding
strength and vigor, the discourse among Christians in North
America—particularly the United States—is filled with expressions of uncertainty regarding the future.

The nature of these doubts is reflected in such questions as
the following:

Have the Churches forgotten that in the life of the Church
the test of authenticity is not success but faithfulness, and has
their outward success been won at the expense of inward
faithfulness?

Is the current statistical strength of the church establishment the result of institutionally self-regarding and self-serving
policies, and does it represent a corresponding failure of that
self-spending movement of the Church's life which aims at a
penetration of the surrounding culture and the transformation
of it?

Have the "victories" of the Churches been in too-easy areas
of conquest (such as the middle-class suburb) while leaving

[1] Benson Y. Landis, "Trends in Church Membership in the United States,"
Annals of the American Academy of Political and Social Sciences, vol. 332,
November 1960, pp. 1-8.
[2] 1961 estimates, in *The World Almanac*, 1963. Cf. *Whitaker's Almanac*,
1963. Figures for various Churches are not on the same basis.

untouched the more decisive aspects of our culture (such as government, mass communications, organized labor, highly urbanized societies, workers in the arts, etc.)?

Has the contemporary prestige of Christianity been proportionate to the degree in which the Churches have espoused a "culture religion" and have abandoned their historic role of mediating judgment upon the existing culture?

What is the significance of the fact that the statistical and institutional strength of Christianity reached its zenith in precisely the period which many theologians and church historians began to characterize as the "post-Christian era"?

Unquestionably there are distinctive problems confronting the Church in North America, as a continent on which Christianity has long been at work. The tendency to identify the "Christian way of life" with the accepted values of contemporary culture, the temptation of the Church to bless that culture rather than living in redemptive tension with it, dullness to the subtler perversions of the Gospel that are characteristic of a society which is openly non-Christian—these are some of the threats which must be taken into account in attempting to foresee the shape of the Christian future.

While there are distinctive problems confronting Christianity and the Christian mission in North America, there are at the same time distinctive openings and elements of very great promise. To say that some aspects of North American life have been de-Christianized is very different from saying that the continent has become anti-Christian. It has not; and that fact carries large significance and hope. Christianity is very much present and very vitally present in some places. It is present in many other places in residuary form. The importance of this fact has been pointed out by T. S. Eliot:

> A society has not ceased to be Christian until it has positively become something else. It is my contention that we have today a culture that is mainly negative, but which, as far as it is positive, is still Christian. I do not think it can remain

negative, because a negative culture has ceased to be efficient in a world where economic as well as spiritual forces are proving the efficacy of cultures which, even when pagan, are positive; and I believe the choice before us is between the formation of a new Christian culture and the acceptance of a pagan one. Both involve radical changes; but I believe that the majority of us, if we could be faced immediately with all the changes that will only be accomplished in several generations, would prefer Christianity.[3]

This preference, which is often latent and inarticulate but the existence of which we can scarcely doubt, is one of the positive allies of the Church in the present scene. The Christian pattern of life, however slight may be its influence upon multitudes of persons, has not been openly rejected by our society. That has occurred in some nations. Some societies, once Christian, have, as Eliot puts it, become positively something else. The fact that in North America we have not come disastrously close to that kind of revolution gives us cause for optimism.

It is clear, however, that any forecast of increasing effectiveness for Christianity for the shaping of North American culture must be a conditional forecast. The outcome will depend on the Church's success in meeting a number of crucial issues and challenges.

There is, for example, the challenge of increasing urbanization. The issue is not the indigenization of Christianity in the urban scene, for when the faith is too readily indigenized in any society it loses its creative power. The problem is one of communication. Can the Church, whose language, symbols, norms of conduct, and standards of ethics have been so largely shaped by a pastoral and rural setting, learn the speech that has become native to man in the typical urban context of today?

One of the studies sponsored by the World Council of Churches puts the problem succinctly:

This is the tragic dilemma of city life—the cross roads between the hope and despair of mankind. All the prime movers

[3] *The Idea of a Christian Society* (London and New York, 1949), p. 10.

in our age, technical as well as spiritual, social and political, are at present based in the capitals of the world. Here, rather than in the villages, contemporary history is written. Here also, with the human race, the churches are put to the test. . .

Nowhere, however, do the institutionalized churches seem to have an answer, adequate in depth and scope, to the spiritual and social needs of the hundreds of millions of town dwellers. Yet, in biblical terms, the old Babylon as well as the new Jerusalem are pictured as large cities, overflowing with human vitality and full of opportunity.[4]

Whether organized Christianity—especially organized Protestantism—can sufficiently transcend its anti-urban bias, the prejudices which are the legacies of its rural origins and its middle-class moralism to enter into authentic dialogue with urbanized man is one of the contingent issues that will determine the prospects of Christianity on the North American continent.

A second momentous question is whether the present tendency toward assigning larger responsibility to the laity can proceed without an attendant disaster which P. T. Forsyth called "the laicizing" of religion. While for Roman Catholicism the laity constitute a continuing problem, being, strictly speaking, unnecessary for the existence of the Church, Protestantism maintains not only the doctrine of the priesthood of the laity but also the laity of the priests. The *laos*, the whole people of God, are both the *locus* and the totality of the Church.

There is increasing recognition that the laity are the true bearers of the Church's mission to the world. It is they who are in the world, who are in daily communication with its secular and unchristianized forces, and who occupy the strategic posts of contact with its decisive centers of power. (It has even been suggested that the decline in enrollment in the Protestant theological seminaries during the early 1960s was due to an "over-emphasis" on the "ministry of the laity" and the implication that training for the professional ministry was not essential to the fulfillment of a Christian vocation.)

[4] Egbert de Vries, *Man in Rapid Social Change* (New York, 1961), p. 170.

As the influence of the laity is given increasing weight in the life of the Church it becomes clear that the maintenance of the Church's theological and liturgical cogency depends on an informed leadership—even an *elite*. A laicized worship will become increasingly a device for inducing moods of religiosity and manipulating the subjective states of the worshipers rather than an office for the adoration of the Most High God. A laicized theology will tend more and more toward the instillation of peace of mind and adjustment to the existing order of society rather than toward the maximization of a faith which continually reminds man of his creatureliness, his contingency, and the requirement for repentance and renewal.

With the emphasis on the responsibility of the laity, some relevant understanding of a reasonable division of labor between them and the clergy must be developed. Unless the clergy can maintain a measure of authority in the conduct of common worship and in the task of giving a biblical-theological interpretation of life there is almost certain to be a serious corruption of Christian teaching.

Third, and most important, few competent observers can doubt that the prospects of Christianity on the North American continent will depend on the resolution of the problem of denominationalism. The denominational system which has characterized religious affairs for the past century and a half is becoming increasingly irrelevant to the actualities of our culture and society. As this irrelevance becomes more visible, the denominations with their enlarged memberships and increased financial prosperity become more self-assertive and tend more and more to dominate the religious scene. Thus the notable material strength of the Churches becomes a strengthening of an order which has less and less pertinence to the realities of society.

All Churches in North America, including the Roman Catholic Church and the "undenominational" Council of Community Churches, are also sects. As the sectarian system becomes stronger and its constituent denominations become increasingly powerful it also becomes decreasingly relevant to the facts of North American life. The so-called religious revival of the last decade needs to be appraised in the light of the decreasing relevancy of the fundamental structure of the Church's life.

One of the facts which diminishes relevancy is the accelerated mobility of the American people. No denomination, not even the largest, is ubiquitous. When people are moving to the extent that the American people have been moving since 1945, many of them settle in places where no church of their traditional denominational affiliation is present. In consequence, many of them change their denominational association. They discover that this can be done without impairing their religious experience. Many pastors of urban churches annually receive by transfer from congregations of other denominations three or four times as many members as they receive by transfer from congregations of their own denomination. It is evident that for many persons denominational loyalty ranks low among the considerations which influence their choice of a local church. Convenience of access, good Sunday school facilities for the children, the general excellence of the church's reputation and program, even availability of parking space may be more important factors than the continuance of an existing denominational affiliation.

A recent survey which included interviews with 4,100 members of the United Church of Christ in all parts of the country revealed that only one member out of three was originally a member of that denomination.[5] The churches studied derived over one-half their present membership from four other denominations: Methodist—18 per cent; Presbyterian—15 per cent; Baptist—11 per cent; and Lutheran—8 per cent. Two per cent of the members included in this study were originally Roman Catholics.

[5] Yoshio Fukuyama, research for doctoral dissertation, University of Chicago.

On the point of the historic theological and ecclesiological controversies which produced the separated denominations, the indifference of the laity is positively monumental. It has increasingly come to be recognized by both clergy and laity that many of the persons who avoid the Church do so not because of the "offense of the Cross," but because they are repelled by the offense of competing denominations.

Can anyone seriously believe that these separated clans and tribes of the Christian family have any relevance to the real problems that humanity confronts in our time, or that their prosperity or lack of it provides any standard for judging the advance of the Christian movement? The statistical records of the denominations are not only notorious examples of the do-it-yourself craft of "how to lie with statistics," but are virtually meaningless as measurements of Christian accomplishments. One reads the recruiting literature of almost any denomination and tries vainly to find some resemblance to the criteria of the New Testament. The motivations to which appeal is made are not essentially different from the apologetic for the Junior Chamber of Commerce or the Neighborhood Improvement Association. They say, in effect:

> Join us because we are a great organization with so many million members and so many thousand congregations. We have a noble tradition; we were brought to this country by passengers on the Mayflower. We have spawned the following well-known personalities. In this nuclear age, when the whole world is a neighborhood, we have missions from northern Greenland to Tierra del Fuego. Furthermore, through the influence of our great personalities and our spiritual teaching we are one of the chief bastions for the defense of the American Way of Life.

When a denomination is asked what is the relationship of this type of self-aggrandizement to Christ's summons to "leave all and follow me" or to "do the things I command you," the answer is, "None whatever." This discontinuity is widely recognized. The response of intelligent persons to the typical forms of denominational propaganda is worse than incredulity; it amounts to boredom.

The movement toward the overcoming of denominational disunity is generated not only by religious considerations but also by sociological factors. At the present moment it is being somewhat retarded by the economic prosperity of the denominations and by the illusions of omnicompetence which this prosperity produces. While there are some four hundred state and local councils of churches representing the cooperative tendencies of Protestantism, the denominations are reluctant to assign to them any real responsibilities except statistically unproductive functions such as work with agricultural migrants, share-croppers, and American Indians. Nevertheless, there is real hope that the sheer senselessness of the present situation, and the impatience of large numbers of church members with its absurdity and ineffectualness, will contribute a powerful drive to the ecumenical thrust which is one of the dominant characteristics of organized Christian life today.

✦ ✦ ✦ ✦ IX ✦ ✦ ✦ ✦

North America, Part II

ROBERT T. HANDY

ROBERT T. HANDY

Robert T. Handy, ordained Baptist minister, is Professor of Church History in Union Theological Seminary, New York. Trained in Brown University, Colgate Rochester Divinity School, and the University of Chicago Divinity School, Dr. Handy served briefly as pastor, as army chaplain, and as educator before completing his doctoral work in theology and entering upon his career of seminary teaching and scholarship. He has devoted himself chiefly to the post-Reformation period and particularly to American Church History. He was elected President of the American Society of Church History, and he is a member of the Editorial Board of The Library of Protestant Thought. Among his published writings are WE WITNESS TOGETHER: A HISTORY OF COOPERATIVE HOME MISSIONS; and, with H. Shelton Smith and Lefferts A. Loetscher, the two-volume survey, AMERICAN CHRISTIANITY: AN HISTORICAL INTERPRETATION WITH REPRESENTATIVE DOCUMENTS.

IX

To try to forecast the shape of any "next period" in the history of Christianity in North America has always been a somewhat precarious undertaking. Over a half century ago President Charles W. Eliot of Harvard, for example, attempted it. Convinced that new scientific concepts had rendered obsolete much of the religious theory and practice of the past, Eliot declared that "the religion of the future will not be based on authority, either spiritual or temporal" and that "in all its theory and all its practice it will be completely natural." Knowing how deep was the attachment of many persons to their historic Churches, Eliot conceded that "the new religion will therefore make but slow progress, so far as outward organization goes," but insisted that the new religion would progressively modify the creeds and practices of all the Churches in decisive ways.[1]

For some years it appeared that Eliot's prophecy might come true; indeed, some felt that judgments like his were too cautious and that the scientific temper would outdate even his genial religious naturalism. The 1920s, a decade of disillusionment with past traditions and of criticism of inherited institutions, was a time of measurable decline in organized religion.[2] William Pepperell Montague could begin his Terry Lectures at Yale at the end of that decade by saying that "the antireligious

[1] *The Religion of the Future* (Boston, 1909), *passim.*
[2] I have attempted to document this in an article, "The American Religious Depression, 1925-1935," *Church History*, XXIX (1960), 3-16.

arguments possess a psychological strength that is due to their profound congruity with modern moods and tempers. It is because of this congruity with the general spirit of the time that the movement against religion is steadily and rapidly increasing in influence." There was widespread belief, he declared, that the "minimum essentials of Christian supernaturalism" had been rendered "antiquated, false, and absurd by our modern knowledge." Science was giving to man the means to conquer poverty, war, and disease. Therefore, as he saw it, "to the modern temper religion is fast coming to seem unnecessary because fear and sorrow are no longer the major themes of our more serious culture."[3]

How could he have known that depression, dictatorship, and war were soon to release floods of terror and fear across the world, and bring aching sorrow to millions? Eliot had foreseen that "the great mass of people remain attached to the traditional churches, and are likely to remain so,—partly because of their tender associations with churches in the grave crises of life." But how could he have foreseen the floods of crises, social as well as personal, which have marked the days of our years since 1930? In trying to describe the impact of the terrible thirties upon him, E. G. Homrighausen once exclaimed, "I saw the evidences of man's lostness: the depression, the constant threat of war, the return to brutality on so vast a scale, the loss of the spiritual substance of life that alone gives society structure, the uncertainty and insecurity of life."[4] In that sentence are given some of the clues that make more understandable the renaissance of religion in North America since 1930. In danger, uncertainty, and insecurity men turned with renewed hope to the Churches, which spoke of eternity, permanence, and changelessness. As all about them change and decay appeared, many men found fresh and profound meaning in a biblical faith that

[3] *Belief Unbound: A Promethean Religion for the Modern World* (New Haven, 1930), pp. 1, 20, 86 f.
[4] "Calm after Storm," *Christian Century*, LVI (1939), 479.

had taken the measure of evil, sin, and death, and yet had confidence in the face of them. The Christianity of the kind which Eliot thought was weakening and which Montague thought was disappearing, Christianity which was increasingly concerned with the authority of Scripture and tradition, Christianity which emphasized not the natural but the divinely transcendent—this Christianity found a new lease on life in troublous times, and Churches were quickened. The religious renewal had its beginnings in the 1930s, it advanced in the war-torn 1940s, and perhaps crested in the late 1950s. Many indices have been cited to chart religion's resurgence: the boom in church building, new heights in church budgets, the voluminous sale of religious literature, the interest in theology on university campuses, and the steady growth of church membership. About two-thirds of the population are claimed as church members in the United States; in Canada the proportion is probably even higher. That many members are nominal or marginal is everywhere admitted, but it is also true that many who are not church members consider themselves Christian. Though the religious revival has of course been given differing interpretations—some rate it highly while others believe that it has been relatively superficial—still it has attracted wide attention and has clearly brought new resources to the Churches. Christianity is flourishing in North America; scholarly observers have provided much evidence on that point. Over ten years ago in his "mid-century report on religion in America" Herbert W. Schneider wrote:

> It is clear that, contrary to what many of our leading historians and sociologists asserted early in the century, religion has not declined in America since 1900. . . . In general, practically all major types of American religion have staged what is vulgarly called a "comeback," and religious leaders are today much less on the defensive than they were a generation ago. . . . Religion has come forward, or at least it has come forth; it has abandoned many of the things which it held

dear fifty years ago and has given new meanings to the things which it still cherishes. It is sobered by bitter experience, less optimistic but stronger.[5]

At about the same time, Robin M. Williams was saying in his treatment of American life that "probably in no other modern industrial state does religion play a greater role."[6] More recently, and basing his statements on careful sociological sampling carried out in a city on the border of the United States and Canada —Detroit—Gerhard Lenski has presented as "the general conclusion suggested by the evidence as a whole: contrary to the views and predictions of nineteenth-century positivists, *traditional religious groups continue to be viable and vigorous organizations*. What is more, they promise continued viability and vigor in the foreseeable future."[7]

The religious renewal of the last three decades which has so clearly upset certain earlier predictions about the future of Christianity has inevitably had to operate in and through the pluralistic "denominational system" which dominates North American religious institutions. The roots of the denominational system go back to the very beginnings of European settlement in the new world. The majority of those who came in the seventeenth and eighteenth centuries accepted the idea of religious uniformity, and Churches were established by law in a number of places—Roman Catholic in French Canada, Congregational in New England, Anglican in the southern colonies. But immigration soon brought representatives of most of the varieties of European Christianity to North American shores, so that religious minorities developed in all colonies—some of them (for example, Pennsylvania) very early became highly complex religiously with no group in clear majority status. By the late seventeenth century the denominational system—multiple

[5] *Religion in 20th Century America* (Cambridge, Mass., 1952). pp. 16 f.
[6] *American Society: A Sociological Interpretation* (New York, 1951), p. 304.
[7] *The Religious Factor: A Sociological Study of Religion's Impact on Politics, Economics and Family Life* (Garden City, N.Y., 1961), p. 50.

Christian Churches living side by side with at least minimal toleration and mutual recognition—had been shaped in England. There the "three old denominations" (Presbyterian, Baptist, Congregational) which arose out of the Puritan movement settled down to legal existence beside the still-established Church of England, protected by the Toleration Act of 1689. In the New World, the denominational system fully matured with the rise of religious liberty, the separation of Church and State, disestablishment (and the end of the clergy reserves in Canada), and the triumph of "voluntaryism" in religion.[8] Currents of religious revival and tides of immigration—both of which continued into the twentieth century—have played a part in contributing further to religious multiplicity.[9]

An important part of the denominational system as it has developed has been the effort to relate the various units to each other to overcome the disadvantages of separation and to provide channels for cooperation and unity. The great voluntary missionary, Bible, and reform societies of the nineteenth century served to do some of this work then. The ecumenical movement with its many agencies, especially councils of churches, does this with official denominational support in the twentieth century. The ecumenical trend seems at last to have reversed the fissiparous bent of several centuries: the twentieth century has seen some significant church unions, both within denominational

---

[8] See two important articles by Sidney E. Mead, "Denominationalism; the Shape of Protestantism in America," *Church History*, XXIII (1954), 291-320, and "The Rise of the Evangelical Conception of the Ministry in America (1607-1850)," in H. Richard Niebuhr and Daniel D. Williams, eds., *The Ministry in Historical Perspective* (New York, 1956), pp. 207-49. For a compact treatment of the rise of the denominational system, see Winthrop S. Hudson, *American Protestantism* (Chicago, 1961).

[9] For extended treatment of these themes consult H. Shelton Smith, Robert T. Handy, and Lefferts A. Loetscher, *American Christianity: An Historical Interpretation with Representative Documents* (2 vols., New York, 1960-63); for the Canadian development, see H. H. Walsh, *The Christian Church in Canada* (Toronto, 1956). It is recognized that there are many differences between Canadian and American religious scenes, but I believe that it is possible to treat them together in a general way.

families (Methodist, Lutheran, Presbyterian) and across confessional lines (United Church of Canada, 1925, and United Church of Christ, 1957). The "para-ecumenical" movement of the last ten years promises a period of considerably closer relations between Roman Catholics and Protestants, though probably without official Catholic participation in councils of churches.

The solid achievements of the ecumenical spirit, however, have not yet seriously upset the denominational system. The principle of "denominational sovereignty" is clearly recognized in councils of churches. Even to list in full the more than three hundred denominations of the United States and Canada would take the rest of the space allotted for this chapter. The following compact summary of the major "families of denominations" with a rough estimate of their memberships in millions, as of 1961, gives the bare outlines of the situation:[10]

United States		*Canada*	
Roman Catholic	42⅘	Roman Catholic	8⅓
Baptist	22	United Church of Canada	3⅔
Methodist	12¾	Anglican	2⅖
Lutheran	8½	Presbyterian	⅘
Jewish	5½	Lutheran	⅔
Presbyterian	4⅓	Baptist	⅗
Protestant Episcopal	3⅓	Jewish	¼
Eastern Orthodox	2¾	Eastern Orthodox	¼
Churches of Christ	2⅕		
United Church of Christ	2		
Christian (Disciples)	1⅘		
Latter Day Saints (Mormon)	1¾		
Evangelical United Brethren	¾		
Reformed	½		

[10] These membership figures are only estimates; it is believed by some that they are quite inflated. The estimates for the United States are based on reports in *The Yearbook of the American Churches*, 1963, as summarized in *The World Almanac*, 1963 (New York, 1963), pp. 705-6. The Canadian figures are reported in *Whitaker's Almanac*, 1963 (London, 1962), p. 698.

The complexity of the denominational system can be more fully recognized when it is remembered that some of the denominational families themselves include many independently organized denominations—in the United States, for example, there are 27 Baptist, 21 Methodist, and 19 Eastern Orthodox bodies under the above single entries for each. Also, some of the fastest-growing denominations on the continent are the small, newer groups, often called sects. For example, there are now over a half million Pentecostalists of one variety or another in the United States and Canada, and nearly as many belong to denominations bearing the "Church of God" name. Hence, despite its power and promise, the limitations of the Ecumenical Movement in really shaking the denominational system can be glimpsed when it is recognized that a majority of Baptists, a third of the Lutherans, the Churches of Christ, and most of the smaller religious bodies are not involved in it in any significant way.

The denominational system is often criticized, but it does have its defenders. One observer forthrightly declares:

> ... the division of Christians into the major families of theological tradition—denominations—is not in itself scandalous. On the contrary, it is seen to be a necessary condition of the fullest understanding of an infinite and inexhaustible gospel which defies containment within any single form of life and expression. Without these families of tradition, or something like them, the Christian movement, past and future, would be permanently impoverished and distorted.[11]

But however one evaluates it, the denominational system is here for the foreseeable future. The religious renewal has operated in and through it, and has been conditioned by it. It has contributed certain characteristics to Christianity in North America, and a fair assessment of the present state and future prospects

[11] Lloyd Averill, "In Defense of Christian Pluralism," *Christian Century*, LXXVII (1960), 666.

must recognize them. A half dozen will be listed here; it will be quickly recognized that these are interrelated.

1.   The denominational system was shaped in the sixteenth and seventeenth centuries, and grew to maturity in the eighteenth and nineteenth. That is, it was developed in a simpler, largely rural, pre-scientific and pre-industrial age. Now it lives on in a radically different world of exploding, highly mobile, and increasingly urbanized populations, a world stamped with the immense power and prestige of science, a world of vast centralization in political, economic and social power. In such a world, the denominations live on with half-forgotten (and often distorted) historical memories from earlier and different times. Denominations still carry birthmarks which may handicap them in rising to the demands the Gospel puts on them in facing today's world. For example, Free Churchmen and Anglicans may become locked in debate over the proper role of bishops, but instead of looking clear-eyed at the Gospel, on the one hand, and the needs of the modern world, on the other, they both get bogged down in struggling over the problems of *seventeenth-century* establishment and prelacy. The perpetuation of the denominational system often forces us to live much of our religious lives in the past as we go back to justify our separations. Patterns of congregational life that have earlier proved useful may now have become largely irrelevant, yet Churches often seem to feel that it is a sacred duty to maintain the familiar ways. It seems as if they can hardly imagine any other patterns than those to which they have been accustomed. But as a perceptive Catholic sociologist explains, "The multiple functions of the old-fashioned, solidaristic, community parish have been attenuated. Like the functions of the family, those of the parish have been largely absorbed by other institutions, and they have been partially replaced by the 'escape mechanisms' of urban society."[12] For the modern congregation properly to do

[12] Joseph H. Fichter, S.J., *Social Relations in the Urban Parish* (Chicago, 1954), pp. 65 f.

its work, many older ideas of what it should be like may have to pass, and many new patterns emerge.

2. The denominational system breeds a certain institutional introversion. The necessity confronted by all the Churches of maintaining themselves on a voluntary basis has forced them to put much attention on internal administration and finance. Controversial questions, even when they are of basic theological matters, are often skirted to avoid upsetting internal balances. The activism and pragmatism of North American life (which no doubt has in part been shaped by the type of Christianity which has been especially strong on this continent) have been absorbed by all institutions, including churches, influencing them to put stress on efficiency and growth. Hence many denominations have grown into impressive institutions but with a strong inward focus. In the complex, urbanized, industrial society which has largely spread over North America, influencing even remote hamlets as well as the great metropolises, introverted institutions can grow to giant size and yet be little seen outside or make much impact on the larger society. A denomination can produce mountains of literature, build impressive headquarters, plant beautiful churches across the land, and maintain able, well-trained staffs—but the institutional vigor is spent to a large degree simply in maintaining itself.[13] How much of the power of the religious renewal of the past three decades has been largely expended within denominations to maintain and strengthen institutional life? Such realities as these are suggested by a famous American historian's oft-quoted criticism of the Churches in the United States: "Never before had the church been materially more powerful or spiritually less effective."[14]

[13] For some good essays on institutionalism in the Church, especially as it relates to ecumenical problems, see Nils Ehrenström and Walter G. Muelder, eds., *Institutionalism and Church Unity* (New York, 1963).

[14] Henry Steele Commager, *The American Mind: An Interpretation of American Thought and Character Since the 1880's* (New Haven, 1950), p. 167.

It is interesting to note that tendencies toward introversion can be seen in the field of Christian thought, too. John Macquarrie was writing about general trends in the whole theological world when he observed that "theologians have equally [with philosophers] tended to become introverted. They have been jealous to defend the autonomy of their subject, to steer away from philosophical interests, and to base their findings on revelation or faith or inner experience."[15] His words are in part illustrated with reference to theology in North America.

3. The denominational system may make certain kinds of distortion of the Christian faith difficult to avoid. Probably all forms of Christian organization have their characteristic dangers, as a survey of church history shows, but those problems that accompany the denominational system are those which bear on the future of Christianity in North America. Robin M. Williams points to one of them in these words:

> Since there is no established church, religious organizations must depend for financial support upon formally voluntary contributions. An extensive *overt* commercialism has thus emerged—for example, businesslike advertising, provision of what were formerly secular services and activities, and formally organized fund-raising activities.[16]

Excessive promotionalism can threaten a denomination's integrity, and the knife-edge of hypocrisy that often accompanies it can undermine its Christian life. Another type of distortion is not unrelated: the tendency of denominations to exploit the (institutionally) "promising" fields and to neglect the more difficult ones, even though spiritual need may be very great in the latter. The way in which Churches push into lush middle-class suburban areas and neglect the difficult inner-city areas has been often analyzed in recent literature. Then, the shaping

[15] *Twentieth-Century Religious Thought: The Frontiers of Philosophy and Theology, 1900-1960* (London, 1963), p. 120.
[16] *Op. cit.,* p. 316.

of denominations along class, nationality, or race lines has long been an accompaniment of the denominational system. The trend is clearly away from this, yet it stubbornly persists, maintaining barriers which the Christian gospel seems explicitly to deny.

4. The denominational system under present political and social conditions leads to a certain isolation of Christianity from life; it tends to compartmentalize religion as a special thing apart. Our sociological analysts have been especially sensitive to this. Williams, who certainly has not minimized the place of religion in American life as an earlier quotation shows, has also said:

> *American religious organizations are extraordinarily segregated from other institutionalized structures.* It is perfectly true that *norms* having religious referents and sanctions run through a wide variety of activities outside of organized religious bodies. But the very fact that religion in our culture is so frequently equated with the churches is a telling indication of the compartmentalization of religious norms. Religious ideas, symbols, beliefs, values have become firmly solidified in definite social organizations having their own specialized personnel, symbols of separate identity, special channels of communication, and segregated group affiliations. In addition, the separation of church and state has tended to isolate the churches from political power and from educational influence. . . . The public generally assigns organized religion a special, circumscribed place as the repository of values that are inherently of the highest good, but that should be safely isolated and restricted to ceremonial occasions ("Sunday religion") so that they cannot interfere too much with the ordinary business of society.[17]

One must not conclude from this that Christianity is irrelevant to contemporary society. Lenski (in a way documenting the second sentence of the above quotation) calls the following the central finding of his study:

[17] *Op. cit.*, pp. 339 f.

> . . . from our evidence it is clear that religion in various ways
> is constantly influencing the daily lives of the masses of men
> and women in the modern American metropolis. More than
> that: through its impact on individuals, religion makes an
> impact on all the other institutional systems of the com-
> munity in which these individuals participate.[18]

The point is that the influence is through individuals; the
Churches themselves tend to be isolated, compartmentalized.
Their social ethical influence is limited. Hence, even as they
influence individual behavior, it is difficult for them to bring
corporate influence to bear on society, though the contending
political and economic giants of today's society may need the
leaven of united action by Christians. Here the cooperative
activity of councils of churches has been helpful, but it has
had to struggle against the tendencies of the denominational
system.

5.   When we look closely at the influence of the denominations
on individual behavior and personal moral standards, however,
we find some ambiguities. The contemporary religious resurgence has not led to moral renewal, a lack which troubles
many religious leaders. Henry P. Van Dusen has called attention
to "the indisputed fact that there has been no corresponding
revitalization in morality. On the contrary, as the curve of
religious interest has risen, the curve of personal morals has
steadily declined."[19] The moral standards of the denominations
were shaped in an earlier age when personal and social problems
were different. Furthermore, they were sometimes shaped in
conscious (or unconscious) counterpoint to the positions of
other denominations. Today in a highly pluralistic society, moral
patterns come into sharp conflict. In certain ways the ecumenical movement itself contributes to the confusion, because

[18] *Op. cit.*, p. 289.
[19] "The Church in the U.S.A. . . . 1961," in H. Wakelin Coxill and Sir
Kenneth Grubb, eds., *World Christian Handbook*, 1962 (London, 1962),
p. 53.

Christians find their standards challenged by those of other traditions who claim to base their views on equally valid Christian principles. The continuation of the denominational system may help to explain why the religious renewal has not been followed by a moral upsurge, and why it has been difficult for Churches to deal more helpfully with the moral confusions of the present.

6. Certain observers have pointed to a disturbing development: the tendency of large religious groupings, often styled "subcommunities," to become the basic units of identity and status in North America. In Canada, the tension between the two major "religious subcommunities" has long been recognized as a serious matter. In the United States, Will Herberg has described and criticized the solidifying of religious subcommunities in his widely read book, *Protestant-Catholic-Jew*.[20] He has found that with the passing of immigration and the fading of self-conscious ethnic groups, Americans tend to identify themselves as belonging to one of the three main religions: Protestant, Catholic, or Jewish. Gerhard Lenski's study of Detroit has in many ways confirmed this; he finds not three but four religious subcommunities: white Protestant, Catholic, Jewish, and Negro Protestant.[21] His book closes with a clear warning of the dangers of the trend toward the intensification of religious subcommunities:

> Our current drift toward a "compartmentalized society" could easily produce a situation where individuals developed a heightened sense of religious group loyalty combined with a minimal sense of responsibility for those outside their own group. In a more compartmentalized society there is good

[20] Garden City, N. Y., 1955.
[21] Lenski shows that in many respects Negro Protestant attitudes are quite different from those of white Protestants. His work reminds the latter in a scholarly way of one of the conspicuous problems before the nation and the Churches—the failure to incorporate Negroes fully into national and church life. Had Lenski studied certain other cities, he might have found a fifth subcommunity: Eastern Orthodox.

reason to fear a weakening of the ethical and spiritual elements in religion, and a heightening of the ever dangerous political elements. Such a development would be a serious departure from the basic ideals of all of the major faiths in America, sharing as they do in the Biblical tradition. Hence, on both religious and political grounds, Americans might do well to study more critically than they yet have the arguments advanced by advocates of pluralistic society.[22]

Inasmuch as the denominations are smaller units than the religious subcultures, it is difficult for them to deal adequately with this situation. Certain types of interdenominational activity might only intensify the trend to a compartmentalized society; happily the ecumenical movement today embraces most Negro denominations (though in too many cases somewhat marginally) and many Orthodox bodies. The present growth of para-ecumenicity and the continuation of cooperation between Christians and Jews are signs of religious maturity.

In conclusion, what may be said about the prospects for Christianity in North America, flourishing as it is, yet organized along the lines of the denominational system? When a student of a religious scene makes his forecast, quite clearly he invests his own hopes in what he offers, at least in part. This becomes apparent when one looks back on past predictions, such as Eliot's *The Religion of the Future*, and is no doubt operative here. The recent resurgence of Christian life in North America has had many genuine elements, has strengthened the life of the Churches, and shows promise of continuing its renewal trends in them in the years ahead. Much of its force, however, has been blunted by the structures of religious pluralism—by the denominational system. The Ecumenical Movement has itself been enriched by these currents of renewal, and has served to channel them further. It has brought many denominations into various types of common effort, has summoned them into deepening dialogue, and has produced several conspicuous illustra-

[22] *Op. cit.*, pp. 329 f.

tions of transconfessional union. While many aspects of the denominational system will inevitably continue and while some new religious bodies will probably yet emerge, still the fissiparous tendency in North American church history would seem to have been checked and the unitive movement to have gained ascendancy. Churches participating in ecumenical endeavor should be able to make some headway against the problems (of which six have been enumerated) confronting Christianity in North America today, more especially as they are enabled to yield themselves more fully to Him who is the only Foundation of the Church, and in Him find fuller unity with each other.

✦ ✦ ✦ X ✦ ✦ ✦

Latin America

JOSÉ MÍGUEZ BONINO

JOSÉ MÍGUEZ BONINO

José Míguez Bonino has been, since 1960, President of the Faculdad Evangélica de Teología (known in English as Union Theological Seminary), Buenos Aires. This interdenominational institution, in which the Methodist share has been major, trains ministers and other professional church workers for the Methodists, Disciples of Christ, Presbyterians, Waldensians, and German Evangelical Synod, in Argentina, Uruguay, Paraguay, Chile, Bolivia, and Peru.

A graduate of that Faculdad, Dr. Míguez served as pastor in his own country and in Bolivia, becoming Superintendent of the Buenos Aires district of the Methodist Church. In 1952 he became Professor of Theology in his alma mater. His advanced training was secured in the Candler School of Theology, Atlanta, and in Union Theological Seminary, New York. His doctoral dissertation was entitled, "A Study of Some Recent Roman Catholic and Protestant Thought on the Relation of Scripture and Tradition." In the World Council of Churches Dr. Míguez is a member of the Committee on the Study of Religious Liberty and of the Faith and Order Commission. Dr. Míguez has been dividing his time between Buenos Aires and Rome, where he is a Delegate Observer at the Vatican Council, representing the World Methodist Council.

X

Latin America is a large and complex entity. There is, nevertheless, a certain degree of homogeneity, particularly so in the area of religion, wherein the main currents and trends have in different measures been common to the whole continent. This area has been understood in our work to encompass practically the whole of human life and history as it relates to the presence and impact of the Gospel of Jesus Christ in these lands. "The prospects of Christianity" must not be simply identified with the ecclesiastical sphere, but must deal with the total attempt to understand and make explicit Christ's kingly and redemptive ministry to the entire continent.

The almost complete lack of monographs or serious attempts at interpretation of local Church history (either Roman Catholic or Protestant) or of the continental scene as a whole, makes a general survey a very difficult and risky undertaking. We have concentrated our attention on the relation of the Church and Christian witness to the social and cultural process. We have tried throughout to point out the tension and encounter between Gospel and world as they have developed on our continent.

I. Structure and Reality: the Settlement of Christianity in Latin America

The missionary thrust to Latin America took place in the sixteenth and seventeenth centuries and came from Spanish

Catholicism. Spain was still totally immersed in the old dream
of "a Christian Kingdom." The conquest and Christianization
of the New World was understood as a new opportunity to
apply the Sacred Temporal Order and the Ecclesiastical Divine
Order, both of them structured to their minor details in
Scholastic thought.

This dream was, of course, never realized. All the realities
of history and geography—long distances, the scarcity of priests,
the persistence of the old indigenous religions and their ability
to take on Christian forms, the hunger of gold and wealth, human frailty—conspired against it. But at least two important
consequences ensued. On the one hand, Christianity never took
root as such in Latin America. Latin America was never "Christian" in the sense that Europe or even North America can be said
to be so. What took place here was a colossal transplantation—
the basic ecclesiastical structures, disciplines, and ministries were
brought wholesale from Spain, and were expected to function as
a Christian order: a tremendous form without substance. Is it
strange that the continent which numbers a third of the whole
Roman Communion has not produced a single outstanding
theologian, or an important order, and very few saints? Moreover, whatever religious forces did develop—and it was impossible that the devout and sacrificial zeal of many a missionary,
or even the superficial, unenlightened and often coercive cate-
chizing by many others would be left without fruits—were out
of touch with the ecclesiastical superstructure and consequently
open to relapse into paganism, whether old or new.

On the other hand, this structure, brought to Latin America
and kept for centuries practically unchallenged, was becoming
more and more estranged from the rest of the world, where the
old Christendom was rapidly disintegrating. The new world of
the Renaissance, the Enlightenment, free trade, and toleration
was the denial of the whole Spanish attempt and came to be
conceived as "the Enemy," which must at all costs be kept away
from America. The colonial order was thus built on a negative

and sterile resistance to the outer world where strange ideas were blossoming. The Church in its institutional form was part of the Spanish dream and consequently foreign both to the reality of the land and the people, and to the realities of the world at large. It was identified with an outmoded and imported order, practically foredoomed to be "reactionary."

II. *Emancipation and Secularization: the Revolt against "the Order" and the Introduction of Protestantism*

The French Enlightenment found its way to the thinking centers of Latin America, either directly from France or somewhat tempered through Spanish thinkers. The new ideas appealed both to the minds of the young Latin Americans and to their interests, hampered by Spanish economic monopoly. Their outlook can be loosely called "liberal." Religion did not constitute a basic part of their lives, and therefore they were not interested in denying or replacing Roman Catholicism. But whenever the hierarchy of the Church identified itself with the old order—and that happened, alas, frequently enough, in spite of the sympathy of many of the lower clergy for the revolution —they fought against it, remaining at the same time nominally "Christian" in a vague and uncommitted way. This is the root of the general acceptance of religious ideas and values accompanied by a profound distrust of the Church and of all the "clerical" attempts to "interfere" in the secular order.

The emancipation of the Latin American countries from Spain took place in this climate in the first decades of the nineteenth century. The revolutionaries had an almost fanatical zeal for education and made enormous efforts to extend the influence of the "liberating" ideas. Moreover, from the middle of the nineteenth century on, a new fact cooperated in this progressive "emancipation" from the Church: immigration. Wave after wave of Europeans—mostly Latins, but also Germans, Swiss, British—were settling in Latin America. In some countries, like

Argentina, they constituted by the turn of the century more than 50 per cent of the whole population. Uprooted from their native soil, and bent on carving out a future for themselves and their families in the new lands, they found the liberal ideas—in a moderate, nonbelligerent form—best suited to their interests and mentality. Some had already caught the secular temper in their home countries; most severed their ties with the ecclesiastical order at the point of sailing from the Old World.

The result of all these influences is the widespread Latin American secularism and alienation from the Church which gives the basic tone to the present religious situation. It is not the secularism born of tiredness and skepticism. It is still an open, mobile, even a fluid secularism. There is nothing absolute today in Latin America, unless it be its own life. The disregard for Christianity is the rebelliousness of a society which does not want to be tied down by a "religion." In Latin American history, religion always rejected movement—and movement is the essence of Latin American life.

This phase of Latin American history saw the coming of Protestantism to the continent. It came from a twofold source: on the one hand, the immigrations to which we have already referred. The immigrants tended to settle as communities and to bring their culture wholesale from Europe, including language and religion. Thus, they constituted for the most part Protestant enclaves in Latin America, sometimes much respected and admired, at other times resented, but without much effective contact with the wider community or influence upon it.[1] On the other hand, there was the missionary and evangelistic work, directed to the Latin American population as such and originat-

---

[1] These remarks apply, of course, to the Protestant immigration and do not contradict the general observations made above concerning the bulk of European (Latin) immigration. Unfortunately there is no careful study of the numbers, importance, types, and influence of Protestant immigration to Latin America. The 750,000 Lutherans reported for Latin America —most of them immigrants or sons of immigrants—give an idea of the significance of these groups.

ing mostly from 1820-60 in British and North American Free Churches and missionary societies related to them.

Protestantism, particularly the Free Church type, was in many ways part of the revolutionary thrust against the old sacred order. It was less institutional, more "liberal" and "modern," closely related to democracy and—supposedly—the champion of private judgment. The liberal intelligentsia of Latin America did not become Protestant. Most of them remained Roman Catholics for complex reasons, not only social and economic—as Protestants have been too prone to assert—but deeper aesthetic and religious motivations. However, they did not conceal their sympathy for Protestantism as a cultural force, and in the practical field they frequently were the champions of religious freedom, disestablishment, and other concrete measures which made the growth of Protestantism possible in our countries.

It is not easy to judge the character and development of Protestantism in the nineteenth and early twentieth centuries in Latin America. Protestantism was not able in this period to make a serious inroad in Latin American societies. The landed aristocracy was a part of the old society and had a definite place in the "sacred order." The intelligentsia felt a certain congeniality to Protestantism, but neither were the forms of the Protestant churches attractive to them nor was their religious interest deep enough to lead to commitment. The Indian masses and the *campesinos* (peasants) were also part, as subordinates, of the traditional order, caught in a web of relations of dependence which, in turn, constituted their only protection. Also, the Protestant worship and message were perhaps too intellectual and individualistic for them. Protestantism was able to enter only at two points. Through schools and educational centers, it exercised a certain cultural influence in favor of democratic and liberal ideas. On the other hand, it drew some membership from the lower—but not lowest—social groups, mostly in the outskirts of the urban society and in certain rural areas. In fact, it did not touch the structure of society; it merely gathered "loose dust" off the surface.

These facts, plus the theological and ecclesiastical bent of the type of Protestantism which came to Latin America, explain a basic characteristic of Latin American Protestantism: its foreignness. The new convert was not encouraged, either by his social position or by the instruction and example of his Church, to feel a strong attachment to his country, his people, or his class. The "world" was evil—both in the teaching of his Church and in his experience of it—and the fewer entanglements with it, the better. Frequently ties of family and friendship, and therefore the whole sphere of social contacts, had to be sacrificed. Work was practically the only link left with the world. And work they did! With the next result of a rapid ascent in the economic ladder, an old phenomenon which has been repeatedly studied in the growth of "proletarian churches." Society retaliated in kind: Protestants were respected, even admired for their honesty, reliability and seriousness, but they were "outsiders" in society, queer in many aspects, and somehow foreign even in the literal sense of the word.

III. *Social Revolution and the "Sects":*
the Twentieth Century

Latin America has suffered from a "compression" of the historical process which has crammed into scarcely one and one-half centuries processes which in the older countries have taken several centuries. When England was living through the Industrial Revolution, our Latin American countries were in the midst of feudalism; as Marx and Engels were writing the *Communist Manifesto*, we Latin Americans did not even have the embryo of the industrial proletariat. In Latin America, the historical process always lags behind, and it is always speeded up from outside. It is not a process of ripening. Nevertheless, a new set of circumstances and factors is giving birth to a new situation, indeed revolutionary in character.

The great waves of immigration at the turn of the century and the growth of the population (the fastest rate of growth in the world) are creating a new demographic reality. The beginnings of industrialization and the corresponding migrations from country to city give rise to new sociological patterns. The low incomes and the failure to keep production up to the level of the population explosion make for acute need. Vested interests, both local and foreign, make it very difficult to enact necessary reforms in the social and economic structure. The social temper is rapidly changing in Latin America. Poverty is a long-standing problem, but the feeling of frustration, "subjective poverty" and, above all, "the revolution of growing expectations" and a grim and reckless disposition to change the present situation— these are new. For the first time in Latin American history, the masses of the population are gaining a sense of their potential power, are beginning to think of themselves as subjects of decision. For the first time reality is facing the structures in a decisive and conscious way.

This breakdown of the old structures raises for the Latin American man basic existential questions. Traditional communal patterns collapse and man is left without a sense of belonging. The accepted moral standards and patterns of behavior do not hold. One could say that the basic "religious" problem is just beginning to emerge. But while this is true, it is also a fact that all these changes seem to have broken the last feeble ties to the Roman Catholic Church. In the proletarian sections of the cities religious practice, even in baptism and marriage ceremonies, diminishes considerably. Attendance at Mass falls below 10, 5, and even 1 per cent of the population. If some practices are kept up, it is without a sense of reality. A Roman Catholic study of the situation in southern Chile concludes that among the workers ". . . in general, the idea of religion is something superimposed on the person and does not spring from anything deep in life itself. It is a tradition, a formula one has; but it does not have practical consequences in habits and in the way of being."[2] The Latin American man does not look to the Church for the solution of his material or spiritual problems.

It is in this situation that the so-called "Protestant sects"[3] are making an impressive impact in Latin America. Their phenomenal growth has come in the last two decades. Their extreme mobility, the considerable turnover, and their almost total disregard for statistics make it nearly impossible to assess their numerical strength, but both secular and Christian observers are deeply impressed by their growth and vitality. We still lack a serious synthetic study of this movement from a psychological, sociological, and theological point of view.[4]

The appeal of the sects to the Latin American masses has been explained in several ways. Father Ireneo Rosier finds in the Latin American man a deep religious desire expressed basically as a search for community. These groups with their vivid sense of solidarity and mutual love minister to this need. The immediacy and warmth of the Pentecostal experience has also been contrasted with the coldness of the historical Churches and the lack of participation of the common Catholic liturgy.

[2] Quoted by I. Rosier in "Estudio del Protestantismo en Chile," *Anales de la Facultad de Teología, Universidad Católica* (Santiago de Chile, 1960), p. 99.

[3] The word "sect" is here used in the sociological sense stemming from Troeltsch's famous distinction and presupposes no theological judgment. Others prefer to speak of "the nonhistorical groups." But whatever the name it is basically the Pentecostal and Holiness groups that constitute this new evangelistic movement. The Pentecostal movement began in Chile in 1910 and numbers today close to a half million (9 percent of the population). In Brazil, where the movement began at more or less the same time, they are today nearing 400,000 active members. In Cuba the Pentecostals began in 1951 and ten years later were exceeding 50,000.

[4] Several articles are devoted to the theme in the issue of 1960 (No. 11) of the *Anales de la Facultad de Teología* of the Catholic University of Chile. For a Protestant point of view see the interesting study of Emile G. Léonard, *L'illuminisme dans un Protestantisme de constitution récente —Brésil* (Paris, 1953).

Urgent personal responsibility for the propagation of the gospel is kindled in the new convert. Other motives may be mentioned: the sense of personal participation, the release of tensions in testimony and public worship, mutual assistance and the security that the group provides. For the first time on the continent, significant groups of the population seem to have found a Christian understanding and interpretation of their existence to which they can confidently entrust themselves. This Pentecostal Church they feel to be their own. This religion shapes their lives, patterns their conduct, ties them in community, and opens up the springs of joy.

IV. What About the Future?

What is in store for the future? One is tempted to quote the sound theological witticism of Karl Barth: "Wait and see." With all necessary disclaimers, a few tentative remarks can be advanced.

1: The future of the Roman Catholic Church in Latin America seems to hinge on a sensitive point: the possibility of its renewal. A Catholic writer, looking intently toward Rome asked recently the question: "Is not this Council the last chance for Latin American Catholicism?"[5] Indeed, there is no lack of signs of renewal.[6] The Latin American Episcopal Council (CELAM), constituted in Rio de Janeiro in 1955 with the express approval of the Pope, made a careful and realistic evaluation of the situation and an appeal for a new missionary effort.[7] German, French, Dutch, Belgian, Italian, and Spanish bishops have set

[5] In *Informations Catholiques Internationales* No. 176 (Sept. 15, 1962), p. 1. Cf. also the critical article published in *Look Magazine* (Oct. 9, 1962), pp. 28 ff. by a Catholic author on "The Catholic Church in Latin America."

[6] I have tried to assess some of these signs in a brief article in *Frontier*, III, No. 5 (Autumn 1962), pp. 491 ff.

[7] Cf. J. Coleman, *Latin American Catholicism: A Self-Evaluation* (Maryknoll, N.Y., 1958).

up or are setting up special programs for the recruiting and training of missionaries for Latin America. Since the Eucharistic Congress of Buenos Aires in 1930 Catholic Action has been gaining strength. Furthermore, the liturgical, biblical, and theological renewal, and the catechetical movement, have set foot in Latin America and are gaining ground in the seminaries.

All these things, nevertheless, do not seem to us to answer the basic question. The renewal of the Roman Catholic Church demanded in the Latin American situation must touch the very character of Latin American Catholicism; its understanding of its place and function in society, its whole relation to the world and to man must be radically modified. Is Roman Catholicism ready to undergo the basic transformation needed to participate creatively in the new free, modern, pluralistic society which is slowly but irresistibly emerging on this continent? Can the Catholic Church shake itself free from the "Sacred Order"? Can it offer itself to the people basically as a message, or better, as a life instead of as a structure and an institution? Can it renounce its centuries-old tendency to shape the life of the people from above, and now consent to wield only that influence which it can command through its message, its service, and its appeal to conscience?

Such conversion is particularly difficult here, where the whole history of the Church militates against it. But in the present revolutionary situation this seems to be the necessary price for the usefulness of the Catholic Church to the work of Christ. There is still a chance for the Church to be heard. But the odds against such a basic renewal seem to be too high.

2. In classical Protestantism—immigrant Churches and the nineteenth-century evangelism—certain changes have taken place. The third and fourth generations are already reaching maturity. These men frequently enjoy economic and social status; they feel at home in the society where they live and are actively interested in it. Their Churches have developed a higher

theological education and are reaching a certain capacity for reflection, self-understanding and cultural and social relevance. The growing contact between the two church types of Protestantism provides valuable cross-fertilization. There is in these Churches an increasing willingness to break away from their ghetto.

But there is also a certain impotence. They continue to grow slowly and there is nothing to suggest that massive growth is likely to take place. Neither the verbalization and restraint of their worship nor the middle-class patterns of their constituency are likely to make great appeal to the masses of population. The awareness of this fact, together with the desire for understanding of their specific vocation, has caused a certain restlessness in these Churches. Without entering in detail upon this question, the present writer would like to suggest that—not minimizing the possibilities of growth and direct evangelism of these groups —their basic contribution may be found in service to the other Protestant and even to the Roman Catholic Churches.

3. Father Muñoz, a Chilean Roman Catholic priest, has predicted that "if they [the Pentecostals] go on increasing as at present, in fifty years the whole country will be Protestant."[8] This prophecy has been echoed in Catholic and Protestant publications all over Latin America. In a careful study the French Carmelite Ireneo Rosier makes an evaluation of this judgment. He concedes the appeal of the Pentecostal movement, and moreover places it at the deepest religious and evangelical level:

> Protestantism has opened a direct access to Christ, while in Catholicism it is as if the authentic face of Christ were veiled by civilization and the complexities of so many centuries. . . .
> Protestantism is more than a reaction against real or imagined abuses of Roman Catholicism. It attempts, in the first

[8] *Mensaje* (Santiago de Chile, 1956), No. 49, p. 166.

place, to give a real answer to the religious and moral needs
of the people. . . . What people really want is Christ. . . .
What fascinates them and answers to the deepest needs of
their existence is not a coherent doctrine but the very person
of Christ or God whose words they find in the Bible. . . .

Their Protestantism is not sentimentality but Christocen-
tric love which makes them capable of great sacrifices of personal holiness and real mutual charity.[9]

At the same time, Rosier rejects Father Muñoz' prediction.
Two of his reasons for this judgment seem relevant to our
problem: (a) the lack of objective control in the Pentecostal
movement; and (b) their "hyper-spiritualism." The first is related
to illuministic tendencies and the lack of an articulated doctrinal
and theological standpoint. It is true that the Bible is always
present and that it provides a certain objective control; but it is
often interpreted in a totally subjective and arbitrary manner.
This subjectivism endangers the very life of these Churches. It
leaves motivation at the level of sentiment, which makes for
passionate commitment, but also for easy withdrawal. There is
also the ever present danger of being carried away into all kinds
of fanaticism and superstition and thus degenerating into the
primitive pagan cults such as are sweeping through some regions
of Brazil and Central America. Most important, the lack of a
coherent doctrine leaves a vacuum acutely felt by second- and
third-generation Pentecostalists in their encounter with an increasingly sophisticated cultural and social environment. Some
Pentecostal leaders are beginning to face this problem, alarmed
by the growing turnover, and are looking for ways to counter-
act it.

But the second problem is perhaps the more serious. Pentecostalism has undoubtedly filled some gaps in classical Protestantism in offering a strong community attachment and
overcoming the purely conceptual forms of worship through a
ritual which engages the whole person in verbal and bodily ex-

[9] *Op. cit.*, pp. 99, 107.

pression. But it shares and even exaggerates the isolationism which we have already pointed out in classical Protestantism. An exaggerated puritanism and legalism create an unreal life, which may be "admired" by the outsider, but which in fact separates the Protestant from society. Worst of all, there is an almost total blindness to the deep social and economic problems of society. The whole realm of political action, social reform and syndicalism is shunned as too worldly for the Christian. The new convert becomes through his conversion to Christ a sober, peaceful, working citizen, but at the same time renounces all direct action in society. He breaks away completely from the interests, needs, expectations, and longings of his own class. There is little in the highly "rarefied" doctrine he receives from his Church—except at the point of mutual assistance—to point him in the direction of service to the outside community. Leaving aside for a moment the theological question implied in this attitude, there is no doubt that such a position is doomed to a final rejection by the Latin American masses, awakened to the need of a social and economic revolution. Whether rightly or wrongly, the decisive human verdict will no doubt be that the Protestant religion is just another form of the "opium of the people."

4. Just as we have spoken of basic renewal as a condition for the usefulness of the Roman Catholic Church, it is necessary to speak of radical conversion in the life of Protestantism—a conversion, with Christ, to the world. This is no less costly and difficult than the other renewal, but also no less necessary. The Christian Protestant Church in Latin America has to learn the road of the Incarnation. Otherwise, how is it to intercede for a people whose preoccupations it does not know, whose joys and sorrows it does not share, whose customs it disdains, and of whose hopes it is ignorant? The evangelical Church in Latin America has looked down upon the sinful flesh of our everyday humanity, and has endeavored to rescue it from outside, without

running the risk of corruption. For this reason it has become ever more incapable of speaking to that humanity—and at the same time ever more incapable of discerning the voice of its Lord. Jesus Christ does not call us to a pious dialogue about our own sweet experiences as believers. He calls us to participate in the dialogue which out there, in other strange terms, he is carrying on with the secularized and disbelieving world. Is the evangelical Church capable of entering imaginatively, creatively, confidently and humbly into this dialogue? This is the conversion demanded of it.

It is in the context of this conversion that a crucial question for Latin American Protestantism must be treated: the ecumenical question. Enough has been said—and rightly—about the scandal of our divisions. The shame and the guilt of it in Latin America is a heavy burden to all sensitive Christians. All the damage that fanatical sectarianism can do is here portrayed in the most grotesque colors. But this is not the deepest ecumenical problem—and moreover, it is gradually being overcome. There is growing cooperation among the "nonhistorical" groups, and a steady grouping together. There is also a growing relationship in study and action among the classical Protestant Churches. The deepest chasm lies precisely at the point of greatest need and opportunity, namely between this earlier Protestantism and the new evangelistic thrust of the last decades. The issue is sometimes put as fundamentalism versus modernism—a wrong approach imported from outside and artificially foisted upon our Churches. One strongly suspects that psychological, sociological, and cultural barriers are much more to the point. But whatever the causes and issues, the problem must be overcome for the sake of the health of Latin American Protestantism and its effective service.

Traditional Protestantism is developing a series of instruments indispensable if the Protestant Church is to fulfill its mission in this continent. It has the doctrinal resources for the development of an interpretation of Latin American society which may provide a point of entry into its life. It can help to provide a coherent theology of secular reality which may guide the Protestant in his life in the world. It can bring to bear on the local situation the whole wealth of ecumenical thought. On the other hand, the new Protestantism has the vitality, the sense of reality, the expansive force which alone can rescue thought from becoming a mere play, a sterile abstraction. It is not a simple question of addition or combination. What is needed is a true encounter on the ground of the basic realities of the Christian Church. These realities are provided in Latin American Protestantism by the Scriptures—which have always played the fundamental role in the expansion of the Church in this continent—and the increasingly felt sense of urgency for the mission of the Church in our rapidly developing society.

5. A final issue confronts us now: Can any fruitful encounter between Protestantism and Roman Catholicism take place in Latin America? And if so, in what sense? The very question would have been unthinkable not long ago. Practically all existing Roman Catholic and Protestant literature speaks in terms of battle and competition. There are problems aplenty in this relationship. The complex problem of evangelization, witness, and proselytism must be honestly and seriously studied. The possibility of conversion from one confession to the other and the need for polemics cannot be easily dismissed. The two confessions cannot conceive themselves as merely complementary to the other. Both the concern for truth and the respect for the freedom and personal responsibility of man compel Protestants and Roman Catholics alike to hold to conversion as an ultimate possibility and even as a demand of the Christian faith.

But other aspects of truth, which have been totally ignored, must be taken into account. One is that the basic task and question in Latin America is the deep spiritual and material hunger of the masses who are awakening to a new day. The Christian task is the heralding of the good news of Jesus Christ who lived and died and suffers and reigns for them. This task relativizes all polemical questions, both in the sense that it postpones them to their due place and in the sense that it defines the possible need and character of polemics by relation to that task. Is it possible for Roman Catholicism and for Protestantism to see themselves and to see each other as related to this task? If so, it will become clear that neither the one nor the other is today fit for this task. Mutual incrimination may give place to repentance; self-righteousness to creative concern. And this may in turn lead to a positive appreciation of some of the Christian values in the other confession and, further on, to intercessory prayer.

The possibility of cooperation may still seem a utopian idea. Yet the very timid openings for dialogue and mutual concern which now occur all over the continent seem to point to something greater. They are merely signs. But to a population which has heard only polemics, abuse, and persecution, they are very meaningful signs. Without shirking the fundamental issues at stake—and they are fundamental—these signs can be multiplied and made clearer. All of this will take place, it seems to us, not so much through a frontal direct approach (which must still be pursued), but in the measure of a real conversion of both Protestantism and Roman Catholicism to their mission. They will find each other as they find Christ, not so much in themselves, or even in each other, but as they come out to Him who watches and works out there, in the turmoil of Latin American history.

The ultimate issue is not the prospect of Christianity as institution or even as religion, but the destiny of the Latin American peoples in God's ongoing purpose and in His work through Jesus Christ.

· XI ·

Australia

HAYDEN MCCALLUM

HAYDEN McCALLUM

The Reverend Doctor Hayden McCallum is Clyde Burgmann Research Fellow and Librarian, St. Mark's Collegiate Library, Canberra. A member of the Church of England in Australia, Dr. McCallum was a Field Secretary for the Australian Student Christian Movement before he entered the service of the Diocese of Canberra and Goulburn as Curate, then Rector and Assistant Registrar of that central and significant Diocese. He also taught in St. Mark's Theological College before completing his doctorate in Union Theological Seminary, New York.

XI

In less than twenty-five years' time, Australia will celebrate the
two hundredth anniversary of the arrival of the first European
settlers and convicts. Christianity came with them under in-
auspicious circumstances, from a mundane Church of England
irrelevant to the new needs of the people. The country was settled on a Sunday, January 26, 1788, but there was no religious
service at Sydney Cove on that day. The first chaplain, Richard
Johnson, was most likely on one of the storeships which did not
go from Botany Bay to Sydney Cove until a day or two later.
Archdeacon A. W. Harris has said that these circumstances
serve as a parable of the place which religion occupies in Australian national life—"kept among the stores to be brought out
when required and always a little behind the times."[1]

This estimate of the significance of Christianity in Australia
has been reinforced recently by the comments of Dr. S. Barton
Babbage, a New Zealander who has carried important responsibilities in Australian Church life. In his opinion, the Australian
Churches, despite considerable real devotion and sacrificial giving, have little impact on Australia as a whole. He believes the
typical cleric is "stuffy, timid, and unimaginative."[2] The Church
has lost any intellectual distinction it may have once possessed,
and its moral and spiritual impact on the community is negligible. "The tragedy is that we are complacent about it."[3]

[1] Letter to the writer, 1961.
[2] *Sydney Morning Herald*, May 8, 1963, late edition, p. 4.
[3] *Ibid.*

By and large, Dr. Babbage's comments were complacently ignored. Australian churchmen as a whole do not believe that what he said is important. This self-deception is perhaps the real centre of tragedy in Australian Christianity.

Many features of Australian Church life are healthy and vigorous.[4] It may be true that not 10 per cent of the population will be found inside the walls of churches on any one Sunday in the year. It may be regrettable that there is a widespread acceptance of nominal Christianity which saps the vitality of a clear-cut witness to the gospel. Yet there is devoted clerical and lay service in parishes and congregations. There are also incredible obstacles of distance and loneliness faithfully met and overcome in such imaginative enterprises as the Australian Inland Mission, working in the "outback" of the country. In conventional and historic patterns, the Christianity of the Australian Churches is acceptably relevant to the needs and life of their members in local situations, engulfed in local concerns. Australian Churches and Christians need little advice on being true servants of the gospel at these pastoral levels.

At other levels, the situation at present and the prospects for the future are precarious. In 1947, Bishop E. H. Burgmann wrote, "At present most people are profoundly ignorant of the teachings of the churches."[5] This fact still holds. Now may be added the further comment that at present most Churches are profoundly ignorant of the moods and felt needs of the large masses of unchurched people. Australia is more than ever a self-

---

[4] The following surveys of Christianity in Australia will be readily available to many readers. This present article does not attempt to duplicate their material.

E. H. Burgmann, "Religion," in C. Hartley Grattan, ed., *Australia* (Berkeley and Los Angeles, 1947), pp. 326-336. Kenneth T. Henderson, "Religious Institutions and Aspirations," in George Caiger, ed., *The Australian Way of Life* (London, 1953), pp. 114-140. J. C. O'Neill, "Letter from Australia," in *Theology*, Vol. LXV (September 1962), No. 507. Cf. also E. H. Burgmann, "Australia," in William E. Leidt, ed., *Anglican Mosaic* (New York, 1963), pp. 111-120.

[5] C. Hartley Grattan, ed., *Australia*, p. 333.

conscious nation, with economic enterprise, social upheaval, and political bewilderment occurring on a national level. Christianity has had little to say or to do about life on this scale. Billy Graham's visit in 1959 created intense interest in the possibilities of a nation reinvigorated by the Spirit of God. The utter absence of any significant lasting effects has produced immense disappointment and disillusionment. What interest there was in religion gave place to a feeling of gross betrayal. The religion offered was the "same old irrelevant stuff" from the culture of another time and place, dressed up in the sleek packaging of the mid-twentieth century. Bishop John Robinson's *Honest to God*[6] has done what Graham failed to do. It has taught unchurched thinking people to think about the Church without false and misleading pressures forcing a hasty decision. Yet one has to ask if many parishes or congregations can take up where Robinson left off, without quenching the freedom of the Spirit which *Honest to God* has brought to many people.

The future is not to be found in noninstitutional Christianity in Australia. This form of faith exists in the main in the vague feeling that Australia is a Christian, as opposed to a Buddhist, Hindu, Muslim, or even a pagan nation. Provision is therefore made for religious instruction in public schools by representatives of the Churches. Combined with this sentiment is the strong conviction among Protestants, not shared by Roman Catholics however, that education in principle should be secular, and that church schools should not receive direct state aid. Most people would hold that no preference shall be shown to one form of Christianity against another in public life. Most churchmen however, would agree that a churchless, common-denominator type of Christianity for public occasions is unacceptable. Most nonchurchmen would feel that even this would be much more than the minimum necessary to preserve the Christian character of the nation. These strange ambivalences are due in part to the correct perception that Christianity

[6] London and Philadelphia, 1963.

is bigger than any of the historic Churches taken by themselves, and also to the dubious assumption that Christianity can be understood and experienced apart from institutional Churches. It is safe to say that the prospects of Christianity in Australia in the future depend largely upon recovery by the Churches of a spirit of adventurous mission.

Christianity in Australia owes its vitality and strength almost wholly to the traditional Christian denominations brought to the country by the early settlers from Great Britain. The Churches have names and titles familiar to Europeans and North Americans: the Church of England in Australia, the Roman Catholic Church, Methodist, Presbyterian, Baptist, and Congregational Churches, and Churches of Christ. There have also been vigorous but numerically small Lutheran and Eastern Orthodox Churches, and a sprinkling of such groups as the Seventh-day Adventists and Mormons. The Salvation Army has provided a worthy public ministry out of proportion to its slender numbers. Small, exotic sects have not made much headway in the country, partly because of the general social intolerance of unorthodox behaviour, and partly because traditional groups such as the Baptists and Churches of Christ have remained close to their primitive origins.

There are encouraging signs that the Churches are beginning to look beyond parochial interests into more comprehensive ecumenical and national responsibilities. The Australian Student Christian Movement has been an ecumenical force since 1896. The Australian Council of Churches brings together nearly all Churches except the Roman Catholic in a living context of common work and study. Proposals for the union of the Presbyterian, Methodist, and Congregational Churches are being carefully worked out and paced to the needs of the most thorough investigation possible. Unofficial Anglican interest may become more articulate as negotiations proceed.

Immigration following the Second World War has contributed a wider outlook and outreach for both the country and its Churches. The 1961 census revealed that 16 in every 100 of Australia's inhabitants were born in other countries. Of these 1,778,000 people, only 556,413 were born in England. Italian, German, and Dutch-born residents totalled 439,000. Italian immigration has been predominantly Roman Catholic, with a mere handful of Waldensians. German immigration has strengthened Roman Catholic and Lutheran Churches. Dutch immigration has prospered Roman Catholic and Presbyterian Churches. One cannot say that the Church of England in Australia has prospered in ratio to the British share in the new arrivals. The sickness of the Church of England in England, in its lack of contact with the daily living of ordinary people, is most apparent when great masses of its nominal members are uprooted and transplanted in soil where familiar restraints and encouragements do not exist.

The Roman Catholic Church has benefitted from post-War immigration in ways far more pervasive than the mere increase in numbers. It is no longer a haven for the inferiority complexes of an Irish minority. It now knows the freedom and lay independence characteristic of some of the continental Roman Catholic countries. It has responded to the plea for a broader understanding of other Churches in the spirit of Pope John XXIII. Yet this Church is still fissured by deep and raw divisions on political matters, which limit the national leadership it could otherwise provide.

Historically, the Church of England in Australia has borne the main brunt of the expansion of Christianity in the country. This Church finally achieved belated autonomy in January, 1962. Nearly 40 per cent of the population reports membership in the Church of England. In many respects it has been saddled with the responsibilities of an established church without possessing any of its rights, for there is no establishment of religion in Australia. The Church of England has had trouble in becoming fully Australian. Its sister Churches, the Presbyterian and

Methodist Churches, received their emancipation years ago, and
the Methodists in particular speak with an unmistakable Australian accent.

At present the Church of England is in two minds about
its relation with England. In the major cities of Sydney, Melbourne, Brisbane, and Perth, there is a powerful continuing
"establishment" of churchmen who have not once seen fit to
appoint an Australian as Archbishop and Metropolitan. By contrast the country dioceses consistently elect Australian-born or
-trained bishops. It is in the countryside that the Church of
England in Australia is most closely identified with the hearts of
men and the soil of the land.

For the next decade at least, the appointments made to
Anglican metropolitan sees will be the measure of the willingness of the Church of England in Australia to take up its inheritance in the country. If Australians are elected, it will be a sign
of growth and maturity and the acceptance of an adventurous
indigenous status. This is not a plea for nationalism, but a concern for cultural relevance. Other countries may decry the identification of religion with culture. Australia must lament the gulf
between the two. All Churches share in some degree in this
isolationism. Why is this so in the present, and what are the
prospects for the future?

An air of unreality broods over the island continent of
Australia. Other countries have their deceptions, their myths,
their escape hatches into unreality when the going gets hard.
But in Australia the going is not hard. Its unreality is born of
the indifference of an isolated, affluent society. Its escape is from
disillusionment with the relative failure of the only creative
social forces in its civilization. Professor Manning Clark writes:

> In one sense it is an age of ruins in Australia and New
> Zealand, for amidst the gaiety and the confidence of a people
> who are creating material well-being and happiness for all,
> there lie the ruins of the ideologies which have fashioned their

civilisation. The three creative influences in that civilisation—
Protestant Christianity, Irish Catholicism, and secular humanism—have lost touch with their original social function.[7]

The unreality is no more keenly apparent than in politics
and religion. Politically, there are significant though stray signs
of alert thinking. Thoughtful questions are asked about Australia's responsibilities and destiny as an archipelago of South East
Asia. There is a stirring of conscience over the welfare and
destiny of the Australian aboriginals. As one of the last remaining traditional colonial powers left in the world, Australia is
exercised on the best ways of bringing New Guinea to independence, though other nations may question the slowness with
which this is taking place. This slender social consciousness is in
great measure derived from the presence of prophetic Christianity in the midst of the common life of Australia.

Yet in the significant pressures of world events, Australia is
a captive nation. The captor is not London. Nor is it Washing-
ton or Moscow or Peking. It is all of them taken together.
Australians know that their future is being decided for them by
these centres of power, without very much thought being given
to their particular destiny. Why, therefore, should one care
about something so pervasive as one's future if one can do so
little about it?

Under these circumstances political concerns tend to become domestic, paltry, and unimaginative. Little thought seems
to be given to the great needs of education, at all levels in the
country, by the people's elected representatives. Many politicians do not appear to be immediately concerned with the im-
pending social revolution being brought about by automation
and cybernetics. Christianity in Australia has limitless possibilities to speak the right word and do the transforming deed in the
midst of paralysing apathy.

[7] *The Observer*, London, Feb. 24, 1963, p. 10, with author's permission.

In particular, Australian Christianity will have to come to terms with the problem of colour. It saturates nearly every social question of any consequence in relation to the aboriginals, New Guinea, and Asia. The major issue is, of course, the discriminatory restriction upon the immigration of non-white persons.

Australia's relations with Asia are important for the prospects of Christianity, because of the relentless way in which exclusionist walls are eventually torn down by the Gospel, or the Gospel goes down with the walls its adherents did not have the courage to attack. This does not constitute an evasion of the economics or other hard realities behind Australian immigration policies as such. Large-scale Asian migration into Australia would make no significant difference to Asia's population problem. One year's natural increase in Asia would provide a population which on present estimates would overwhelm Australia and Australians. Yet some limited form of open Asian migration would stabilize long-term relations with Asia, and provide a necessary corrective to Australian fears.[8]

It is difficult to convince an average Australian that colour is an outmoded way of distinguishing between one man and another in the twentieth century. The unconscious prejudices in favour of the white man are securely rationalized. Christianity has a responsible future in preparing the conditions under which Australians may learn to live dangerously, by a radical re-examination of the fears and prejudices which form barriers to Asian culture and society. It is true, by and large, that there are no current, obvious racial strains or prejudices within Australia, apart from occasional misunderstandings between white Australians and aboriginal Australians. But Asia will soon become a much more vocal and viable foe of Australian exclusionist immigration policies or any other device which makes colour a division between men. Few Australians, Christian or otherwise, realise that Australia has no friends, except possibly South

[8] *Control or Colour Bar?* (The Immigration Reform Group, Melbourne, 1960).

Africa, on the unconscious issues behind her historic immigration rules; and South Africa's friendship on this point may prove
embarrassing. One cannot ignore the probability that if all the
refugee inhabitants of Hong Kong were white they would be
admitted to Australia on the most urgent compassionate
grounds, whether or not they were economic burdens or social
misfits. But they happen to be coloured. At the root of most of
the problems and the necessary as well as unnecessary compro-
mises in Australia's immigration policy is the stark, terrible, un-
formed, inarticulate fear of colour.

It is true that immigration policy avoids for the present the
worst manifestations of racial conflict, such as open revolt and
social discrimination and segregation. Yet who has the bigger
problem? The community where open conflict is a reality, where
perhaps at least small moderate groups are working for reconciliation in the proximity of the problem? Or the community where
rationalized fear prevents the problem from being faced until it
is too late, until the reality of the common bond in God of all
races and colours is forced home in the midst of tragedy and
remorse? In this area alone, Christians in Australia have a super-
human task.

✤ XII ✤

Japan

MASAO TAKENAKA

MASAO TAKENAKA

Masao Takenaka is Professor of Christian Ethics and Sociology of Religion in Doshisha University, Kyoto. A member of the United Church of Christ in Japan (Kyōdan), he has served that body in various fields, notably through its Commission on Industrial Evangelism. Dr. Takenaka is a graduate of the Kyoto University and of the Theological Department of Doshisha. He later took complete theological training in Yale Divinity School. He is Vice Chairman of the World's Student Christian Federation; Chairman of the Committee on Witness of the Laity, East Asia Christian Conference; and, in the World Council of Churches, member of the Committee of the Division of Ecumenical Action and member of the Working Committee of the Department of the Laity. In 1962-63 Dr. Takenaka was Henry W. Luce Visiting Professor of World Christianity in Union Theological Seminary, New York. He published in English RECONCILIATION AND RENEWAL IN JAPAN; and his chief Japanese work is entitled SHINJIN NO KYŌDOTAI (Community of True Humanity).

XII

I. Place of Encounter

In many ways Japan is a fascinating country. On closely cramped islands, with a total area less than the state of California, more than ninety million people struggle for life. Active traditional cultures carry the impact of past heritage upon contemporaries; but at the same time there is rapid and enormous development of modern technological civilization. Japan is now known in the world for transistor radios rather than for silk embroidery. We find a complex and unique combination of various cultures in Japan, not only the meeting of old and new in traditional culture and modern industrial civilization, but also the encounter of East and West alike in the spiritual and in the political sense, plus confrontation of men of other faiths by the Christian Gospel. Let us examine several facets of Japanese society in terms of the ground of encounter before we discuss the present status and future prospect of Christianity in Japan.

First of all, we find in the society and even within one personality a rather surprising degree of cultural assimilation. One of the characteristics of the Japanese is their ability to harmonize themselves with new cultural imports. During the course of history, a certain process of cultural transformation has been achieved by the Japanese in making other cultures a part of their own rather than leaving them to continue as foreign and strange. The transformation of Hinayana Buddhism and the development of Mahayana Buddhism which took place in Japan are classic examples of cultural assimilation. Moreover, an attitude of tolerance and harmonious living rather than of rejection and protest informs the predominant ethos of Japanese mentality. In relation to Christianity, these facts raise two challenging questions. One is the question of indigenization of Christianity and the other is the question of general tolerance and common life among people who differ in religious belief. How can Christianity contribute to the development of an open society which not only genuinely respects the existence of different religious and ideologies but also encourages them to work for the common good of mankind, without diminishing effective freedom for Christianity to make its unique claim?

Second, we recognize the interesting phase of encounter between the traditional culture and the modern technology. One finds with a sense of wonder, on the rooftop of a super-modern industrial firm in Tokyo a small Shinto shrine before which the employees meet every morning for a brief ceremony. Many of the hectic taxi drivers in Osaka hang in their cars for protection a talisman issued by a Shinto shrine. In an ordinary Japanese home in the rural village it is not unusual to find a Buddhist family shrine above a television set in the living room. There is a rapid and wide trend of industrialization transferring population from rural areas to industrial and urban centers. Now approximately 70 per cent of Japan is urban. Tokyo is the largest city in the world, with a population of nine million. Even the pattern of rural life has been changing drastically. The number of farmers who engage exclusively in farm occupations had decreased radically. Furthermore the change of physical location and the new pattern of employment and living both challenge and modify the traditional culture. What makes the unique Japanese encounter exciting is the quality of two components therein. Industrialization in Japan is not the elementary or intermediate industrialization of earlier periods, but is that of the most advanced technological and organizational systems including automation, and the cultural background is not that of modern

Western culture but rather of millennial Eastern culture. Here is a challenging question for the Christian movement, namely, how can Christians participate in the process of interaction between technological forces and traditional cultural values? What is the pattern and shape of the new man whom the Christian Gospel directs and nourishes in the concrete situation of industrial Japan?

Third, the tense struggle for modernization in Japan has been a double process. One drive is to regard modernization as the means to strengthen the national power, especially military, economic, and political power of the empire. The other impulse is to regard modernization as the process by which to transform the old enclosed self into open maturity both in the Japanese community of persons and in the world community of nations. Until the Second World War, Japan took the former course with the exclusive nationalistic emphasis. Since 1868, Japan has undergone, with severe discipline and patriotic fervor, the rapid process of nation building in every aspect of her life, achieving a high rate of literacy, industrialization, military development, medical and social services. We recognize the impact of Christian missions in the process of modernization in Japan, especially in the field of social service and education. But we must not overlook the limitation of the Christian Church which failed to play a prophetic role in protesting against the danger of absolute nationalism during this period. Both the contribution and the failure of Christianity during the course of modernization in Japan constitute valuable experience to be shared among the Churches in areas of rapid social change where the problem of nation-building is acute.

Fourth, there is in Japan a concern to foster the confrontation between East and West not only in terms of spiritual encounter but also political encounter. This is different from a naïve pacifism or idealistic neutralism. The actual struggle of life in the world is certainly too harsh to allow wishful thinking. On the other hand, it is increasingly necessary and important to guard against the narrow absolutization of particular national interests; and to fight against self-complacency and apathy, constantly seeking mutual understanding and reconciliation in the community of nations. A recent best-seller in Japan is a book called *The Sword and the Cross* by Michio Takeyama. The author, a well-known scholar of Western history, makes a provocative attack on Christianity. Surveying the development of so-called Christian nations he maintains that Christianity tends to divide the world sharply into two camps, black and white, and to persist in crusading on the basis of religious conviction. Thus he establishes the interdependence of sword and cross. Of course, one could reply by pointing out the development of pacifism based on Christian faith and by distinguishing between the notion of a just war and a crusade. Nevertheless, one must admit that Christianity has tended to be too timid and too self-concerned to make a new step out of the vicious circle of power conflict. Among Japanese after the defeat in 1945, there has been a strong concern to struggle for peace and reconciliation with the people throughout the world. Article Nine of the present constitution explicitly renounces the development of military force. This was adopted not only because of the influence of the occupation forces but also with the enthusiastic support of Japanese. Both in terms of geographical location and of actual contact a unique role must be played by Japan in relation to China, for the restoration of needful relationships and for mutual understanding and reconciliation. This will require not only patience and wisdom but also anguish and courage, for the Cross is not the sign of privilege but the badge of suffering through which the dividing wall of hostility is broken down (Eph. 2.14).

II. *The Present State of Christianity*

The total number of Christians in Japan, according to the (Japanese) *Christian Year Book* for 1962, is 725,445. They are divided into three groups: Roman Catholic, Orthodox, and Protestant.

1. *Roman Catholic.* The Church begun in Japan by the mission of St. Francis Xavier in 1549 endured nearly three centuries of persecution which ended only in the latter half of the nineteenth century. Today it includes 323,599 members. There are three notable developments in recent years. One is the increase of open contact and incipient cooperation with other Christian Churches in Japan. Even before the Second Vatican Council the Roman Catholic student organization was interested in dialogue with the leaders of the Protestant Student Christian Movement. In 1961, and again in 1962, prominent professors of Protestant seminaries were invited as guest lecturers at the Roman Catholic national assembly. Just after the New Delhi Assembly of the World Council of Churches in 1962, the *Japan Missionary Bulletin,* the best Catholic periodical in Japan, published a special number on "Ecumenical Issues," inviting five Protestant scholars and pastors to contribute articles. Several informal yet intimate study fellowships have been formed in various cities, meeting regularly for study and prayer together on behalf of Christian unity among Roman Catholics, Orthodox, and Protestants.

Another significant advance in Roman Catholic work is the strategic planning and development of Christian schools. At the university level, the Catholics have only three fully accredited universities, while the Protestants have eighteen. The Protestant universities with their large number of students face the dangers of secularization and of lowering academic standards, while the Catholics try to concentrate their resources in order to maintain both academic and religious quality. When we come to secondary and primary education, the Catholics have more schools than the Protestants. On the secondary level, there are 100 Catholic schools, 89 Protestant; and on the primary level, 60 Catholic, 32 Protestant. There are no satisfactory data for comparing the Catholic and the Protestant schools in quality of education. But a study made in five cities shows rising academic levels for the Catholic secondary schools.

Finally, there is an interesting development in the renewal of Christian art in the Catholic Church in Japan. The Martyrs' Memorial Hall on the high hill overlooking Nagasaki is a contemporary expression of Christian faith through artistic creativity and imagination. Together with the Protestant groups in the last five years, the Catholics have encouraged the development of classical *Noh* plays based on Christian themes such as the Resurrection.

2. *Orthodox.* The Orthodox Church was founded by the courageous effort of Father Nicolai in 1861, on behalf of the Russian Orthodox Church. It now includes 35,431 members. In 1946 the Orthodox Church of Japan renounced its ties with Moscow and established relations with the Autocephalous Russian Orthodox Church in the United States of America.

In general the Orthodox community in Japan has not yet fully recovered from the difficult relationship with the mother Church in Russia during and after the Second World War. In addition one cannot deny the existence of a static atmosphere in the Church. There is very little active participation of young people in its life. The Church is more or less maintaining the tradition, without making a courageous effort at living dialogue and sacrificial service in rapidly changing Japan.

3. *Protestant.* The total number of Protestant believers in Japan is 403,846. The immediate reaction to the Protestant scene is distress over division. In spite of the existence of the United Church of Christ in Japan (the Kyōdan) which consists of nearly one-half of the total Protestant population, there are more than 89 different denominations. Half the denominations are small sectarian groups having not more than 1,000 members each. Only seven of them hold more than 10,000 members. In this country where the number of Christians is less than 1 per cent

of the total population, the unity of the Church is the most urgent issue. The outsider is very quick to note whether Christians manifest visible unity or not. In the missionary situation the disunity of the Church may easily become a stumbling block before the Church is able to present to non-Christians the real stumbling block of the Gospel. Two factors mark the trend of disunity among the Protestant Churches in the postwar period in Japan. First came the reaction to the United Church of Christ which had been formed during the period of nationalistic control in 1941. Not a few Churches were moved to leave the United Church. This is in one sense an inevitable development, since true unity will not be manifested under compulsion, but rather by voluntary acceptance of His gift with freedom. Those who decided to remain in the union have striven to establish a sound foundation for the United Church, especially through the adoption of the Confession of the United Church in 1954.[1] They have made progress in unity, thankfully bringing to realization the sincere concern and earnest effort for the oneness of the Church maintained since the beginning of the Protestant mission in Japan, and recognizing that even within the unhappy nationalistic pressure God has continuously called his people to manifest oneness in Christ.

Another factor of division is the postwar development of the various foreign missions operated in Japan. Partly due to the changing situation in China, which had been one of the largest fields in the modern missions, a number of new denominational missions came to Japan in the postwar period. The conditions created during the occupation period also stimulated many independent foreign missionaries, singly or in groups, to come to Japan as to a field ripe for harvest. With a few exceptions, the progress of most of the Protestant Churches in the last four years is not so rapid as was anticipated in the period immediately

[1] For the historical development see Ken Ishinara, "The United Church of Christ in Japan," in Nils Ehrenstrom and Walter G. Muelder, eds., _Institutionalism and Church Unity_ (New York, 1963), pp. 235-252.

after the war. We are entering a new stage, passing from the years of naïve optimism to a time of sober realism, in developing true conversation with the existential issues in Japanese society rather than carrying on a one-sided spiritual monologue.

III. *The Emerging Directions*

This leads us to examine some of the immediate issues and emerging directions to be noted especially within Protestantism in Japan.

First of all, there is a strong concern on the renewal of the Church. In 1959 the Protestant Churches celebrated their centennial. This provided an opportunity to re-examine the experience of one hundred years both appreciatively and critically and to reformulate the new missionary strategy for the second century of the Protestant enterprise in Japan. The Rev. Isamu Omura, Moderator of the United Church of Christ, expresses the Protestant concern in the following terms:

> Looking back over this hundred-year period, the conclusion drawn by most Japanese Christian leaders is that it was a "centripetal century." That is, Protestant Christianity in Japan was then largely introverted. The United Church, as she stood at the end of this century and examined herself, had to confess that she had too long been a receiving church. She determined, therefore, to make the second century of Protestant Christianity in Japan a "centrifugal century," to make of herself—under the leadership of the Holy Spirit—a fully responsible and contributing partner in the world-wide mission of the church. What was—and is—called for today is a renewal of the church.[2]

The United Church after a thorough discussion which extended over eighteen months finally approved the "Fundamental Policy of the Mission of the Kyōdan," which carries a strong

[2] "The United Church Today," *Bulletin,* United Church of Christ in Japan, Ecumenical Department, Research Institute on the Mission of the Church, Vol. I (Spring 1963), No. 1, p. 12.

note of the renewal of the Church so that the Church may fulfill her calling "to serve the world as Christ served the world and to remember that daily life is the arena of evangelism and to share the suffering and burden of the life of the ordinary people with the spirit of solidarity in Jesus Christ." The note of renewal also reminds us to consider the quality of Christian presence in the world rather than merely to think of quantitative gains. It is a hard fact that the Christian community is a tiny minority in Japan, less than 1 per cent of the total population, as we noted earlier. Since we are a minority, the true question is what kind of minority are we? Are we an isolated minority enclosing ourselves in a religious shell, and thus forming a Christian ghetto? Are we an adapting minority, adjusting ourselves to the secular trend of national life, thus to conform with the world? Or are we a creative minority, constantly maintaining a distinctive secular presence in the ordinary Japanese society, thus to become the salt and light of the world?[3]

Second, if the Church pursues emphasis on renewal, it must take seriously the challenging issues which exist in Japanese society. Here we see the significance of the attempt of the Churches in relation to the industrial workers in Japan. There are three factors which definitely indicate the necessity and significance of courageous effort for Christian involvement in industrial society. (*a*) It is an immense and pervading fact that rapid development of industrialization proceeds in Japan. The Church cannot be the Church in the world unless it takes seriously the reality of the actual lives of men and women in the industrial sphere. (*b*) The membership of the Churches in Japan is heavily weighted by and toward the intellectual and middle classes. Therefore it is highly important to seek a bold and concentrated involvement among working people. (*c*) By and large Christianity is still regarded in Japan as either a religion of the intellectuals or a religion of the West. The whole

[3] Masao Takenaka, "A Pattern for the Creative Minority," *Japan Christian Quarterly*, XXVII (July 1961), 159-65.

background and expression of Western Protestant Christianity in general and its ethics in particular need radical re-examination in the light of the development of industrial society. What is the relevant social structure of responsible society in Japan? What is the positive pattern and style of Christians living today in the changing industrial society in Japan? Unless we are certain on these questions, Christianity will not be able to meet the challenge of Communism in Asia.

Throughout its fourteen districts, the Kyōdan has for a full decade been developing a program of Occupational Evangelism by information among pastors, observance of Labor Sunday at the end of April, sponsoring labor schools in the various cities, and above all training the laity for their witness and service in daily work. Together with two theological seminaries, three districts of the Kwansai area have engaged in courageous experimental projects in which four full-time labor pastors together with various laymen, such as sociologists, journalists, industrial workers, and social workers, carry on a flexible and mobile group ministry in that highly complex industrial region.

Third, along with the emphasis on the renewal of the Church and Christian involvement in industrial society, we see increasing interest in the indigenization of Christian faith and practice among Japanese Christians. Three faulty types of indigenization are to be avoided: One is narrow nationalistic indigenization which we had during the war when some Christians tried to identify Christian faith with the nationalistic ideology and spirit of the Empire. Another danger is to interpret indigenization as artificial amalgamation with other religions and theologies. The third temptation is to consider indigenization in a superficial way without thorough understanding of the Christian gospel as embodied in the Bible and continuously confirmed through the experience of history. With these cautions in mind we must pursue the way further. There are promising indicators of valid indigenization within the Christian community in Japan. We here depict three aspects of the signs of hope that the Gospel is to be known and to be expressed in and through Japanese society and Japanese culture.

1. The starting point of indigenization is not, I believe, theological thinking. Theology is not formulated in a vacuum. Indigenous theology will develop within a living dialogue with actual problems in society. Unless Japanese Christians take seriously the responsibility to wrestle with common problems in ordinary life, there will be no natural expression of indigenous Christian faith. In this sense, the present emphasis on the ministry of the laity in the world is the right point for thinking on indigenization. Through the searching questions coming out of striving in secular participation, theologians will develop deeper and penetratingly meaningful theological formulations in the Japanese situation.

2. Reflecting the needs of the situation in recent years, there have been fruitful beginnings of theological discussion on indigenization among Japanese Churches. The United Church of Christ of Japan sponsors an annual institute for a highly selected group of ministers, followed by the regional institutes in the fourteen districts. The theme of the institute in 1961 was "Indigenization of the Christian Gospel." If one compares the theological climate with that of ten years ago, remarkable change is evident. Having rather solid theological learning and a high standard of academic discipline the Churches in Japan have a unique opportunity to develop an exciting indigenous theology if Christian thinkers maintain dialogue with the living issues in Japanese society through personal and social involvement in them.

3. There have been stimulating efforts to express Christian faith through various new artistic forms. Some of them are still not beyond the experimental stages, but we see the definite signs of renewal. Rinzo Shiina is a well-known novelist, formerly a member of the Communist party, who was converted to the Christian faith. His writing describes a style of man who radiates a measure of hope and humor in the ordinary struggles of daily

life. Two of the largest newspapers and outstanding *Noh* artists have cooperated with the drama project which was jointly supported by Protestants and Roman Catholics. Futaba Hanayagi, one of the finest classical dancers in Japan, also experienced adult conversion in the midst of her career. She dedicated her dancing to the expression of her new-found faith. Sute Ota, a teacher of flower arrangement, is now making a courageous attempt to express Christian faith through one of the treasures of Japanese traditional culture, namely the art in which she is profoundly skilled. Also we have a first-class artist, Sadao Watanabe, who produces biblical figures such as Moses, laborers in the vineyard, a Good Samaritan, through a distinctive process of stencil print.

Fourth, there has arisen a substantial interest in the role and the contribution of the Churches in Japan to the world-wide mission of the whole Church in this ecumenical period. Three factors support the challenge to such service: (*a*) We recognize increasingly the interdependence of one world, in which the Mission must become a movement from all peoples to all peoples. (*b*) In relation to the countries of Southeast Asia, there is deep concern to manifest full reconciliation through sending Japanese Christian workers—most of them skilled laymen such as doctors, nurses, agricultural specialists—to render the service demanded by most urgent human needs. (*c*) Japan is one of the exceptional countries possessing a surplus of ministers, if that is understood to mean the presence of a number of theologically trained men larger than the number of organized parishes or congregations. We must continually be aware of the great mission field in Japan itself; but it is a real blessing to be able to respond to invitations from abroad by sending dedicated and qualified men and women from Japan. Each Church has a unique gift to share, and each Church exists for the world.

The United Church of Christ in Japan established in 1956 a Commission on Overseas Missions. Since then more than a dozen missionaries have gone forth to nine different countries.

Some are fraternal workers responding to needs and invitations in Asian Churches, as in India, Nepal, Thailand, Indonesia, Taiwan. Others are trained pastors sent to serve Japanese congregations abroad, as in Canada, the United States, Germany, Brazil, and Bolivia.

Finally, I would like to touch briefly on the reform of the structure of the Church in Japan. Both the (Christian) Non-Church Movement (*Mukyokai*), and the Communists challenge constantly the present institutional structure of the Church. Both operate without heavy investments in buildings; and with few paid or professional leaders. Also, some of the new religions like Sokagakai emphasize the importance of nonprofessional leaders and the establishment of a nucleus fellowship in the milieu of ordinary people. On the other hand, in the Christian Church the rigid normative idea of the institutional church has been kept up, practically saying that unless you have a church building and a full time professional minister you will not have the Church of Jesus Christ. Here the idea of the tent-making ministry is suggestive. We must find the way to make the Christian Church not a static, building-centered religion but a people's movement, a company of new humanity making a joyful pilgrimage on earth.

On the other hand, in facing the challenge of the complex modern society, both religious and social, the Church must make concentrated efforts to understand the reality of the world and to be ready to enter into meaningful dialogue. In this sense the work of the Research Institute on the Mission of the Church, which was established by the Kyōdan in 1954, promises to provide valuable factual and theological information on the important questions which the Church faces today. In the encounter with non-Christian religions, two centers are worthy of note: the International Institute for the Study of Religion, in Tokyo; and the Center for the Study of Japanese Religions, organized by the National Christian Council. In meeting the need for a new type of lay training and for developing real conversation and encounter among different groups of people in modern society, the Nippon Christian Academy has been working experimentally for six years. It is now centered in Oiso outside of Tokyo, where a house is maintained for Christian and for non-Christian groups. This is timely and important work. It will develop if we try not to impart a Western movement into Japan but to make a strenuous effort to discover a Japanese pattern in the spirit of hope and solidarity which are given in Jesus Christ.

Japan as a country of encounter presents endless possibilities of confrontation and dialogue among various groups of people and differing ideas. May the Church not forget the attitude of patient listening and suffering service in the world!

✦ XIII ✦

China

M. SEARLE BATES

M. SEARLE BATES

M. Searle Bates is Professor of Missions in Union Theo-
logical Seminary, New York. Trained in history at Oxford,
Harvard, and Yale, he later was for two years a Visiting
Fellow at Yale Divinity School, working on his major book,
RELIGIOUS LIBERTY: AN INQUIRY. Dr. Bates was sent by
his Church, the Disciples of Christ, as a missionary to
China 1920-50, where he was assigned to the interde-
nominational University of Nanking as Professor of History.
He was a member of the China Council of Christian
Higher Education 1924-50, and of the Executive Commit-
tee of the National Christian Council of China 1946-50.
He carried various duties for the International Missionary
Council within the period 1938-58; and, since 1950, for
the Division of Foreign Missions in the National Council
of Churches, U.S.A. Dr. Bates also serves that Council and
the World Council of Churches in their organs concerned
with Religious Liberty and with International Affairs. He
has been President of the Association of Professors of
Missions.

XIII

We are here concerned with mainland China, now the People's Republic of China, whose seven hundred million souls are sixty times the population of Taiwan, considered in Chapter XIV of this volume. The present situation and prospects are comprehensible only in terms of what was revolutionized; and then of the Revolution itself, with 1949 as the date of Communist triumph.

I. Yesterday Evening: The Human Scene, National and Religious

Twentieth-century attempts to modernize the bulky, tradition-bound, largely peasant society of China broke down in their own weaknesses, long aggravated by Communist political and military activity and by vast Japanese aggressions. The historic culture, distinguished of old but hardly valid in the modern world, was destroyed by educational and social changes more confusing than complete. Tens if not hundreds of millions were aroused to new wants; but nearly all Chinese remained victims of poverty and warfare, in disease and ignorance inadequately attacked. The "Nationalist" regime ingloriously bore the blame for complex and miserable failure in conditions of immense difficulty. Moreover, the dismal and utter collapse of the brittle compound of feeble Confucianism, dictatorship in semifascist style, pseudo-constitutional forms and liberal words associated with American and related "imperialism" and even more remotely with Christianity through the tenuous contacts of Chiang Kai-shek, discredited all these elements of pre-revolutionary China. By contrast, the Communists presented themselves increasingly as irresistible power, total virtue, perfect wisdom, to which challenge was impossible and active support was, under fateful sanctions, required. These claims were close to the attributes of deity.

The Protestant Churches comprised some 800,000 communicant or full members, and further touched enough inquirers, pupils, and family members to suggest, by extension, a total "Christian community" of possibly 1,500,000. They were sadly divided by denominations and by varied missionary or sectarian origins, though a number of consolidations had been achieved and some three-fifths of them cooperated in the useful National Christian Council. Thirteen colleges and universities, nearly 250 middle schools, some 230 hospitals, varied publications among which the Bible and a good union hymnal were prominent in the Protestant life and in its figure before the public. Roman Catholics reported more than 3,000,000 members, but were less extensively developed in the institutions and services just named. They surpassed Protestants in the number of primary and catechetical schools closely related to the Churches; in the provision of charitable institutions, notably foundling homes and orphanages; and in the influence of six daily newspapers, two-edged in their sharp anti-Communism soon to be a perilous memory.

Protestants had, in the majority of church bodies and related organs, advanced far in the assuming of responsibilities and leadership by Chinese personnel. Missions and missionaries were conspicuous, however, in major cities and in some prominent organizations and institutions. Funds from abroad counted much more heavily and obviously in central organs and institutions than in local churches and services; and Chinese dependence upon them was prolonged and enhanced by the destructions and dislocations of the long international and civil wars.

The Roman Catholic circumstances were not radically dissimilar. But foreign missionaries were still numerically important in the total clergy and especially so in the episcopate despite the elevation of a Chinese to the rank of Cardinal. The international composition of the missionary body, in which Americans were a small minority not found in large regions of China, was a relative advantage, but not so great as it appeared in Western opinion. For the Communist propaganda assault made the most of the unitary organization of the Roman Catholic Church under authority situated outside China but expressed through the Apostolic Delegate; and of the well-known hostility of the Church, transferred from European experience of Communist and other totalitarianisms.

II. The Early Morning of the Revolution

Very small fractions of the Chinese people were pro-Communist in advance of the Communist triumph with its resultant comprehensive organization and re-education of all. But many were worn out by long years of war and distress. With force and skill the Communists overcame material and ideological resistance, until for ordinary folk there was no choice. As much or perhaps more than others, Christians explicitly desired and required peace and order, and felt that some kind of accommodation between the government and the Communists was a humane necessity. Important elements of Protestant leadership quietly but firmly conveyed to Chiang Kai-shek (1947) their refusal to assist in an "entire mobilization" of every resource for all-out war against the Communists, on the grounds that the people could not endure the prolongation of war and would not respond to such a call from the government (unreformed and ineffective) that was ignoring their greatest need. On the other hand, Archbishop Paul Yu-pin, the most prominent Chinese publicist among the Catholics and himself a member of the Central Executive Committee of the (government) Party, strove boldly to rally opinion for total war.

Some elements among educated Christians had been attracted to the Communist claims of complete understanding of life in social terms, of dedication to the development of the needy masses, of freedom from the exploitation by "ruling classes" notorious in China and attributed to capitalists-militarists-imperialists outside China. The irresistible forces of history were advancing. Those who stood in the way were by definition responsible for war, destitution, and every evil. Christians could enter and contribute worthily to the great cause of justice, brotherhood, and fullness of life; or they could remain aloof in self-seeking individualism and parasitic otherworldliness, futile, and suspect of serving the condemned order under the guise of religion. Enough of fact or plausibility could be found in this picture of destiny to complete the alienation of many from the discredited past, and to lead them to feel that the disciplined, apparently competent Communists, now the *only* movement of power that could promise the pearl of great price—decisive peace and order—and subsequent tackling of omnipresent poverty, should have their chance to make good.

A small group of Protestants had for years accepted the Marxist critique of modern society and of the National regime. As the point of national decision drew near, they prepared for the difficult and dangerous role of communication between the oncoming order and the Churches. This meant explanation and persuasion of the validity and the opportunities of the Revolution, with an unpredictable factor of manipulation, intimidation, and even coercion, to bring as much as possible of Christian strength into the new line. Conversely, the same leaders would seek and expect to secure some measure of practical toleration for the Churches, even under the antireligious ideology and in the face of thorough attacks upon everything that could be associated with imperialism and with the old regime. Under the name of the Three-Self Reform Movement, these men and prominent Christians including some bishops and other high officers of Church bodies whom they were able to persuade or push into acceptance of the rightness or the necessity of their program, directed with considerable success the transition of 1950 and thereafter. ("Three-Self" is the capsule term for the century-old missionary objective of self-government, self-support, self-propagation, now employed with nationalizing and isolating stress.) The Three-Self Reform Committee displaced the National Christian Council as the switchboard and the public voice of Protestantism; and the denominational mechanisms seem to have lost much ground through various privations and some forced changes of leadership. The Committee has included a number of persons whose integrity is indubitable.

Playing with tremendous persistence upon the nationalist and anti-imperialist chords so moving to Chinese emotions because of the country's experience in former generations and the decades of propaganda by Sun Yat-sen and Chiang Kai-shek, the Communists and the intermediary Three-Self Committee were able to induce among the chief and many lesser Christians a flood of repudiations of the American and other "imperialist" connections of Christianity, often personalized in well-known missionaries. More serious were the compelled "confessions" of imperialist and antirevolutionary taint on the part of hundreds, even thousands of individuals, frequently required to be accompanied, as proof of "sincerity," by accusations of colleagues or seniors for similar errors criminal in import. The pressures were wickedly devised and terribly potent. One result, whether or not it was a major objective of such procedures, was a shaking of ethico-spiritual foundations, of inner confidence and of mutual trust, among the confessors and accusers, among all other Christians who saw, heard, and read in terror and in doubt. Who knew now what was right, what was true? Who could be trusted, even among the leaders and pastors? And was it too dangerous, at least for the time being, to be associated with them? Whose turn next?

Moreover, the Communists and their youthful pupils infiltrated everything, offering food, jobs, advancement, and protecting power to malcontents, ne'er-do-wells, professional wreckers, anonymous denunciators. Every actual and imputed weakness in present or past of Christian Churches, organizations, and personnel was ruthlessly revealed and often vengefully exploited. Not a few lost employment or educational opportunity because they were Christians. In the land reform a high percentage of rural churches was closed and not infrequently their chief members were "liquidated" as landlords though they usually were farmers who worked with their own hands. Colleges, schools, hospitals, service enterprises with scarcely an exception save the privileged YMCA and YWCA, were promptly made over into Communist agencies.

III. The New Day Unfolds

On the basis of very scrappy information, it has appeared that perhaps one-fourth of the Protestant Christians in some discernible fashion soon left the Churches. Loss of faith and of commitment may, of course, have been more, or less, widespread than is implied by our flimsy indicators. It has been understood that the early losses or dislocations were followed, 1953-57, by some measure of recovery. Yet we may be misled by hearing of particular congregations in cities, where faithful effort was rewarded even by accessions; and of rural districts reporting the reopening of chapels long closed by public requirement (as late as 1962 we hear of such a district). The general story, particularly from 1958 onward, is more and more clearly marked by signs of pressure, attrition, and decline of visible Christianity.

The totalitarian organization of education and of all health and welfare services brought about wide redistribution and powerful ideological and administrative control of the many teachers, nurses, doctors, and supplementary staffs who had been significant elements in hundreds of congregations. Many other Christians, especially those with training and valuable skills, were sent off to distant enterprises, with disastrous effects on parish life. Pastors and other professional or trained Christian workers have been forced into "production"—factory or other ordinary labor often far from home and church. Few hours and little energy have been available to anyone for "unproductive" activity. Even the elderly and those housemothers not employed have been exhausted by tedious efforts to secure and prepare food under difficulties, and to care for workers and children.

Publication was sharply cut down. We know of little more than token printings of Bibles and hymnals, and of anxious care to salvage those used in churches closing or closed. *T'ien Feng,* the periodical of the Three-Self Committee, has been reduced from a weekly to a fortnightly and now to a monthly; with some Christian calendars, it is about all that we can be sure of as current publications. *T'ien Feng* stresses guidance to Christians as citizens. It has regularly carried a sermon or meditation which is genuine religion, cautiously segregated from public problems. In recent years Church news has dwindled practically to zero, leaving the impression that there was not much which the editors felt free and eager to report. Theological institutions rapidly declined and were combined for economy or for convenience of control, till we now know only of the Nanking Theological Seminary, product of complex unions and transfers, and much less clearly of the Spiritual Training Institute *(Ling Hsiu Yuan)* in Shanghai. It is cause for gratitude that some earnest and qualified teachers have been able to continue in this truncated function; and that several scores of young men and women have been engaged each year in preparation for Christian ministries so precarious in outlook.

Published materials show a good deal of conformity to the new order, so inimical to traditional church life, and so comprehensive in its antireligious education. Some of this conformity undoubtedly began in conviction and even in enthusiastic Christian welcome for a kingdom of concern for the masses, though difficult to maintain through years of hardship or disillusion. More of the conformity has been characterized, probably, by passive acceptance and by recognition that education and health services have been urgently extended, economic problems energetically tackled, albeit with methods and accompaniments damaging to many persons and their values. An unknown measure of essentially silent submission, as corroborated by various Communist statements and acts, has been reluctant and resentful.

For a brief moment in 1957, inaugurated by Mao Tsetung's poetic allusion to "the blooming of a hundred flowers," the regime permitted or encouraged Christians, like other groups with educated leadership, to declare their anxieties and criticisms. Probably because they were shocked at the vehemence and depth of disapproval, the authorities quickly shut down the experiment and used the products in long campaigns, for the edification of the people, against the persons and the views rashly disclosed. Complaints by prominent Christians, often known to us only through publication of verdicts or censure upon the complaints, centered around the theme that Christians were injured and discriminated against to such a degree that they could scarcely be loyal citizens. Dr. Marcus Cheng, long Vice-Chairman of the Three-Self Reform Committee, even insisted in the most conspicuous national forum, the Chinese People's Political Consultative Conference, that the antireligious campaigners were "imperialist missionaries," a bold reversal of charges which obviously involved the Russians, the Party, and the government. Other prominent Christians were accused of asserting that four-fifths of the farmers had been alienated, that the Communists had swiftly outdistanced their predecessors in deceiving the people and in corruption, and ought to forfeit their control of the nation; that "freedom of religion is manufactured as a show" for foreign visitors to observe, and that the Bureau of Religious Affairs was in reality a police office. Not so many complaints from Buddhist and Muslim sources are known to us, but they were so closely similar as to suggest nationally directed prompting or editing, though a broad base of common resentments is probable.

The attrition of city churches, amid forces already suggested, made plausible by 1958 a program of abandonment and consolidation under the doubtful slogans of offering to the government inadequately used buildings, and of winning the long struggle for Christian unity against the divisions deliberately established by missionary imperialism for the perpetual subjection of Chinese Christians. We may surmise that there was also a political decision to cut down the activities of churches, as part of the campaigns against anything "nonproductive" and against superstition and barriers to scientific and social progress. At any rate it was public fact that the 240-odd Protestant churches in Shanghai were reduced to about twenty; the sixty-odd in Peking and likewise in Canton, in each case to four; the ten to twenty in each of several other important cities, to one or two. We have nothing like a comprehensive recent picture for most cities and large towns, or for any province, or for any denomination. It can only be guessed that the full story of radical shifts and reorganizations of rural China, with bureaucratic mobilization of persons, occupations, time, and buildings, has brought grievous losses, if not disaster, to many a humble Chinese Christian group.

A considerable fraction of Protestants has distrusted or even opposed the Three-Self Committee and the many Church leaders who supported or accepted it. The open opposition has included fundamentalists who accused the Committee of "modernism," although certain prominent conservatives have marched in its front rank; and sectarians who have always fought shy of the traditional Churches and of large-scale cooperation and organization. It seems that the Three-Self Committee has felt it necessary to be severe in its treatment of nonconformity; and also that a retreat of dissidents and sectarians into household prayer-meetings has been sufficiently important to call forth governmental prohibitions and police controls, limiting freedom of worship to regularly and openly announced services in authorized church buildings.

The structure and the stance of the Roman Catholic Church delayed adaptation to the Revolution, although from the beginning there were some laymen, Chinese priests, and missionaries who felt they should or must come to terms with it, for the good or even for the very existence of the Church. Communists intrigued and infiltrated, cajoled and threatened, organized mobs and contrived crude accusations with imprisonments and tortures. A Three-Self Movement widely raised the issue, but it was largely countered by the Encyclical *Ad sinarum gentem* (1952). The nationalist theme was intermittently pressed by the Communists and by "progressive" Catholic personnel, until political selection supplemented by fraud and coercion brought eleven bishops, more than seventy priests, and one hundred and fifty laymen to establish a National Patriotic Association of Chinese Catholics, unsuccessfully banned by the Vatican. Roman authority was the pivot of struggle, with control of the hierarchy the prize before the Communists. The Patriotic Association identified itself as the real Church, denounced as schismatics and political traitors all who refused to participate, and set out to replace the ex-missionary and dislodged Chinese bishops with conforming men. Within a year the remnant of old bishops was outnumbered by twenty illicit consecrations. An Encyclical of 1958 excommunicated the new appointees, declared them and all priests adhering to them to be without jurisdiction, and asked all Catholics to depart from them. Thus the visible hierarchy and Church were anti-Church, and the disarray was tragic for many a faithful priest and believer. Building up of the banned hierarchy has proceeded, and responsible Catholic sources have published reports that few churches are open. But information is slight indeed, and sometimes clouded by differing definitions of what is to be called a church.[1]

IV. And Is There a Prospect?

What is the prospect for that which is scarcely discernible through present haze; minimally known during the past dozen years of drastic, totalitarian revolution; difficult to comprehend even as it was in the confused and warring decades prior to the catastrophic transition?

The nonreligious, entirely human answer, institutional and sociological, is gloomy—but not utterly so. It must take into full account the disruptive and negative forces, the all-pervasive forces of the totalitarian society and its strenuously antireligious ideology, driving to dominate not simply the acts but the minds and emotions, collective and individual, of all who live within it. Buddhism and Taoism have suffered more severely than Christianity. For them, organized life has nearly ceased.[2]

Islam as a community religion among border peoples has a shelter, though a precarious one; but as a faith it is under effective pressure. Christian sects that never knew missionary tutelage have been persecuted, even broken up. Yet the Communist regime has not employed all its resources immediately to destroy the Churches. Marxism carries a thread of authoritarian self-restraint in the idea that individuals ought not to be too rigorously punished for futile and antisocial superstitions due to the

---

[1] Abundant publications abroad carried select elements of the Roman Catholic experience up to 1957 or thereabouts, sometimes cherished for edification rather than for comprehensive understanding. Two highly informing essays are "The Tragic Situation of Chinese Catholics," a summary review for 1950-58, in Father Eleutherius Winance, *The Communist Persuasion* (London, 1960, from the French); and Father John Fleckner, "The Catholic Church in China," in the final year of the Catholic journal Asia (Hong Kong) XII (1960), No. 7. *Ad Apostolorum Principis* (1958) reveals the tragic dilemma of Rome, desiring both to avoid schism and to maintain discipline.

[2] The best concise survey is "Buddhism under the Communists" by Holmes Welch in *The China Quarterly* (London, 1961), No. 6.

bad social environment of the past; especially since the advance
of science and production under the Communists will automatically reverse the environmental determinants. Moreover, as
in Russia, the Communists did not think it politically astute to
press all religious folk into desperation, so long as they largely
conformed to State requirements in economic life and made no
trouble. It is not yet clear how far the Communists intend to go
or will actually go, by stages of relaxation alternating with fresh
severities, in their campaigns against religion. The experience of
the Russian Church, immense in extent and intimately bound
up in the national and cultural development of centuries, is
little guide to the future of the tiny and essentially recent
Chinese Church, derided as a foreign import. Nor, in the politics
of 1963, can one expect the Chinese Communists to use as a
model Russian Communist policy regarding religion, which is in
itself a series of changes.

The answer of Christian faith, if not bound to human fact,
is incompletely satisfying, even to the inquirer who is a devoted
believer. For we want to know where and how faith lives and
works in the concrete situation, in China a hard situation indeed. At the maximum, Christians of all sorts and in widest definition approached 1 in 100 of the population. The realization of
the Church and the experience of Christian community had
been achieved here and there, but not abundantly. Protestants
were widely scattered and divided, though gaining in considerable cooperation and in partial unions. Protestants were relatively strong in the Chinese Bible and hymnal and their wide
distribution, relatively weak in theological scholarship and understanding. The pastorate was not equal to its responsibilities,
and was deficient in the younger age-brackets where numbers
and standards of training should have been rising vigorously. On
the other hand, many pastors, other workers, and faithful lay
folk had endured creditably the exhausting strains of the wars,
and their tested commitment would not lightly be set aside. The
sudden loss of educational and service institutions, of missionary

collaboration and assistance, of international Christian fellow-ship, was crippling. It could have been constructively offset by a new sense of responsibility and a new concentration on the tasks and life of the Church as Church only in a freedom of being and of service which the Revolution did not permit.

Our concluding word should be spoken by Chinese. It must be admitted that few treasures of Chinese Christian thought and effort have made their difficult way into print, and those prior to 1958. The excellent witness of Bishop K. H. Ting, made in 1957 to hearers and readers all too few, directly challenged atheist positions in an able and timely treatment of "Christian Theism." "How many men there have been since the beginning of history," said Ting in an instruction directed primarily to seminary graduates, "who have drugged themselves by a denial of God's existence, so that they could continue in sin, avoid responsibility, and stifle the reproaches of their conscience."[3] One of the more significant reports brought from China by Christian visitors is that of Professor Walter Freytag of Ham-burg, a valued scholar of Christian missions and a leading ecumenical figure. In intimate fellowship with a group of Chi-nese pastors, he reminded them that friends abroad would ask him for what they should pray when remembering their Chinese brethren. The pastors promptly and unitedly urged that the prayer should be, "That the Gospel shall grow in China."[4]

The prime leader of the Three-Self Reform Movement, Dr. Y. T. Wu, published in 1954 an appeal to Chinese churchmen perplexed about the prospects for Christianity in China, as we are at this moment:

[3] For a fuller presentation of Bishop Ting's published address, see Francis P. Jones, *The Church in Communist China: A Protestant Appraisal* (New York, 1962), pp. 138-144. This book is a first-class study by our best authority, who from 1951 to 1962 edited the *China Bulletin*, devoted to gathering information upon this subject. Dr. Jones has also edited *Documents of the Three-Self Reform Movement* (New York, 1963), an important collection of source materials.

[4] Walter Freytag, "Meeting Christians in China," *International Review of Missions*, XLVI (1957), 410-416.

Since Liberation we frequently hear Christians asking, "Has Christianity any future?" That is a strange question to be upon the lips of a Christian. What has happened to his faith? Does he believe that the eternal God who made heaven and earth exists today and will not exist tomorrow? Has he forgotten that the Christ whose life was full of mercy and truth is the same yesterday, today, and forever? Does he believe that the Holy Spirit who has hitherto enlightened and guided his heart will now suddenly stop working? Not so. The eternal Triune God does not change with the times. It is not the faithfulness of God that we need to be concerned about, but our own faithfulness. If we have deeds to match our words, if we make an effective witness for Jesus Christ, then all our anxieties will be found to have been needless.[5]

⋆ XIV ⋆

India

DAVID GNANAPRAGASAM MOSES

DAVID GNANAPRAGASAM MOSES

Dr. David Gnanapragasam Moses, Principal of Hislop College, Nagpur, is one of the Presidents of the World Council of Churches. He took his B.A. and M.A. degrees, with Honors in Philosophy, from the Madras University; and later the M.A. and Ph.D. degrees in Religion and Philosophy in the Joint Program of Columbia University and Union Theological Seminary, New York. He had become Professor of Philosophy at Hislop College in 1926, and Principal in 1939. Dr. Moses' major publication is RELIGIOUS TRUTH AND THE RELATION BETWEEN RELIGIONS. He has been active in the councils of Nagpur University and in other professional bodies concerned with higher education. A member of the United Church of North India, he has been at various periods Moderator of the Nagpur Church Council of that body; President of the Student Christian Movement of India; and, since 1959, President of the National Christian Council of India. For more than twenty years Dr. Moses has been serving, in various capacities, the International Missionary Council, of which he long was Vice Chairman; the World Council of Churches; and the Joint Committee of the two Councils, which directed their cooperation and prepared for their integration. He was Henry W. Luce Visiting Professor of World Christianity in Union Theological Seminary in 1954-55.

XIV

Christianity in India has a very long history, extending 1,900 years. Tradition has it that St. Thomas came to India in A.D. 52 and established a church in Malabar in Cochin, now part of the Kerala State. Whatever we may think of this ancient tradition, there is no doubt that from the fifth century onwards flourishing Christian communities, numerically small, existed in Malabar, the Southwest coast of India. They had their own bishops and were in communion with the Patriarchates of Antioch and Alexandria. From these stem the modern Syrian Churches.

The next stage for Christianity in India begins with the arrival of the Portuguese in 1500. The Roman Catholic Church is strongest in the old Malabar coast area, including Kerala State and Goa, which area has roughly 44 per cent of all Catholics in India. There are sixteen archdioceses and fifty-five dioceses, covering every state in India. The Catholic hierarchy has grown rapidly since 1935, especially in the large number of nationals to be found in every category of the clergy and auxiliaries.

The arrival of Protestant missions, beginning with the Lutheran missionaries Ziegenbalg and Pluetschau who landed at Tranquebar in 1706, marks the next stage. But the real inrush of Protestant missions from the West began with the turn of the eighteenth century, which coincided with the establishment of the British rule in India. As a result of the manifold activities of these missions, the Protestant Christian population in India today is over five million, about a million less than the Roman

Catholics. Protestants and Catholics taken together form 2.6 per cent of the total population of India, which is 438 million.

It might appear that Christian missions have been a failure in India, if after centuries of Christian work in this great land only 2.6 per cent of the population profess this faith. On deeper analysis we discover that the very existence of a Church in India is a standing miracle. India's is an ancient civilisation of about 4,000 years, with innumerable sects, every one of them accepting as an axiomatic truth that there are many ways to God and all of them equally valid. In this vast society men found the necessary supports of common life within one of the endless number of castes and subcastes authorised and validated by the religious scriptures. Then consider if it was at all easy for anyone who sincerely felt that there was something unique in the new faith to leave his caste and become a Christian.

In the first place, the intellectual difficulty was to recognise Christianity as a new way to God; if this were overcome there was the further difficulty to prefer it to his own faith when it could, with much less strain, simply be regarded as one other of the many ways to God. Next, the insuperable difficulty of giving up the caste in which he and all his forefathers for generations had had their being, lived, and died.

But, thanks be to God who giveth us the victory in Jesus Christ, there is in India at the present time a genuine Church true to its original character. It has withstood the genius and fundamental characteristic of Hinduism to absorb every new faith that comes within its reach. Dr. Radhakrishnan says, "Hinduism killed Buddhism by a fond embrace." It has taken Buddhism more than 2,500 years to come back to its home land and to be recognised as different from Hinduism. Even now it is not regarded as really different from Hinduism but as one more room in that many-mansioned edifice. That this has not happened to Christianity is an arresting wonder even though many of the articles of the Christian faith have found a harmonious place in Hinduism. There are two reasons for this survival: One

is the personality of Jesus Christ. The other is the doctrine of
the Church as an integral part of the Gospel. Ideas can be
absorbed but a historical person resists assimilation. The Church
as the Body of Jesus Christ, as the fellowship of the redeemed
new humanity in Him, has prevented Christianity from becoming the religion of "the friends of Jesus," one more sect within
Hinduism.

I. *The Strength and "Weakness" of Christianity*

The strength of Christianity consists not in any one article
of its faith but in the whole *Gestalt* of its beliefs, doctrines, and
its declaration that in Jesus Christ as the final revelation of God,
the universal predicament of man has found a solution. Parallels
can be found for many of its doctrines. But the saving act of
God in Jesus Christ, in other words, the cross, is nowhere found.
The *idea* of the cross being at the very heart of God is sometimes
talked about by some Hindus and it is also a common belief that
God comes to the rescue of man from his heavenly abode. But
anything resembling the cross as the act of God in Christ,
reconciling the world to Himself, is not to be found in Hinduism
or any other religion.

Moreover, it is in the light of the righteousness and holiness
of God that sin becomes such a stark reality and demands the
saving power of God as exhibited in the cross. In Hinduism,
modern or ancient, there is no sense of sin in terms of its
heinousness and death-dealing character. To call man a sinner is
blasphemy. Sin is due to an ignorance or *avidya*, and therefore is
something that can be remedied by knowledge or *vidya*, though
this knowledge is understood as a nonlogical, intuitive, mystical
experience. The inadequate understanding of sin also accounts
for the failure to comprehend the costliness of salvation, even
among some Bhakti sects of Hinduism where there is a wonderful recognition of the free grace of God. Nowhere do we detect
any signs of the Christian belief that while creation can be by

word of mouth, salvation can only be by the complete self-giving of God.

Another point of strength in Christianity, meaningful in the present perplexing and promising day in India, is its doctrine of history, that this world is God's world, that He is a God of history, acting in, and through and above history fulfiling His eternal purpose in Jesus Christ to sum up all things in Him. The Hindu has always had a very slight sense of history. Recent events in India however, have made him alive in a strange new way to the meaning of history and its metaphysical significance. Not only is he conscious that he is an active partner in the making of history; he is also conscious of living in an age of universal history. The significance of history has come to India by way of the Communist philosophy of life. It should really have been given by the Christian faith. That it did not shows how poor Christian communication has been in this land.

In *Asia and Western Dominance*,[1] the historian and publicist Dr. K. M. Panikkar mentions four weaknesses as reasons for the meagre success of Christian missions in Asia. First, "the missionary brought with him an attitude of moral superiority and a belief in his own exclusive righteousness." "The doctrine of the monopoly of truth and revelation . . . is alien to the Hindu and Buddhist mind." This criticism is more or less valid of the presentation of the Gospel to the non-Christian by the first missionaries. But it must be remembered that the beginnings of the Protestant Christian missions coincided with the low-water mark of Hinduism. Knowledge of the higher forms of Hinduism and its ancient literature were unavailable. What they saw in Hinduism was so dark that they were tempted to regard the whole of Hinduism as the work of the Devil and their own faith as all light and holiness. But Panikkar's statement that the missionary believed "in his own exclusive righteousness" is a gross misunderstanding. No missionary believed in his own righteousness; his very faith demanded the recognition that he

[1] London, 1953.

was as much a sinner as any man, but that the righteousness and love of God in Jesus Christ have saved him.

Panikkar's second reason is "the association of Christian missionary work with aggressive imperialism." It is an unfortunate historical accident that the beginning of Christian missions in India and the whole of Asia coincided with the arrival of the Western Powers. It is also true that some missions used the political power of their own nations to increase the number of Christians. But Protestant missions in India were free from this unholy alliance. They often started their work without the support or even approval of their governments. Moreover, conditions in India are not as they were in 1700 and 1800; today India is a sovereign democratic republic. The last imperialist power has withdrawn from India. The Christian Church can now proclaim her message without this confusing embarrassment.

The third reason for the meagre results of Christian missions is stated to be proclamation of the Gospel with an "unconsciously inculcated" but nevertheless clear feeling of the "cultural superiority of the west." This again was not totally untrue. The error was due to the attempt to identify Christianity with Western culture and to assume uncritically that singing the praises of the Gospel was also to lift up European culture as the highest and best. Many valid elements of European culture do stem from the Hebrew-Christian tradition, and there has been an enriching relation between the two. We now understand more clearly that the Gospel is *sui generis* and cannot be identified with any culture, Western or Eastern. The creative seed of the Gospel can be planted in the soil of any culture and it has the power both to grow and to assimilate, to judge and to discard from every culture. If this were not so the universality of the Gospel would be a fiction.

Panikkar's fourth reason is that "the wide variety of Christian sects, each proclaiming the errors of others handicapped missionary work." In this he puts his finger unerringly on the weakest point of the Christian enterprise in the eighteenth and nineteenth centuries and to a certain extent in the twentieth century. The Christian Church in India has been painfully conscious of the scandal of its divisions and in the twentieth century has started to heal these divisions. Panikkar's book was first published in 1953, and six years before that the first great united church, the Church of South India, had been inaugurated, bringing together the Congregationalists, the Presbyterians, the Anglicans, and the Methodists. Panikkar should at least have referred to this first effort at Christian unity.

We have dwelt at some length on the analysis by Dr. Panikkar of the causes of the failure of missions in India and the East, for it is good to see ourselves as others see us and to learn from their criticisms, even when onesided or misinformed. The weaknesses of Christianity are not inherent in the faith but the result of historical circumstances in which the missions started their work.

Undoubtedly the work of Christian missions constitutes one of the important transforming forces that have created the New India. Christians have always been in a minority, but the gospel they preached was an explosive power tearing away ancient evils such as *sati*, infanticide, child marriage, enforced widowhood, *devadasis*, untouchability and polygamy, and laying low hoary lies. They proclaimed the fatherhood of God and the brotherhood of man and the infinite worth and dignity of the individual. They believed and affirmed that every child of God had the right to a full and abundant life, and acted upon these truths by founding educational institutions, dispensaries and hospitals, homes for fallen women, institutions for the handicapped and disabled, all concrete expressions of the love of God for all men and women, and of their own Christian responsibility in the midst of human need. Some Hindus criticise these institutions as "baits" used to convert the non-Christian and to increase the number of Christians. This cannot be denied; but such cases were exceptions. All the service institutions of both

the Roman Catholic and Protestant missions were a result of
the constraint laid upon the Christian missions by the example
and teachings of their Master, that He had come "not to be
ministered unto but to minister." This work and teaching roused
the conscience of thinking Hindus. Dr. K. M. Panikkar in his
latest book, *The Foundations of New India*, writes:

> If the effort of the missionaries failed in the field of
> religion, in other spheres their work has had notable success.
> Especially their educational institutions introduced a new
> spirit of understanding, a better appreciation of life in the
> community and gave an added impetus to the rethinking of
> values.

Again:

> In the field of social service also the foreign missions have
> a fine record of achievement. The inspiration of many activi-
> ties, notably of the advocates of social reform both in their
> desire to raise the moral standards of the people and in their
> narrow philistinism and intolerance, can be traced directly to
> the missionaries. . . . The one field where missionary activity
> had a positive result was in relation to the untouchables and
> the aboriginal tribes.

And finally:

> . . . perhaps the most important contribution of Christianity,
> though indirect, was the sense of communal solidarity that
> it gave to Hinduism.[2]

This reluctant but substantial tribute from a Hindu historian
amply corroborates what we have said about the transforming
influence of the Gospel in many aspects of Hindu life.

Along with the directly Christian factors, Western liberal
education, commerce and technology, Western stimulus to nationalism, have been working their changes for a full two cen-

[2] Chapter III, "The Christian Tradition," pp. 48, 49. (London, 1963)

turies, with the inherent resilience and strength of Indian
civilisation responding. Modern India has emerged. It is the
scene of multiple revolutions, political, economic, social, and
religious, all simultaneous. Free India was born in 1947 when
British power withdrew. But the achievement of independence
is just the beginning of the political revolution. More than four
hundred million people belonging to different castes and communities have to be welded together into a single nation. Thanks
to the long British connection and their administrative practice,
the ideals of democracy are deeply embedded in the minds of
the people and it is this that has saved India from accepting any
form of totalitarianism. Then there is the economic revolution
to change over from a purely agrarian economy to an industrial
economy. Thirdly, there is the social revolution, with the consequent changes in social structures and behaviour patterns of
Indian society.

In the earlier decades of the freedom struggle not many
Christians participated actively, though the large majority of
them shared in the general upsurge of the nationalistic feeling.
Their greatest political contribution to the new democratic
India was their voluntary giving up of special privileges as a
minority community. This produced a very favourable impression among their co-patriots and it was this that influenced the
Constituent Assembly to include in its formulation of the fundamental right of religious freedom not only the practice and
profession of one's religion but also the right to preach it.

This new India with its rising tide of nationalism and the
spread of democratic institutions in the country has had its
natural impact on the Christian Church. Missions all through
the centuries have had a paternalistic character about them. In
India nearly 80 per cent of the Christians were from the de-
pressed classes and with their low literacy and poor economic
capacities it was difficult to develop indigenous leadership. The
missionary was necessarily the source of authority and the centre
of influence in the early days. But now that most Christians are

of the second or third generation and have advanced in their education and in their economic status, they have come to desire that the conduct and control of the affairs of every Church should be in the hands of nationals. The transfer has been a long process, and its latest form is what is called the integration of the mission and the Church. Not everywhere has this process been properly understood nor has it happened in every Church. Many nationals have seen integration as the mere transference of power from the mission council to the Church council, instead of realising that it is the handing over of responsibility to the Church for the task of evangelism. The real independence of the Church is still nominal, insofar as the enormous sums of money needed to run the institutions founded by the missions still come from the parent Churches. In the new India the Christian faith will have very little chance to grow and to be in dynamic relation with the world around until the Churches are genuinely and fully independent, not in the political sense but in terms of the biblical understanding of the selfhood of the Church.

Tendencies towards building a narrow, nationalist Church have been happily absent among the large majority of Christians. This is because all the Churches in India were already in close communion with either their respective world confessional movements or with the International Missionary Council and the World Council of Churches. The coming into being of the East Asia Christian Conference in 1954 "as an organ of continuing cooperation among the churches and councils in East Asia" has further strengthened the supranational character of Christ's Church. These associations have given the India Christians new insights into the nature of the Church, its mission to the world, and the necessity of carrying forward this mission in unity.

The Indian constitution has granted the Christians full religious liberty to profess, to practice, and to preach their religion, and it has not only been on paper but an actual reality.

Except in certain states where fanatical and militant Hindu organisations have had a large following, and in certain princely states where the entrance of missionaries was prohibited, persecutions have been absent. But it must always be remembered that while Hinduism claims to be tolerant of all religions, what it cannot tolerate is any religion that declares it has a unique Gospel, a final revelation. Wherever there have been difficulties the new Christians have been loyal to their faith and borne them gladly and victoriously.

II.   *The Resurgence of Hinduism and the New Apologetics*

The new life of modern India is very evident in the field of religion. Religion in some form has been the soul of India and her whole life has been governed and controlled by her religious beliefs. Many of the age-long social institutions and practices from which she is breaking away were considered to have religious sanctions. But Hinduism has been a dynamic religion, with a succession of great reformers such as Ram Mohan Roy (1772-1833), Ramakrishna Parahamsa (1836-86), and Swami Vivekananda (1863-1902). In our own day the two great names connected with a reinterpretation of Hinduism are Mahatma Gandhi and Dr. Radhakrishnan. Dr. Radhakrishnan is regarded by many as the exponent of Neo-Hinduism, though he himself will assert that it is the eternal religion of the Hindus re-expressed. His attempt is to show that Hinduism is adequate to meet the needs of emergent India and that it is also the one universal religion which can meet the spiritual needs and desperate plight of modern man. For the first time in the history of Hinduism, it has become a religion with a consciousness of world mission. Hindu missionaries are crossing the seas and spreading their message in the West. Ancient religious classics are being published today with commentaries to show their relevance for the modern world.

It is agreed by most fair-minded scholars that all these new ideals and goals and in fact the whole reinterpretation of the Hindu faith have been the consequences of *(a)* the nationalist reaction of Hinduism to Christian missionary effort, *(b)* the permeation of Western liberal ideas in the minds of the educated, and *(c)* the advance of science and technology. But what is of particular significance to the Church in India in this revitalisation of Hinduism is the compelling fact that Christian Apologetics in our day has to be undertaken in this new context. All our old methods of commending the Gospel to the educated Hindu have become out of date. Doctrinal comparisons are unavailing because no Hindu doctrine is now understood in the sense in which it was expounded in the original authoritative scriptures. *Karma* is no longer a fatalistic determination of the individual; it is only the law of cause and effect in the moral world. Indeed, *karma* now implies conditioning rather than actual determination. *Maya* does not now mean the illusoriness of the world; it simply affirms the transitory character of the world and its fashions. The absolute Brahman is no longer an indeterminate, indefinable, passionless Nothing; he is both the personal God of devotion and the ineffable Godhead.

The line of commending the Gospel as the source of higher morality and purity of life has also become of doubtful validity because Hinduism can point to scores of highly moral and nobly self-sacrificing individuals among its votaries. On the other side, many members of the Christian Church and nations which call themselves Christian have not shown themselves to be models of virtue.

How is the apologetic task of the Church in India to be carried out? In the East Asia Christian Conference has arisen the valuable new suggestion that instead of starting with the concept of revelation and the doctrine of God, Christian apologists should begin with the new concept of man that has become prominent in all non-Christian religions, as evidenced in their revolutionary social and political reforms. The Christians in East

Asia were asked to carry on a continuous and sympathetic dialogue with their non-Christian brethren on the common issues of the religious life and in terms of their living faiths. The Christian Institute for the Study of Religion and Society in Bangalore is the practical outcome of this suggestion. Another fruitful suggestion comes from the profound work of Dr. A. G. Hogg, former Principal of Madras Christian College, which he calls the principle of "challenging relevancy." He says, "In the modes of presentation there must be always a challenging relevancy. There must be challenge, for it is a unique Gospel that the church is commissioned by its Lord to declare. But if the challenge is to be made effectively, it must be concentrated on key positions and not dissipated by being spread over every point where Christian and Hindu ways of thought diverge."[3]

The prospects of Christianity in India particularly among the educated classes are dependent to a large extent on the Church in India concentrating its thought on a clear exposition of the finality of Jesus Christ and including in it the biblical view of the relation between religions. The Indian Church needs a typically Indian expression of the authentic Christian faith. There are difficulties and dangers involved in this venture. It may fail to be authentically Christian or it may fail to be truly Indian. But if after two hundred and fifty years of Christian experience and nurture it is impossible to work out an Indian expression of the Christian faith, it would mean either that we are still strangers to the depths and profundities of the Christian faith or that we are ignorant of Indian culture and its genius.

III. *Other Winds of Doctrine*

There are other systems of thought claiming the allegiance of men. One is secular humanism, the view that recognises ethical values, such as human brotherhood, integrity of charac-

[3] *The Christian Message to the Hindu* (London, 1947), p. 11.

ter, and world peace, but is silent about God. It pins its faith
for the remaking of Indian society on science and technology.
It is difficult to estimate the number of its adherents, for very
few proclaim themselves openly as secularists and humanists in
this land where religion is still the dominant force. But many
among the educated are inclined to this philosophy of life because of their experience of the inhibiting effect of religion on
social and economic advancement and, on the other hand, their
knowledge of what science and technology have done and are
doing in their own and other countries for a fuller and better
life. The turn away from a contemplation of happiness to be
achieved in a future life, towards the realities of the present life
and a new assessment of its value and possibilities, is salutary.
The Christian Church in India has a relevant message to this
growing class of Hindus. Christianity has been described as "the
most materialistic of religions," in that, at its centre is the doctrine of the incarnation, God in Christ coming into the world to
give life and life abundant, to all believers. Christianity must
support all this new interest in this world and its affairs, approve
all the endeavours to right ancient wrongs and to provide
opportunities for a fuller and better life. But it has also to give
its message of the priority of God and His Lordship over all the
world. It must give the warning that when man is placed at the
centre of the universe and humanity is regarded as the final
value, by a strange paradox humanism may become destructively
inhuman.

IV. What of the Future?

Will India become Christian? Will she come under the
Lordship of Jesus Christ, within a reasonably measured time?
When the kingdoms of the world will become the Kingdom of
Our Lord Jesus Christ is a mystery of the inscrutable will of
God. But we can say with certainty that if the Church in India
can steer clear of certain deadly dangers and strive earnestly to

use the opportunities before her, the Lord of the Church will
bless her efforts.

One danger she must avoid, a danger which arises just because of her minority position in this land, is to turn her attention in upon herself and forget that she exists not for herself but
for the world. Another danger, and one which she has faced
from the very beginning of her history, is any attempt to compromise the Gospel and fall a prey to syncretism. New ways should
be found to lift up the gospel of Jesus Christ in our day of
resurgent Hinduism. But this does not mean, whatever our
apologetic method may be, that we can in any way give up the
uniqueness and finality of Jesus Christ.

Many opportunities of service summon the members of the
Indian Churches. The parent missions were pioneers in various
forms of social service. Now the welfare state has entered all
these fields and covers larger portions of the country with infi-
nitely more facilities. But the very development of India presents
new opportunities for service in the economic, political, and
social sides of Indian life. Two changes are required in our
understanding of service: (*a*) We must regard our service not as
instrumental to mission but as integral to mission, and itself a
form of witness to the Servant Lord of the Church. (*b*) Our
service must be really Christian, exhibiting the characteristic of
sacrificial costliness. Many a Hindu sings the praises of the old
missionaries because he remembers their complete self-giving in
their service. The Roman Catholic Church has a natural advantage in this regard. They have the orders of priests and nuns who
take their vows of celibacy, poverty, and obedience. They bear
on them the marks of absolute surrender to the service of our
Lord; and their influence in the Roman Catholic colleges and
seminaries has been tremendous. Without sacrificing the principle of the priesthood of all believers, the Protestants need to
move in this direction.

But the prospects of the Indian Church will be bleak indeed if she does not set her own house in order and acquire the
true marks of Christ's Church:

1. She must really become One Church. Unions have been accomplished, and others are patiently sought. But there are still about two hundred denominations in India. Can true and effective witness possibly be given by these splintered Churches?

2. The whole Church, clergy and laity, men and women, should be engaged in the missionary task. Every member of the Church in his particular station and duties is called to obedience to the Lord of the Church in his situation. Christian workers have earned the name of being a professional class, paid for preaching the gospel. This impression cannot be removed unless every Christian is a messenger of our Lord, witnessing to Him in word and in deed and in humble service. It is to the credit of many of our churches in India that they have sent men and women from their churches to cross the frontiers and work in other lands, and they have supported them from their own funds.

3. The Indian Church should extricate herself from too great a dependence upon foreign money. It is true we all have the conviction that Christian Churches all over the world are members of one World Fellowship and that it is the privilege of the Churches to have the grace both of giving and of receiving. We are also advancing towards the conception of Joint Action for Mission, that missions and Churches all over the world should join together to fulfil the calls for new forms of service. But non-Christians are quite aware that the major efforts are not the result of the self-sacrificing giving of the Indian Church. It is true that the economic capability of many Christians in the villages is very poor, but even allowing for that it cannot be said that the Church in India is giving enough. In this situation, Joint Action for Mission may become a snare and a positive handicap.

4. The Indian Church should hasten to become as indigenous as possible. She has a rich religious heritage in the past of this country, but she has not made it to serve her Lord and to sing His praises. She has been afraid of it and has clung to the forms of worship, hymnology, and styles of church architecture brought

to her by missionaries. Many thoughtful people are realising that
the present structure of our Churches has been completely
Western and that it is not able to meet either the needs of the
spiritual nurture of the congregations or the new evangelistic
opportunities. The Mar Thoma Church in Malabar and the Syrian Orthodox Church, and also certain Protestant Churches have
made some use of the Ashram method of witnessing to the
Gospel. This genuinely indigenous method makes a strong
appeal to the Hindus. A great deal can be learned by discerning
study of the devotional manuals of Hindu sects, and adapted for
the development of the interior life of the Christian believer.

Finally, as I have written elsewhere, the Church in India is
called to new realisation of the truth that

> our God is a living God, and He that entered history in the
> Person of Jesus Christ to create a new humanity, is working in
> the new India of today. This will save the church from both
> pride and despair, from pride because what we do will not be
> our own doing but His through us, from despair because He
> cannot be defeated. It will rebuke the all-too-human tendency
> to seek our own security in splendid isolation and will launch
> the Indian church into joyous involvement in the whole life
> of our fellow human beings.[4]

---

[4] "India: Changes Pose New Demands," *Christian Century*, LXXIX,
Oct. 3, 1962: 1188-91.

✦ XV ✦

Indonesia

ALAN C. THOMSON

ALAN C. THOMSON

Alan C. Thomson is on the staff of the Theological College of Malang, East Java, supplied since 1961 as a fraternal worker by the Commission on Ecumenical Mission and Relations of the United Presbyterian Church in the U.S.A. The Theological College is maintained by five of the eight church bodies—all within the Reformed tradition, but constituted by region and by language—on the populous island of Java. Before acquiring his theological training in Union Theological Seminary, New York, Dr. Thomson taught for three years in Iran. He has had good opportunity for study and consultation on the condition and outlook of the Churches in Indonesia.

XV

For the Church of Christ in Indonesia, the present situation made its appearance not as a gradual development from observable causes, but rather as a sudden explosion. Perhaps nowhere, other than in lands wholly or partially under Communist administration, was the shock so sudden and severe. Surely only Christians in China, in Germany, in Korea, in Vietnam—and most recently in the Congo—have undergone contemporary transition in as violent a manner as have the Christians in Indonesia.

I

Because the Indonesian Churches have developed in a distinctive situation, some notes on their historical background may be helpful. The peoples of the Indonesian archipelago have known a whole series of religious invasions since the early centuries of our era. Their indigenous mystical animism has been confronted with Buddhism and Hinduism, and marks of both are still visible in Java and Bali. Islam, the only religion not primarily imposed by a conquering power, conducted by far the most successful of these campaigns. The Portuguese entered the Indies in 1511 and brought with them the Iberian passion for the Christian faith and the Roman primacy. At the beginning of the seventeenth century the Dutch fleet of the United East India Company began to test the Portuguese dominance, and

by 1619 Djakarta—then Batavia—was founded as the headquarters of the Company's operations. The Dutch conquerors
established the Church of the Indies, which was no missionary
agency, but rather an extension by the Company of the Dutch
State Church for the convenience of its employees. It is a mark
of the power of the gospel that in fact a Christian community
was gathered by this body. Never was the Spirit so completely
quenched as by this Erastian, bureaucratic, and under-staffed
agency. Nevertheless, by the end of the eighteenth century the
greater part of the inhabitants of the areas of early European
occupation—the islands around Ambon, Timor, and the north-
ernmost tip of Sulawesi (Celebes) called Minahassa—had come
under its care. Curiously enough, there has often been real vigor
in the resulting independent Churches.

The situation changed radically in the nineteenth century.
At its beginning the evangelical-pietist movement of northern
Europe produced a series of missionary societies, including
(1797) the Netherlands Missionary Society, the *Nederlandsche
Zendelinggenootschap*. At the end of the Napoleonic period
the Indies, by this time a crown colony, received regular missionaries for the first time. The religious policy of an officially
neutral government played no favorites among confessions—
now including the Roman Catholic—laid down strict comity,
and closed off certain areas regarded as fanatical or unruly. In
practice, most of Java (for a time), northern and western
Sumatra, and the islands of Bali and Madura were forbidden to
missions. The most spectacular ecclesiastical development of
this period was a number of mass movements, among the Bataks
of Sumatra, on Timor, and at the beginning of the present
century in central Sulawesi.

The first independent Church was the Huria Kristen Batak
Protestant in 1930, followed immediately by others. Plans for
the disestablishment and independence of the Protestant
Church of the Indies were approved in 1934, and fully carried
out at the time of the withdrawal of the Dutch civil authorities

in 1949. The Second World War meant an end to mission work and outside support, some persecution of Christians at the hands of Muslim groups and the Japanese, and considerable loss of property and personnel. However, the war was only the beginning of her time of troubles. Indonesia had to fight for independence, achieved with United Nations intervention in 1949. The Indonesian Churches were without effective outside assistance for almost a decade. And the following years continued perilous disorder. The dissolution of the interim Republic of the United States of Indonesia, set up under the independence agreement, provoked a revolt in the midst of the eldest of the Christian communities, Ambon. Another wave of regional revolts beginning in 1956 involved the Bataks and the Church of Minahassa. While the rebels were officially pacified in 1961, murderous harassment of Christians by outlaw Muslim elements, which began at the conclusion of the war, is not yet at an end.

II

The present state of the Church in Indonesia is of necessity conditioned by its social, political, and religious environment. There is great variety in the Indonesian social scene, with deep cultural diversity among the various islands and groups thereof. Populous Java is a complex country in itself; whereas among the less-populated islands there are those which have been in continuous touch with European civilization for more than three centuries, and others where neither Dutch nor Indonesian administration has ever been a reality. In Bali the evangelist confronts a closed village community in which a convert can hardly continue normal life, whereas in Central Java the "gathered church" has always been possible.

In the political sphere, the Churches find themselves in a State in which religion is honored and privileged, in which freedom of religion is officially and sincerely proclaimed. It is customary to say that such freedom is more real in Indonesia than anywhere else in Southeast Asia. The *Pantjasila*, the Five Fundamental Principles of the Republic of Indonesia, begin with "Belief in God." Even the Communist Party dares not openly flout this principle. On the other hand, this declaration could point toward an ideology of benevolent religious comprehension on the Hindu model; that all religions are the same is a standard maxim of casual conversation. Following the Dutch example, the government exercises paternal supervision over church affairs through a Ministry of Religion. The leadership, searching for a unifying principle adequate for this largest of island regimes, divided culturally, ideologically and religiously, is inclined to lean upon compulsory indoctrination which could ultimately bring forth something like a national cult. "Indoctrination"—so labeled—is a regular subject in all schools, including theological schools, and a passing mark in it is required for graduation.

It has been estimated that Indonesia is 85 per cent Muslim with a Christian community of 5,000,000 as the second group, followed by 1,500,000 Hindus in Bali, and the rest animists and Buddhists—the latter including both Chinese immigrants and some indigenous survivals. All these groups are deeply divided except the Bali-Hindus. Islam possesses an old school which has made great concessions to mystical animism. The new school is relatively more orthodox but is dominated by a reformist-modernist body called Muhammadiah, perhaps inspired by Ahmadiyya. The Christian group consists of 3,500,000 Protestants and 1,500,000 Roman Catholics.

A fanatical element in Islam took advantage of the interregnum between the Dutch and the Japanese in 1942 to ravage Christian villages in the northern part of East and Central Java. Others, who had hoped the Republic of Indonesia would become a Muslim state, went into revolt at the time of independence, and remnants continue active after seventeen years. A deadlock over an Islamic versus a secular State was one of the causes of the dissolution of the Constituent Assembly, so that today the Republic operates on the revolutionary constitution promulgated by President Soekarno in 1945. There are signs of a resurgence of anti-Christian sentiment among Islamic groups, possibly with Communist connivance. Thus the Church lives amidst real though veiled hostility from some Muslim elements and from the Communist Party, which is the largest and perhaps the only really functioning political association in the Republic. At the same time there is the constant question, in all relations with the government, as to when national ideology becomes national cult.

The Protestant community which faces this situation is—relatively speaking—large, well-rooted, advanced in matters of self-government and support; and by tradition Continental-Reformed. It is, indeed, the largest of all fields worked primarily by Continental missionary societies. Indonesian Protestantism is second in size only to that of India throughout Asia, and perhaps carries relatively the more weight since it is much more homogeneous. It is well-rooted in the sense that it has both a long history of more or less continuous growth and also because it is an accepted part of the Indonesian community today. Since it has never known an oversupply either of missionaries or of trained clergy, it has long been accustomed to depend on lay leadership in its congregations. Generally speaking the churches pay their pastors' salaries and support their own local programs, but large projects, such as higher educational institutions, require outside assistance. Some Christian schools, as well as others, receive government subsidies.

The Protestant Churches in Indonesia fall into two classes, the thirty-one members of the Indonesian Council of Churches, comprising three million persons and the others, estimated in 1958 as a half-million. The "others" consist of Continental Pentecostals and Adventists who came in before the Second World War and a larger group of newer movements, mostly Anglo-Saxon in origin. This group includes Southern Baptists,

Assemblies of God, Jehovah's Witnesses, and various non-denominational missions. The "ecumenical" Churches can again be divided into three types: the inheritors of the Church of the Indies, confederated in the Protestant Church of Indonesia; the Churches which arose from major Dutch, German, and Swiss mission work between 1800 and 1942; and several smaller Churches of Dutch Mennonite, American Methodist, and Pentecostal background. Thus the Reformed tradition accounts for at least three-fourths of the Protestant community.

However, denominationalism in the Anglo-Saxon sense is almost nonexistent, partly as a result of the homogeneity of missions at work in the area and partly through government-enforced comity. In fact there is no Indonesian translation for the word "denomination." The dominant tradition is "Reformed," primarily expressed in liturgy and polity. Most of these churches adhere to a polity referred to as "presbyterial-synodal." In general the synod exercises considerable power in a rather centralized church-structure. With two exceptions the only confessional formulation in official use is the Apostles' Creed. The exceptions are churches of *Gereformeerd* background, which use the Heidelberg Catechism, and the Batak Federation of Churches.

The latter-named body, the largest Protestant Church in Indonesia, is an exception to many generalizations concerning the "ecumenical" Churches. Its baptized membership of 691,000 (in 1960) rose from the brilliantly effective work of the Rheinische Missionsgesellschaft, a "Unionist" mission with a strong Reformed element. The Batak Church is one of the most successful of all examples of mass evangelism, a tribal group acceding almost whole and with its customary law intact. This Church was given a structure which one of its leaders has referred to as "presbyterial-feudal," with regional synods in addition to a General Synod, and a presiding bishop, the Ephorus, elected for a six-year term and exercising patriarchal authority. The Bataks are remarkable also in that in 1952 they adopted their own confession of faith, the first such in Indonesia. This confession is influenced by the Augustana and also cites the Barmen Declaration, but is very much an indigenous document, dealing with specific local demands and problems. Furthermore, the Batak Federation of Churches has joined the Lutheran World Federation, becoming the only Indonesian Church in world confessionalism.

III

Indonesia makes a good impression in ecumenical circles partly because of her sheer size among the Asian Churches, but also because of the unquestionably indigenous character of her leadership, the degree of self-support she displays, and the high quality and thorough training of her small group of leaders. Yet this Church has been described in a "state of shock."[1] The great machine of the Church has been working only at reduced capacity since independence. The Church seems not wholly to have caught up with its present state.

The primary instrument and instigator to unity is the Indonesian Council of Churches, founded in 1950. Relations with missions from overseas are conducted through the Council's Commission on Mission. This body has Continental and English-speaking associate secretaries who are appointed by the Netherlands Missionary Council and by the Far Eastern Office of the Division of Foreign Missions of the National Council of Churches in the U.S.A., respectively. The third article of the Council's constitution states: "The object of the Indonesian Council of Churches shall be the establishment of a united Christian church in Indonesia." Thus it is perhaps unique among national councils as being overtly an agency to promote organic church union. At its third general assembly in 1956 the

[1] Winburn Thomas, "Indonesia and the Indonesian Church in Today's World," Missionary Research Library *Occasional Bulletin* Vol. IX, No. 2, Feb. 10, 1958.

Council defined its "common task" more precisely as "the establishment of one church of Christ in Indonesia with one confession of faith and one basis of church order." The Bataks have since dissented, proposing instead federal unity through the existing agencies; but the Council continues to uphold its original position.

In point of fact, only one church union has been consummated in the postwar period. This is especially striking in view of the generally conceded absence of theological issues. On the other hand, for Churches coming from a single European tradition, the Indonesian Churches have shown remarkable hospitality toward new groups requesting entrance. The Commission on Mission is prepared to receive new and nondenominational missions as associate members, and at present the Salvation Army, the Overseas Missionary Fellowship, and World Vision have accepted the invitation. One bright spot in the ecumenical picture is the unexpectedly good relations with the vigorous and amazingly liberal Roman Catholic community. This Church has been less affected by the difficulties between the Dutch and Indonesian governments than have the Protestants, even though it has an overwhelming preponderance of foreign priests and workers. Many of these workers applied for Indonesian citizenship during the most difficult period. The Roman Church received a full-fledged hierarchy in 1961.

The Protestant Churches have been active in the ecumenical movement. Ten Indonesian Churches became members of the World Council of Churches at the Amsterdam Assembly. Immediately following independence many Churches hoped to be able to carry on without outside assistance, but from 1950 this experiment was reluctantly given up and missionaries were again invited, with mixed feelings. However, in the crisis of 1958 the Council of Churches and most individual synods were valiant in the defense of Dutch colleagues, who, though diminished in numbers, continued to work throughout the period of political difficulties. When they have been antiforeign, Christians have been so with a bad conscience.

The Churches continue to grow steadily, and some spectacularly, many doubling in membership since the war. In the early postwar period the Protestant community was estimated at only two million. The Roman Catholics have perhaps tripled in membership in the same period. The sects also are growing rapidly, in East Java constituting a full third of the Protestant population. Mass movements continue on the island of Timor and among the Toradjas of Central Sulawesi, despite the most adverse conditions in Indonesia, with active persecution and sometimes a total lack of civil order. With churches established in every district of Sulawesi, and the Minahassa area said to be "105 per cent Christian," it has been prophesied that the entire island will become Christian. The Bataks have long been conscious of their evangelical calling and have had their own home mission board since the early years of the century. The ancient Church of Ambon, which has a long history of evangelistic work on other islands, pledged in her "Synod of Repentance" in 1961 new efforts within and without her own territory. In view of their solidly Muslim environment, the churches of East and Central Java continue to be remarkable for their steady growth. The statistics for the Indonesian Churches took a sudden leap on May 1, 1963, with the transfer of sovereignty over West Irian (New Guinea). The Evangelical Church of West Irian claims that in a population estimated at between 700,000 and 800,000, Christians number 300,000. Since the Muslims claim another 150,000, there are at least 350,000 animists—a group which has hitherto formed a ready field for evangelism. The Evangelical Church operates 469 schools, most of the educational institutions of the area. What will happen with the change of regime remains to be seen.

In the colonial period the Dutch educated pitifully few, but educated them very well. Theological education in Indonesia reflects this background. The eight theological schools conducted by member Churches of the National Council stand alone in Southeast Asia in upholding a European pattern of training. The higher theological schools teach Greek, Hebrew,

English, Javanese (classical and modern), German, Latin, and in a newly proposed curriculum, Sanskrit. However, entrance to these schools is from the twelfth grade, from which base they offer five years of heavily biblical and linguistic training leading up to the equivalent of an M.A. in theology. At present two schools are in this "higher" category, with the six others receiving students from the ninth grade. At least three of the latter are planning to change to the twelfth-grade level in the immediate future. All these schools are small, with a total enrollment of about 650 students. The Christian Literature and Bible Societies are active and well-led. The former has published over three hundred titles since the war, including excellent original theological texts. The latter has portions of the Bible in thirty-one languages, and is in the midst of a new translation of the Indonesian Bible.

The government recently suppressed all international organizations in Indonesia and all independent youth movements, darkening the future of Christian associations. In 1961 the Christian Boy Scouts were merged with a new national youth organization, the Pioneers. The most striking of all Christian organizations is the Protestant political party, *Parkindo*. In the only general election held thus far, in 1955, *Parkindo* ran sixth among the twenty-seven parties. Its leading figure is the Ambonese physician, Dr. Johannes Leimena, who became, in the present Presidential Cabinet organized in 1957, one of the several deputy premiers, and has on several occasions served as acting president in Soekarno's absence. It is claimed that the strongly ideological or religious character of all existing parties makes necessary a specifically Christian expression in politics. The Roman Catholics also have a small party. The necessity for close and sympathetic cooperation with the present regime in its "guided democracy" makes increasingly heavy demands on Christian political leaders for conformity. They seem to feel that the identification with the national welfare thus achieved is worth the price, and place great faith in the freedom-of-religion clause and in the benevolent attitude of the government. Throughout its course the Indonesian revolution has had strong Christian support.

There is an extensive network of Christian schools and hospitals. The former culminate in three institutions of higher education, the Christian University in Djakarta, Satya Watjana University in Central Java, and Nommensen University in Sumatra, with a combined enrollment of about 2,700. There are thirty hospitals and almost two hundred clinics; but only nine Christian doctors work full-time in these institutions.

IV

The Church of Christ in Indonesia is still engaged in consolidation and stock-taking for the most part, still testing the possibilities of her new environment. Although progress continues along older lines, a really new departure must now be made if her mission is to be performed faithfully in this time. What is continually impressive and exciting in Indonesia is not the grandeur of the long past, but rather the immensity of the opportunities immediately at hand. Thus it is deeply exasperating when the Church, wrapped up in the problem of consolidation, contents herself with housekeeping.

Five very bright possibilities for witness and service seem to me to present themselves at present. The first is the more intensive pursuit of a task long labored at, the evangelization of the remaining animists. This is especially urgent as they, with a faith which offers no real alternative to whatever curious gospel is on the lips of the authorities, come under the direct influence of the central government.

A second evangelistic opportunity is that of proclaiming, to the many principalities and powers who have not yet been directly confronted, Christ crucified. In addition to animists, secularized Chinese and nominal Muslims, the Church must speak to the major varieties of Islam, to the secularism of the new intellectual, to the Communist and his many fellow travelers, and to the new and sometimes sophisticated forms of Javanese mysticism.

A most urgent third calling is that of breaking the impasse in church union. Present issues often appear as low-level disputes about ecclesiastical dignity. Despite the large measure of co-operation achieved by the Council of Churches, the problem is pressing because Christianity tends to take an ethnic shape among the larger Christian bodies and because of frequent tensions of a semitribal character—as, for instance, in relations with the Churches of Chinese background. For, sadly enough, the Churches are not wholly free from the anti-Chinese attitudes which are causing civil disorder at present.

A fourth point, which depends in part upon outward circumstances but more upon the zeal of the people, is that of taking a more positive and active part in the opportunities for service offered in ecumenical Christendom. The vision is there but it is not yet widespread.

Finally, it would seem that the Church in Indonesia is in an admirable position to embody the ecumenical concern and fellowship to those churches estranged from that fellowship by ideological issues, or perhaps restrained by their governments from participation in an active way in the common concerns of the World Church. Specifically, the Indonesian Council of Churches appears to be excellently situated to extend Christian hospitality to the Church in China, as rather cordial relations between the two countries now exist.

✦✦ XVI ✦✦

South East Asia

JOHN R. FLEMING

JOHN R. FLEMING

John R. Fleming is Executive Director of the Association of Theological Schools in South East Asia, and of the Foundation for Theological Education in South East Asia (which now succeeds the Nanking Theological Seminary Board of Founders represented in Asia by Dr. Fleming since 1957). He is Editor of the SOUTH EAST ASIA JOURNAL OF THEOLOGY and assists in various undertakings of the East Asia Christian Conference, the important regional group fostering common concerns and activities among the Churches from the Indian peninsula to Japan.

Theologically trained in Glasgow, Heidelberg, and Union Theological Seminary, New York, Dr. Fleming served his Church of Scotland as a missionary in Manchuria 1938-50. There he taught several years in the Moukden Theological College of the Church of Christ in China. From 1951 to 1957 he was General Secretary of the Malayan Christian Council, and concurrently taught in Trinity College, Singapore, a union institution which is the one important agency for ministerial training among the Protestants of the Singapore-Malaya region and for some Chinese far beyond.

No person, past or present, has equalled Dr. Fleming's experience in continual visitation and consultation among the Church leaders and the theological schools of South East Asia.

XVI

I. The Environment of the Church

The term "South East Asia" commonly includes Burma, Thailand, Vietnam (North and South), Cambodia, Laos, Federation of Malaysia, the Philippines, and Indonesia. For the purposes of this essay we ignore Indonesia, which is dealt with in a separate chapter, but add Hong Kong and Taiwan, since the Churches there are connected with South East Asia in a number of ecumenical operations, and are centres of Chinese life and culture with many relationships among the large Chinese communities resident in South East Asia.

Each country in South East Asia has its own particular setting, but there are some major factors common to all that provide the backdrop to the life of the nation and the life of the churches:

1. *Nationalism and Nation Building.* The most powerful dynamic of change in the last twenty years in South East Asia has been nationalism—the desire to be independent and free of colonial controls and to build a new nation with a new life for its people. Since the end of the Second World War Burma, Vietnam, Cambodia, Laos, Malaysia, Indonesia, and the Philippines have all emerged from political dependence. But national independence, as the new nations have discovered, is but the first step in the complicated task of nation building, of filling the rice bowl, of achieving national unity, of developing effective leadership and honest administration, of meeting the real needs of the people.

2. *Population Growth and Age Composition of Populations in South East Asia.* The problems of nation building are today more complicated by phenomenal population growth. This has been due to sharply reduced mortality rates and to an unchanging fertility in South East Asia, bringing the population from 155,000,000 in 1940 to 175,000,000 in 1950 to 214,000,000 in 1960 with an annual increase of between 2 per cent and 3 per cent. Also significant is the increasingly large percentage of the population under fifteen years.

3. *Education and Potential Leadership.* The nations of South East Asia are determined to open to their children doors of literacy generally closed until yesterday. In Taiwan in 1960, 94.8 per cent of primary-school-age children were in school. The Karachi plan, in which all the South East Asian countries participate with others, aims at seven years' free and compulsory primary education by 1980. Malaya and the Philippines plan to achieve this much earlier.

4. *Technology, Science, Industrialisation, and Urbanisation.* Asia has seen the power of science and technology in the West and the new nations are determined not to be left out of this "brave new world." The best students are going into scientific and technical higher education. There is everywhere an emphasis on the need to industrialise—to provide work for the growing population, to produce the goods formerly imported from the West, to export into the world's markets. South East Asia's traditionally agricultural population, though still large, is slowly moving towards the cities, sometimes to a rootless existence deprived of the old sanctions of village community life.

5. *Secularism.* Secularism is capturing the minds of the scientifically and technologically trained Asians and the workers in the factories. To such, a pietistic, otherworldly message merely gives point to the Marxist interpretation of religion, and confirms men in their determination to build life on what can be seen and handled, and accomplished by man "himself—alone."

6. *Cultural Cohesion, National Unity, and Asian Religions.* Much has been written about the resurgence of Asian religions, as part of the Asian revolution. Some aspects of this resurgence stem from genuine religious renewal or from reformations in the light of modern knowledge or even in the light of Christianity. More often, however, this religious resurgence has had a strong utilitarian and political motivation on the part of national leaders. The old religions are called upon to provide cultural foundations for political cohesion. "To be a good Burman is to be a Buddhist."

Is Christianity, in the particularities of each country, really aware of the trends and forces in its situation, and the need to preach and live a relevant Gospel?

II. *The Prospects of Christianity in South East Asia*

1. *The Outlook in Burma.*   The common problems of new nations in South East Asia are well exemplified in this country of more than twenty million, with over twenty tribal and language groups. Since the military coup of 1962, the national course is the "Burmese Way of Socialism" in which Buddhism is no longer the official religion, all religious groups receive grants from the Religious Affairs Department, foreign missionaries find it difficult to get visas, banks and a good many private businesses have been nationalised, and many Christian leaders fear that nationalised schools will follow. Probably the main reason for the coup was the fact that the five major tribal groups in the Union of Burma were raising the question of becoming separate states in a federation. Some interpret the new government policy as the first steps to a Communist state. Others believe that this is unlikely in a Buddhist country with many national leaders sincere practising Buddhists.

One of the major difficulties facing Christianity in all this is that in the minds of the majority racial group—the Burmese who are Theravada Buddhists—Christianity is associated either with white people like the British who conquered Burma and opened it up to Christian missions both Roman Catholic and Protestant, or with "wild and uncivilised" tribal groups like the Karens, Chins, or the Kachins. It is among these tribes that the gospel has had greatest success, while it has met with much resistance from the Buddhist Burmese, among whom there are only about 5,000 Christians. In addition the Karens are associated in the minds of the Buddhist Burmese majority with rebellion against the central government. As a Burmese Christian reports: "If you say you're a Christian, you are immediately asked: 'Are you a Karen?' " This is true of the Roman Catholic Church (Christian community *ca.* 250,000) as well as of the Protestant Churches (Christian community *ca.* 700,000, among whom Baptists are reckoned to have 207,000 members and a Christian community of 600,000). Many individual Christians have been making outstanding contributions to the life of the nation, both in the independence movement and in the subsequent nation-building period still continuing. But as a leader said, "The Church as a whole has lived a more or less ghetto existence, out of which she is only now being challenged to move."

Several major problems and needs are clearly sensed by far-seeing Burman Christian leaders themselves: There is need for more and better-trained ministers and pastors. Many congregations have no trained leadership at all. Christian education, lay training, and the task of relating the Gospel and the Scriptures to the daily life and to a changing society and nation have still to be done. Among the tribes, their own myth of a divine book lends itself to literalism and biblicism in relation to the Christian Scriptures.

While indigenous leadership in some of the Churches is of a very high calibre indeed, it has been observed that the Burman leaders of the Churches are too involved in questions of property and administration, taken over from Western missions, to have much time for evangelism and a forward movement. Another charge is that they are overnationalistic, and in their acceptance of the Government's line of "Burma culture" imperil the integrity of the Christian message.

It is recognised that Christians need to know much more about Buddhism from the inside, and that too little has been done in this direction. One knowledgeable leader said, "It is my thought that Christ and the Buddha have not yet really met in this land."

Burma's population is increasing at the rate of nearly a half million per annum. The ratio of Church growth is nothing like this. The proportion of youth in the population is high, but Christian youth work is still very inadequate.

These and other serious situations confront the Churches. Besides being a minority group (Roman Catholic and Protestant Christians together would be about 5 per cent of the population) they have not solved their own ecclesiastical and racial problems of disunity. Humanly speaking, the outlook is not very promising. "There are more dangers than opportunities," said a leading pastor and theological teacher. But dangers are opportunities for Churches aware of their resources and their mission. Events are giving the Churches in Burma that kind of opportunity.

2. *Thailand.* Thailand is most conspicuously a Buddhist country, with its 20,000 Buddhist *Wats* or monasteries, and about 250,000 monks, among its twenty-eight million people. Buddhism is less aggressive, more polite and refined than in Burma; but there is no question about its cultural impact and influence on the national life.

Thai Christianity is still weak, and in its history has made slow progress. More than three centuries of Roman Catholic effort have resulted in a Christian community variously reported as 50,000 to 100,000. In 1952 of 171 priests 77 were indigenous. In 1958, 38 seminarians were in training.

Protestant work has also been difficult. The first Thai convert was won after thirty-one years. After fifty years there were more missionary graves in the cemetery than there were Thai Christians in the Church.

A new era in mission–church relationships began in 1929 with the formation of the Church of Christ in Thailand, a Union of Presbyterians and Disciples, which in the course of the years has attracted other missions in association, such as the Marburger, the United Church in the Philippines, the Church of South India, the Kyōdan of Japan, and others.

But at the beginning of the Second World War there were only about 7,000 Protestant Thais, of whom some 2,000 were soon lost. Indigenous Christian responsibility grew in the war period, and led to a strong lay movement of witness and evangelism in the postwar years. In fifteen years the numbers had trebled to 20,000, of whom about 15 per cent are Chinese.

Taking advantage of the good community relations built up by Christian schools, hospitals, and leprosaria over the years, Thai Christian laymen have now made a significant effort to bring in their Thai neighbours. But the Church of Christ in Thailand has barely forty pastors, of whom only fifteen have been theologically trained. There are 135 congregations in the Church, which means that nearly one hundred of them are looked after by untrained laymen. The Executive Committee of the Church, apart from two foreign missionary representatives, includes only one theologically trained pastor.

Since 1958 the mission has been genuinely integrated in the Church, but the Thai Church has not been able to assimilate the large missionary structure and apparatus. A Thai pastor said, "The centre of power sometimes tends to be the mission office rather than the headquarters of the Church." Instead of an increased pressure in the Church to assume responsibility, to develop the potentialities of stewardship and self-support, to follow through with more systematic plans of lay training in the different areas of Thai society, there is a new tendency, for financial, social and cultural reasons, to appoint Western missionaries as heads of institutions and departments of the Church's work. In the absence of trained theological leadership, this is not surprising, but foreign missionary help may smother the Church's initiative and leadership.

In general, the picture is one of open doors, no strong political pressures, and a fairly friendly Buddhism not easily converted, but tolerant of Christianity as a cultural enrichment in spite of its being spiritually heterogeneous and divergent from Thai traditional culture and the demands of Thai nationhood.

3. *Cambodia, Laos, and Vietnam (North and South).* These four independent countries, formerly French Indo-China, have had distinctive experiences in the events following the Second World War, and the subsequent struggle for independence, stable government, and a developing nationhood.

Christianity is regarded very much as a foreign religion in the Theravada Buddhist kingdoms of Cambodia and Laos, though it has government favour in the Chinese-Buddhist (Mahayana) and Confucian-influenced republic of South Vietnam. Of the Church in the People's Republic of North Vietnam (population 16,000,000) too little is known, though some of its difficulties can be surmised from the mass murders during the Communist Agrarian Reform Campaign. Cambodia (5,000,000), has a socialist regime, impregnated with Buddhist thought. It keeps a wary eye on its neighbours Thailand and Vietnam, both of which "regard Khmer neutrality as a Communist Trojan horse in the region." The kingdom of Laos (2,000,000) has had still greater difficulties in working out its problems of independent nationhood and unity, both in relation to its constituent ethnic, social, and tribal elements and to its connections with France, the United States, and the Soviet Union. A neutral status for Laos was agreed upon by the fourteen-nations conference at Geneva in 1962, but foreign pressures continue to enhance the internal political rivalries.

South Vietnam (14,000,000) has from the start faced military, political, and economic difficulties of extraordinary severity. The greater part of Vietnam was in the hands of the

Communist Viet Minh, and the remainder mostly controlled by three armed groups, two of them indigenous religious sects, the Cao Dai and the Hoa-Hoa, each with an army, and the third a bandit force. By 1956 President Ngo Dinh Diem had secured control of South Vietnam. The Viet Cong—Communist guerrillas—the major open opposition to President Diem's regime, is able to attract the support of many who are resentful of his party and his police, in spite of what his government has done for material prosperity and advancement of education.[1]

This then is the situation in which a fairly large Roman Catholic Church and a much smaller Protestant Church lives. The former, with a Christian community of about two million, is a Church that has survived some of the most severe persecutions in modern church history, when tens of thousands of Christians were massacred. It has put forth concentrated effort to train an indigenous clergy. There are 9 training institutions and around 1,500 native clergy and 400 foreign clergy. Roman Catholic authorities on missions regard the achievement in Vietnam as one of the four or five best outside Europe and America.

The Protestant movement is smaller and weaker, with a Christian community of about 45,000, yet through the effort and policies of the Christian and Missionary Alliance (c.m.a.) it appears to be the most nearly self-supporting and self-propagating Church in South East Asia, with 90 ordained nationals, 265 lay national workers, many of them licensed as preachers, and some 34 foreign missionaries. The Evangelical Church in Vietnam was set up in 1927, but the c.m.a. retained a fairly rigid control. In spite of numerical weakness, and a rather biblicist evangelicalism that is unlikely to attract students and the educated, this is a vigorous Protestant Christian movement that emphasises evangelism, lay witness and training, steward-

[1] Editors' Note: The Diem government was overthrown in November, 1963, by military men who profess better treatment of the Buddhist population and more effective opposition to the Viet Cong.

ship, self-support, and production of Christian literature. Related efforts, smaller in scale, proceed in Cambodia and in Laos.

Geography, politics, and mission policy tend to isolate the churches of the three countries from Protestants in neighboring lands, despite some desire among Vietnamese Christians for ecumenical fellowship. Also, there is the further weakness of otherworldly piety deflecting Christians from responsible obedience in their complicated national problems. Christianity has been most successful among the tribal mountain peoples. Special efforts have been made in recent years to win students and intellectuals, but the level of education of ministers and church workers needs to be raised for this, and for meeting with Buddhism in Laos and Cambodia. Nevertheless, here is a Church on strong foundations with a high level of literacy, and encouraged to be independent, in contrast to many in South East Asia that have been enervated by mission subsidies.

4. *Malaysia.* In 1963 the latest new nation came into being, joining the Federation of Malaya (independent in 1957), Singapore (self-governing in 1959), Sarawak and Sabah (North Borneo, both British Crown Colonies), as the new Federation of Malaysia. This new nation of ten million is interracial with Malays, Chinese, Indians, Sea and Land Dayaks, and many more racial groups. The Malays are Muslims, and Islam is the official religion of the new nation. Freedom of religious practice and propagation is guaranteed to other religions by the constitution, except in relation to the Malays, who have been protected from non-Muslim religious teaching since the Treaty of Pangkor in 1874. Tensions exist between the politically dominant Malays and the economically dominant Chinese, but the new Federation constitution and its safeguards offer a reasonable basis for peaceful development.

Malaya and Singapore. Kept apart from the indigenous Malays, Christianity has grown mainly among immigrant communities from China, India, and Europe, many of which had the attitude of sojourners in Malaya. The Protestant Christian community now numbers about 130,000; the Catholic, about 75,000.

Congregations were naturally formed on the basis of language or dialect, and this, with denominationalism to compound it, has introduced a disunity in the Churches which weakens their whole witness in a multiracial society. The "orientation to the homeland" also affected the growth of theological education and the rise of an indigenous ministry. Ministers and priests were brought from China, India, or England. It was not till 1948 that the main Churches began to train local ministers in Singapore. The level of training is rising steadily, but still higher standards are required if the ministry is to be as well educated as a great many laymen in the Churches. National leadership has not been very strong in the Churches. Self-support is inadequate, though a great deal of money from local sources has gone into new church buildings in recent years. Some Churches are still too much led and influenced by Western missionaries, and have failed to emerge from a position of tutelage to the full self-understanding of themselves as the Church in the land with responsibility for mission in all its aspects. The Gospel, held with conviction and sincerity, is often a limited one, concerned with personal piety, a puritan morality, and the next world. The demands of obedience as citizens of the Kingdom in relation to the secular spheres of daily life are scarcely understood. A considerable number of small Christian sect groups have come in recently—zealous for the Gospel narrowly interpreted, and sometimes much opposed to the larger denominations.

On the other hand, there are other more hopeful signs. The Churches are now trying to orient themselves to the Malayan situation and to the demands of mission in it. There is a growing sense of their need of renewal. Trinity College, in which Methodists, Anglicans, Chinese Christian Church, and Lutherans cooperate, has over eighty students for the ministry. The same four Churches are planning for 1964 a mobile training team to operate in a large rural area where there are insufficient trained pastors and evangelists. The Malayan Christian Council has over the last few years conducted training courses for lay people in the villages, for Sunday school teachers and church workers. Though hopes of church union are not very good, there is a slowly growing sense in the Churches of the *skandalon* of disunity, as Churches become more aware of their tasks in relation to the changing social and political situation.

Sarawak and Sabah (North Borneo). These two small territories with populations of 655,000 and 419,000 respectively, are made up of Dayaks and other tribal groups, a few Malays, and considerable numbers of Chinese divided by dialects.

Features in the development of Christianity that bear upon prospects for the future are: (*a*) the comparatively rapid growth of the Methodist Chinese Church among the Foochow people; (*b*) slower and more difficult growth among the Hokkiens and Hakkas in the Anglican area, groups which had a stronger Buddhist background; (*c*) small-scale mass movements among the Sea Dayaks or Ibans and the Land Dayaks; (*d*) only individual training of clergy till 1954, with dependence on Christian schoolmasters who were preachers in their spare time.

Weaknesses in the Methodist Church reported from among pastors are too great dependence on mission-board generosity, which has been excessive and debilitating; and the failure of the Foochow Chinese to break out from a closed community or clan concept of the Church, to take the Gospel among other Chinese dialect groups and tribal neighbours. In contrast, the Basel Mission and Borneo Evangelical Mission policies have laid responsibility for leadership, self-support, and evangelism on the indigenous Church *from the beginning.*

Much in the external situation is favourable, many opportunities are before the Church and little direct opposition. The creation of Malaysia may bring the Churches of the four territories closer together, if they really want to overcome denominational and regional separateness. But this is not likely to happen unless there is a greater realisation that effective witness to the new nation demands that Christian obedience be shown in terms of the nation's life, and in terms of the one people of God created by the gospel.

5. *Philippines.* The Philippines, with a population nearing thirty million, is today 81.5 per cent Roman Catholic, the result of massive Roman Catholic activity in missions begun in 1559 by Philip II of Spain. A unique Christian group is the Aglipayans, or Philippine Independent Church, which broke from the Roman allegiance in 1902, not on doctrinal grounds but in defence of indigenous leadership in the Church. Its community is about one and one-quarter million, and most significantly, its priesthood is being trained in the Protestant Episcopal Seminary of St. Andrew's, Manila.

Protestant Christianity was able to enter only with the American conquest in 1898, and over the years American Methodist, Presbyterian, Baptist, Protestant Episcopal, and other missions have been at work. Today non-Roman Christianity is represented by 113 different groups or sects, reporting a Christian community of one million and a quarter, collectively described thus:

> Protestantism in the Philippines has on the whole represented the Puritan strain in ethical matters. Conscious of their rivalry with Catholics, Evangelical Protestants have sought to outdo them in righteousness and so have tended to avoid such practices as smoking, gambling, drinking, dancing and the like. They have also sought to avoid identification with Catholicism in matters of public worship and other religious demonstrations, which in part explains the plainness of their buildings, informality and lack of colour in their services, and a negative attitude to *fiestas*. Though individual Protestants have attempted constructively to influence the social and political life of the Philippine nation, the Protestant churches generally present an unimpressive record of concern and action in affairs beyond their own internal organisation and problems.[2]

[2] Gerald H. Anderson, Peter G. Gowing, and Agustin E. Masa, "Philippine Christianty in Outline" (unpublished conference paper), p. 4.

A Filipino Christian leader further enumerated the weaknesses of Protestant Christianity in the Philippines as follows: (a) Divisions and divisiveness. (b) Theological lacks. Biblical and theological thinking do not govern the decisions or actions of the churches and individual Christians. (c) Self-support is deficient. The effect of missions and missionaries has too often made for paternalism and financial dependence. (d) The impact on the national life is generally poor.

Rivals to Christianity in the Philippines are not so much Communism (confined to Central Luzon) or Islam (in Mindanao among the Moros, and now being influenced by considerable numbers of Christian immigrants), but the secular humanism of the educated and intelligentsia, and the materialism of the bourgeois. Against this, only a Christianity that is "materialistic" and not merely "spiritual" can expect to make headway.

The late Valentin Montes, a pioneer in concern for lay training with social emphasis, in the last article he wrote stated this:

> The pathetic lack of social consciousness among the whole membership of the Church is both a challenge and an opportunity. A challenge because the laity is not necessarily allergic to social thinking. All they need is to be challenged. The Church must be made real to them as a vital part of the community, a part of all that occurs in the social relationships of people. It needs to be clearly shown that as the laity they are a vital and necessary part of the Church, that they have a ministry to perform in the world.[3]

A syncretistic rival to Christianity is found in the Philippine indigenous sect called the Iglesia Ni Cristo, founded in 1914 by Felix Manalo. This movement is very attractive to its members, who find within it a place of importance and responsibility; it is self-supporting and has impressive material resources; it is strongly authoritarian, and it works on fears of hell-fire and

[3] "Social Thinking of the Churches in the Philippines," *South East Asia Journal of Theology*, Vol. IV, No. 1 (July 1962), p. 42.

destruction. It condemns all other Churches as apostate; its view of Christ is Arian; and its interpretation of the Scriptures subjective and arbitrary. But it has flourished and claims to have over two million members, though a critical estimate puts the membership at 250,000.

Thinking of the prospects of Christianity in the Philippines, once more the vital question is not so much what is facing the Churches, but whether or not they have within themselves the real resources of the Spirit to meet the tests of the new situations.

6. *Taiwan*. Taiwan has a population of about eleven million—80 per cent Taiwanese, descendants of Chinese who crossed the Straits from the adjacent mainland; 2 per cent mountain tribes similar to other aborigines in the Philippines and Borneo; and 18 per cent Chinese from various provinces who crossed to Taiwan after the mainland was taken over by the Communists.

The defeat of Japan in 1945 opened the way for a strong movement of consolidation and expansion of the Christian Church. The familiar Presbyterian Churches in the north and the south grew rapidly. At the close of the Japanese period, it was discovered that in the mountains a flourishing Aboriginal Church had come into being despite prohibitions and persecutions. The Presbyterian Church has now 385 congregations with 72,000 people among these mountain tribes, and a theological training institute for them.

The Taiwan Church started in 1955 the significant "Double-the-Number Movement," looking both to congregations and to members. The plan was to double the Church in the ten years up to 1965, the first century. This was no mere statistical effort, but was solemnly undertaken as ". . . our offering of sacrifice and thanksgiving to God our Father." Three promises were made by members supporting the Movement: "To give in prayer every day; to give in money at least NT$10.00 [New Taiwan Dollars] every month; to give in work by helping fellow Christians, by witnessing to and helping non-Christians, by bringing others to Church, and by praying for others." Congregations have increased from 230 to 432, and membership from 59,467 to 104,002. In 1962 when these increases were reported, a further decision was taken to plan to have 1,000 churches by the centenary year 1965.

Although the Church has grown largely among the rural population, Christianity has had a strong influence on educated and professional men, third-generation Christians, whose minds are also influenced by science and technology, by secularism and by the materialistic values all around. In some cases it is the humanism of neo-Confucianism that is most influential in their thinking, or Buddhist ideas of self-salvation.

In the light of all this, one can see the significance of improved theological education, the work of Tunghai University, the training institute for aborigines at Mount Morrison, and plans to use and support a possible "surplus" of theological graduates by sending them into a variety of nonconventional ministries in society. Some of the most significant Christian and theological thinking in South East Asia has been done by Church leaders in Taiwan, both in relation to traditional Chinese thought, and in relation to new industrial developments in society. The experimental Church and Industry Study (1959-62) is significant. Although its conclusion was, "The Church is not ready to do this kind of thing seriously," this study has given a new orientation to theological training, and has roused a number of younger pastors. Generally speaking, however, this social emphasis and obedience in the light of Jesus' teaching of the Kingdom of God is confused with the old liberalism, and "liberal" is a bad word in most Chinese churches in South East Asia.

Christian disunity, not conspicuous before 1945, has been complicated by sudden migration from the mainland and by the postwar influx of about forty sects, many of them narrow, theologically ultra-conservative, biblically literalist, and unconcerned for any witness of Christians in the world. On the other hand, a recent Faith and Order meeting in Taichung was attended by about thirty representatives of twenty-four different church and mission groups. The host church was the True Jesus Church, the Chairman was a Southern Baptist, the leading speaker was a Chinese Roman Catholic priest!

There is true life in a Church that is assuming responsibilities of mission. There is hope too, in lay training and theological education that really face the world, in the new developments towards Christian cooperation and unity, in the improved relations with Roman Catholics, in the efforts to produce more Christian literature and to make better use of it.

7. *Hong Kong.* This small Chinese island and its adjoining area of Kowloon and the New Territories, the last remaining outpost of British colonialism in Asia, sits on the doorstep of Communist China.

Hong Kong is a place of feverish building, and there are still 600,000 squatters in tin and cardboard shacks on the hillsides. It is a place of rapid industrialisation. It is a place of labour tensions, where labour unions are too many and too political, and wage a struggle between Peking and Taiwan. It is a place of youth and the need for education where nearly half the population is under fifteen. Since 1946, private organisations including churches, usually with large public support, have opened more than 1,000 schools; and now a new school is opened every two weeks. It is a place of drug addicts, of tuberculosis, where 60,000 hospital beds are required and 2,000 available.

In all this area of need, overcrowding, degradation, hunger, homelessness, unemployment and misery, the efforts of the Hong Kong government in welfare and rehabilitation, education and housing have been prodigious. The contribution of Christians has been steady and continuous—in money and manpower, coming from the Hong Kong Churches and through them from Christian agencies round the world.

The Hong Kong Churches, like everything else in Hong Kong, have been growing fast—about 13 per cent each year. Protestant Christians number about 140,000 persons in more than 300 congregations, and the Roman Catholic numbers are about the same. Together they represent 9 per cent of Hong Kong's population.

Though one is impressed by the zealous evangelism, church extension, and Christian service going on in Hong Kong today, there are disturbing features, such as a certain denominational competitiveness, as well as division; the tremendous burden of relief work, taking the energies of pastors from other tasks of building up congregations; weaknesses in theological education, divided into a number of small and understaffed confessional seminaries.

Something of the dilemmas of Christianity in Hong Kong is caught in Dr. Andrew T. Roy's words:

> Hong Kong is filled with sturdy, wonderful people. It is also filled with the hunted, the haunted, and the broken. War, revolution, and political struggle produce both types. The Church must be open to both. But membership and partaking of the sacraments involve decision and a change of life. Can the Church maintain its spiritual vitality and the purity of its witness if it fills its pews with those who have been broken morally? It can, if the whole congregation understands its mission.[4]

III. A Conspectus of Prospects

Earlier in this essay the question was raised, "Is Christianity . . . really aware of the trends and forces in its situation, and the need to preach and live a relevant Gospel?"

In attempting to estimate the prospects of Christianity in the light of the strength and weaknesses of the Churches in South East Asia, it can be said:

[4] *On Asia's Rim* (New York, 1962), p. 150.

1. Many places appear to be weak in the understanding of the Gospel of the Kingdom. Generally, Christianity tends to be individualistic, with a puritan ethic, and often otherworldly. This has tended to make the Churches ingrowing in their attitudes, and to foster the characteristics of a defensive, self-preserving minority group.

2. This narrow, pietistic understanding of the Gospel minimises the impact that Christianity might make on changing society, if it understood the Gospel not only in terms of individual salvation, but also in terms of the acceptance of God's rule in the whole of life, wherever committed Christians are called to live and serve.

3. Weaknesses in ecclesiology follow. If the Gospel is understood and preached only in terms of individual piety and personal salvation, the full understanding of the Church's mission and function in the world cannot be grasped.

Signs of renewal and rediscovery are to be found in many places, perhaps especially in emphases and insights connected with the work of the East Asia Christian Conference set up in 1959 by the Churches and Christian Councils in East Asia. It could be that the theological climate of the Churches may change in the next ten years, with improved theological education of pastors and leaders.

There are signs, too, that some of the younger men in the Churches are grappling with the problems of a truer and fuller indigenisation of Christianity in Asia, to develop out of what is at present largely a nationalising of Christianity. The indigenising of Christianity in South East Asia, in terms of worship, cultural expression, thought, and theology is a task still on the threshold.

What then is the prospect? "It depends . . ." It depends on the Church understanding her mission. It depends on the laity knowing its call to live by and under the reign of God in all the situations of secular life. It depends on congregations knowing that they are the place where people are prepared for answering that call and that whatever does not contribute to the living answer is irrelevant. It depends on a clergy that sees its task directly related to the teaching and training of such a people, being part of it themselves. It depends on taking seriously the fact that God through the Gospel of Jesus Christ has made Christians one people, and that we disobey His will by maintaining our divisions that hide the Gospel of reconciliation from the world.

There are signs of these things happening in South East Asia—perhaps not very powerful signs, but they exist. Trusting that in them is the work of God's Spirit, and sensitive both to our weaknesses and to new directions in which He is leading, we can be soberly hopeful, leaving the outcome to Him.

Index

A

Africa, Southern   121 ff.
Africa, Sub-Saharan   107 ff.
African Church History Society
   115
African revolution   118
Afrikaner Nationalist Party   122,
   124
Ahmadiyya   250
All Africa Churches Conference
   118
Ambon   249, 255
Angola   131 ff.
Apartheid   122, 124, 127, 129
Atheism   57, 59, 61, 114, 225
Aubert, Roger   36
Australia   185 ff.
Australian Inland Mission   186

B

Babbage, S. Barton   185 f.
Bali   247, 249, 250
Bangalore   240
Bantu Education Act   130
Baptists:
   in Angola   132
   in Russia   62 f.
Barrett, C. K.   40
Barth, Karl   44, 175
Basil the Great   97

Batak Federation of Churches
   252 f.
Beauduin, Lambert   37
Beirut   92
Bible   35, 70, 181, 206, 224, 264
Bible translations   36
Bible printings in Russia   55, 58
Birmingham   26
Birnbaum, Norman   15
Boer War   122
Bonhoeffer, Dietrich   69
Booth, Charles   23
Borneo   269 f., 274
Brahman   239
Brazil   178
Broadcasting   109
Britain   15 ff
Brogan, D. W.   40
Brunner, Emil   44
Buddhism   198 f., 223, 230, 247 f.,
   250, 263, 269, 271, 275
Bultmann, Rudolf   47
Burgmann, E. H.   186
Burma   263 ff.
"Burmese Day of Socialism"   263

C

Calvinism   123 f.
Cambodia   267 f.
Campesinos   171
Canada   149 ff., 161

Cao Dai 268
Cévennes 45
Cheng, Marcus 220
Chiang Kai-shek 214, 215, 217
China 203, 213 ff.
Christian Council of South Africa
  129
"Christian Pro-Existence" 77, 82
Chrysostom 97
Church of Christ in Thailand 266
Church of England 16, 19, 32, 40,
  41, 190
Church of South India 234
Church of the Indies 248
Church membership:
  in Australia 187 ff.
  in Britain 16 ff., 21 f.
  in Canada 138, 151 f., 154
  in China 214, 224
  in Hong Kong 276 f.
  in India 229
  in Indonesia 250, 251, 255
  in Japan 200 ff., 205
  in Malaysia 270
  in Near Eastern countries 85,
    94
  in the Philippines 272 f.
  in Russia 54
  in Scandinavia 43
  in Soviet Satellite countries
    71 ff.
  in South Africa 121, 127
  in South Vietnam 268
  in Switzerland 44
  in Taiwan 274
  in Thailand 264 f.
  in U. S. A. 138 f., 143, 154 f.
Clark, Manning 190
Collectivization 79, 82 f.
Communism 35, 53 ff., 68 ff.,
  75 ff., 81 f., 213 ff., 224, 273
Communism in Africa 128
Communism in China 215 ff.,
  224
Confirmation 67

Confucianism 213, 275
Congar, Yves 38
Copts 92
Cottesloe Statement 125
Cragg, Kenneth 97
Cross 103, 231
Cullmann, Oscar 44
Czechoslovakia 67 ff., 72, 78, 81

D

Dayaks 271
Decline of Christianity in China
  218, 221
Decline of church attendance:
  in Australia 185 f.
  in Britain 22 ff.
  in Latin America 170, 173
  in U. S. A. 139
Delayed Action 124, 125
Denominationalism 142 ff.,
  152 ff., 243, 252, 270
Detroit 152
devadasis 234
Dibelius, Otto 47
Diem, Ngo Dinh 268
Double-the-Number Movement 274
Dutch Reformed Church 124 f.

E

East Asia Christian Conference
  237, 239, 278
Ebeling, Gerhard 47
Economic freedom 80
Ecumenical movement 28, 38 f.,
  45, 129, 153, 160, 162, 180,
  188, 208, 254, 258
Education 26
Egypt 85
Eliot, Charles W. 149 f., 162
Eliot, T. S. 139 f.
Encyclical *Ad Sinarum Gentem*
  222

Encyclical *Divino Afflante Spiritu* 36
Encyclical *Humani Generis* 37
Ephräem, H. 97
Evangelical Academies 47
Evangelical Church in Vietnam 268
Evangelization 181, 206, 257

F

Family-worship 46
France 37, 44 ff.
Fraternal Messenger 55
Free Churches 17, 23, 170
Forsyth, P. T. 141
Freytag, Walter 225
Free German Youth 71
Foochow Chinese 271

G

Gandhi, Mahatma 238
Geneva 33
Germany 37
Germany, Eastern 67 ff., 73 ff., 76 f., 81
Germany, Western 32, 47 f.
Ghana 113 ff.
Goa 229
Graham, Billy 187
Grandmothers 61 f., 93

H

Häring, Bernhard 36
Hakkas 271
Hamel, Johannes 76
Hanayagi, Futaba 208
Harris, A. W. 185
Hauge, Hans Nielsen 42
Herberg, Will 161
Highet, John 15, 19
Hinde Street Methodist Church 18

Hinduism 230 ff., 238 ff., 247, 250
History, meaning of 232
Hoa-Hoa 268
Hogg, A. G. 240
Hokkiens 271
Homer 94
Homrighausen, E. G. 150
Honest to God 41, 187
Hong Kong 193, 276 f.
"House Church" 42
Hromadka, Josef 73
Humanism 240 f., 273
Hungary 67 ff., 74, 78

I

Iglesia Ni Christo 273
Immigration:
    to Australia 189, 192
    to Latin America 169 f., 173
India 229 ff.
Indigenization of Christianity 206 f., 226, 240, 243, 266, 278
Indonesia 247 ff.
Indonesian Council of Churches 253
Industrial chaplaincies 42
Industrialization 39, 128, 173, 191, 198, 205, 236, 262
Industrial Revolution 123
Interracial fellowship 126 f.
Ireland 32, 34
Islam 86, 88 f., 96 f., 98, 247, 249, 250, 255, 273
Iona 42
Italy 34 f.

J

Japan 197 ff.
Japan Missionary Bulletin 201
Java 249 ff.
Jehovah's Witnesses 54, 252

John XXIII   100, 117, 189
John of Damascus   97
Johnson, Richard   185
Joseph II   72
Journal of the Moscow Patriachate
   55

K

Karachi plan   262
Karma   239
Khrushchev   57
Kowloon   276
Kraemer, Hendrick   46
Küng, Hans   39

L

Laity   37, 141 ff., 207, 267 f.
Latin America   167 ff.
Latin American Episcopal Council
   175
Lebanon   85, 88, 92, 94, 101 f.
Leimena, Johannes   256
Lenin   55, 59
Lenski, Gerhard   152, 159, 161
Lewis, C. S.   40
Levantinism   89 ff.
Ling Hsiu Yuan   219
Liturgy   86 f., 93 f., 98
Liturgical Movement   37
London   23

M

Macquarrie, John   158
Makhlouf, Sharbel   103
Malabar   229, 244
Malayan Christian Council   271
Malaysia   269 f.
Manalo, Felix   273
Mao Tse-tung   220
Martyrs' Memorial Hall   202

Marxism   55 f., 59, 69, 75 ff., 95,
   216, 223, 262
Masaryk, Jan   72
Maya   239
Methodists:
   in Angola   132
   in England   41
   in South Africa   127
Minahassa   249
Mindszenty, Josef   74
Missions   48, 99 f.
Missions:
   in Africa   107 f., 114 f.
   in China   214 f.
   in India   229 ff., 232 f., 242
   in Japan   198, 203 f., 208 ff.
   in Latin America   167 ff.
Modernization of Japan   199 f.
Montague, William Pepperell   149,
   151
Montes, Valentin   273
Moscow   58 f.
Mozambique   131 f.
Muhammadiah   250
Music, African   110
Muslims   16, 88 ff., 96 f., 98, 107

N

Nagasaki   202
Nanking   Theological   Seminary
   219
Nationalism   112 f., 122 ff., 131 ff.,
   190, 199, 236, 261
National   Christian   Council   of
   China   214, 217
Near East   85 ff.
Netherlands   32, 45 f.
Netherlands   Missionary   Society
   248
New Guinea   191 f., 255
New York   91
Niemöller, Martin   47
Nippon Christian Academy   210
Noh plays   202, 208

Non-Church Movement (*Muky-osai*) 209
Norway 42 f.

O

Omura, Isamu 204
Orthodox Church:
  in Near East 85
  in Japan 202
  in Russia 54 f., 58
  in Syria 244
  in U.S.A. 155
Ota, Sute 208

P

Pangkov, Treaty of 269
Panikkar, K. M. 232, 235
Pantjasila 250
Parahamsa, Ramakrishna 238
Parkindo 256
Patristic Studies in Britain 41
Paul VI 39
Pentecostalists 21, 43, 54, 155,
  174 f., 177 f., 178, 251
Philippines 272 f.
Philippine Independent Church
  (*Aglipayans*) 272
Planning, total 79
Poland 32
Preaching in Russia 60
Protestantism in Latin America
  170 f., 174, 176 f., 179 ff.
Presbyterianism in Twaiwan 274 f.
Pro Veritate 125

R

Racial conflict 192 ff.
Racial discrimination 125
Racial justice 133
Radhakrishnan, Sarvepalli 230,
  238

Religious liberty 32, 34, 114, 153,
  220 f., 236 f.
Religious pluralism 160 ff., 198 f.,
  230
Religious renewal 151, 161, 206,
  278
Rheinische Missionsgesellschaft
  253
Robinson, John 41, 187
Roman Catholicism 55, 141
Roman Catholicism:
  in Angola 131 f.
  in Australia 187 ff.
  in Britain 20 f.
  in China 214 f., 222
  in Czechoslovakia 72
  in India 229, 242
  in Indonesia 254
  in Japan 201 f.
  in Latin America 168, 169, 173
  in Philippines 272
  in Scandinavia 42
  in Scotland 18 f.
  in South Africa 121, 127
  in Thailand 265 f.
  in Western Europe 32 ff.
Rosier, Ireneo 174, 177
Roy, Andrew T. 277
Roy, Ram Mohan 238
Russia 53 ff.

S

Saintliness 102
Salvation Army 21, 188, 254
sati 234
Satory, T. A. 38
Saxony 80
Sayers, Dorothy 40
Schneider, Herbert W. 151
Scotland 18 f.
Secularism 262, 175
Science 150, 262
Science and Religion 56 f., 62, 63
Sheffield 42

Shiina, Rinzo   207
Shintoism   198
Singapore   269 f.
Soekarno   251
Sokagakai   209
South East Asia   261 ff.
Southern Rhodesia   131 ff.
Spain   32, 34, 35
Stacey, Margaret   15
Stalin   54, 57
Stalinism   70
Suburban ministry   26 f.
Suffering   103
Sulawesi   248, 255
Sumatra   248
Sun Yat-sen   217
Sweden   43
Switzerland   32, 33
Syncretism   242
"Synod of Repentance"   255
The Sword and the Cross   200

T

Taichung   276
Taiwan   262, 274 f.
Takeyama, Michio   200
Taoism   223
Television   25
Thailand   265 f.
Thernvada Buddhists   263, 267
Thils, Gustave   38
Thomas, St.   229
Thomas Aquinas   94
T'ien Feng   219
Ting, K. H.   225
Three-Self Reform Movement   217,
     220, 221, 222, 226
Timor   248
Toleration Act   (1689)   153
Tradition, Christian   97 f., 102,
     110
Tranquebar   229
True Jesus Church   276
Tunghai University   275
Turkey   85

U

United Church of Christ in Japan
     (*Kyōdan*)   202 ff., 206, 208
United East India Company   247
U.S.A.   137 ff., 149 ff.
Urbanization   140

V

Van Dusen, Henry P.   160
Vatican Council II   33, 37, 39,
     201
Vietnam   267 f.
Villain, Maurice   38
Visser't Hooft, W. A.   46
Vivekananda, Swami   238
Vocation   79 f.
Voluntaryism   153

W

Wales   19, 25, 27
Watanabe, Sadao   208
"Wee Frees"   19
Wilgespruit Fellowship Centre   131
Williams, Robin M.   152, 158,
     159
Wilson, Bryan   15
Winter, Gibson   26
World Council of Churches   58,
     101, 124, 125, 129 f., 140,
     201, 237, 254
Wu, Y. T.   225

X

Xavier, Francis   201

Y

York   22
Yu-pin, Paul   215

Z

Ziegenbalg, Bartholomäus   229